VAUGHAN WILLIAMS ON MUSIC

VAUGHAN WILLIAMS

ON MUSIC

Edited by
David Manning

OXFORD
UNIVERSITY PRESS

2008

OXFORD
UNIVERSITY PRESS

Oxford University Press, Inc., publishes works that further
Oxford University's objective of excellence
in research, scholarship, and education.

Oxford   New York
Auckland   Cape Town   Dar es Salaam   Hong Kong   Karachi
Kuala Lumpur   Madrid   Melbourne   Mexico City   Nairobi
New Delhi   Shanghai   Taipei   Toronto

With offices in
Argentina   Austria   Brazil   Chile   Czech Republic   France   Greece
Guatemala   Hungary   Italy   Japan   Poland   Portugal   Singapore
South Korea   Switzerland   Thailand   Turkey   Ukraine   Vietnam

Copyright © 2008 by Oxford University Press, Inc.

Published by Oxford University Press, Inc.
198 Madison Avenue, New York, New York 10016

www.oup.com

Oxford is a registered trademark of Oxford University Press

Library of Congress Cataloging-in-Publication Data
Vaughan Williams, Ralph, 1872–1958.
[Literary works. Selections]
Vaughan Williams on music / edited by David Manning.
  p. cm.
Originally published in various sources.
Includes bibliographical references and index.
Contents: Musical life and English music—
Continental composers—Folk song—British composers—
Programme notes on Vaughan Williams's music—
Programme notes on the music of other composers.
ISBN 978-0-19-518239-2
1. Music—History and criticism.
1. Manning, David, 1978–   II. Title.
ML60.V285 2007
780.9—dc22   2006050654

9 8 7 6 5 4 3 2 1

Printed in the United States of America
on acid-free paper

ACKNOWLEDGEMENTS

THE WRITINGS COLLECTED in this volume are reprinted with the permission of Ursula Vaughan Williams and R.V.W. Limited. I thank Ursula for the kind support she has shown towards this project, and acknowledge the help of Hugh Cobbe as Director of R.V.W. Limited in processing the permission request. Permission to reprint Chapter 64, co-authored by Vaughan Williams and Bert Lloyd, is also granted by Caroline Clayton.

Chapters 4, 13, 25, 28, 29, 34, 47, 49, 59, 66, 68 and 69 are reprinted with permission of Oxford University Press. Chapter 7 is reprinted with permission of the Royal College of Music. Chapter 21 is reproduced by kind permission of the Governing Body of Charterhouse. Chapter 42 is used by permission of the City of Birmingham Symphony Orchestra. Chapter 46 is reprinted with permission from *Encyclopædia Britannica*, © 1929 by Encyclopædia Britannica, Inc. Chapter 57 is reprinted with permission of the International Council for Traditional Music. Chapter 60 is reprinted with permission of the Diocese of St Edmundsbury and Ipswich. Chapter 61 is reprinted with permission of the Merlin Press Ltd. Chapter 63 is used with permission of the Society for Ethnomusicology. Chapter 64 is reprinted with permission of the English Folk Dance & Song Society. Every reasonable attempt has been made to identify and contact the relevant copyright holders for the items in this collection. The author would be pleased to hear from any individual or organization he has been unable to trace.

A constant source of reference during this project was Peter Starbuck's valuable dissertation, 'Ralph Vaughan Williams, O.M., 1872–1958: A Bibliography of his Literary Writings and Criticism of his Musical Works' (Thesis for Fellowship of the Music Library Association, 1967). An abridged version of this bibliography is reprinted in Michael Kennedy, *A Catalogue of the Works of Ralph Vaughan Williams* (2nd edn, Oxford: Oxford University Press, 1996), 282–94.

Helpful advice was received at the proposal stage from Alain Frogley and Byron Adams. I thank them for sharing with me their considerable knowledge of Vaughan Williams's writings and music. At Oxford University Press, Kim Robinson and Norm Hirschy skilfully supported me from first thoughts to the finished book, and I am very grateful for their patient advice.

CONTENTS

ABBREVIATIONS

EFDS   English Folk Dance Society
EFDSS English Folk Dance and Song Society
KC   Michael Kennedy, *A Catalogue of the Works of Ralph Vaughan Williams*
          (2nd edn, Oxford: Oxford University Press, 1996)

CHRONOLOGICAL LIST OF CONTENTS

VAUGHAN WILLIAMS ON MUSIC

Introduction

RALPH VAUGHAN WILLIAMS (1872–1958) enjoyed a long career as a high-profile and successful composer. He first aroused public interest by writing popular songs for the Edwardian salon. 'Linden Lea', his first published composition, appeared inside *The Vocalist* in 1902, one of many musical magazines in circulation at that time. Over the remaining fifty-six years of his life Vaughan Williams's published *oeuvre* steadily grew, eventually including nine symphonies, four concertos and another twenty orchestral works, five operas, dozens of works for chorus and orchestra, a significant repertoire of smaller-scale vocal and choral music, and eight chamber works. In addition, a large number of compositions remained unpublished in the composer's lifetime, such as the early chamber and orchestral works, and the film scores. A list of works, however, can only reveal one aspect of Vaughan Williams's activity. He may have gained a lasting reputation as a composer, but in his lifetime Vaughan Williams was also a folksong collector, musical editor, teacher, conductor, music historian, polemicist, and administrator. His achievements in these fields include editing the first edition of *The English Hymnal*, teaching as a professor of composition at the Royal College of Music, conducting the annual Leith Hill Musical Festival for fifty years, and collecting a substantial corpus of English folk songs. It is clear that Vaughan Williams possessed energy, enthusiasm, and an unswerving commitment to work throughout the whole of his life. What is less obvious is how, or whether, all of these activities are related, and why, given that Vaughan Williams

3

was passionately committed to original composition, he spent so much time engaged in other work. One might imagine Vaughan Williams as a workaholic, collecting tasks to occupy every waking moment; this would be a mistake, for there was a central purpose to all that activity which is revealed most clearly in his writings.

In a short article titled 'Who wants the English Composer?' (Chapter 7), published in 1912, Vaughan Williams tackles the fundamental aesthetic questions facing the emerging creative artist. He expresses frustration with contemporary music and musical culture in England, complaining that established and popular continental composers are dominating the tastes of audiences, and unduly influencing the musical style of native composers. To write genuinely original music, he explains, the English composer should focus on his own country and its culture, rather than attempt an imitation of the 'great' composers. There is no merit, either, in the contemporary composer attempting to detach himself from the world, enacting the romantic stereotype of an artist struggling with his materials. These observations prepare the ground for Vaughan Williams's central claim:

> The composer must not shut himself up and think about art, he must live with his fellows and make his art an expression of the whole life of the community—if we seek for art we shall not find it.

Now it becomes clear: attending choral society committee meetings, adjudicating musical competitions, teaching aspiring composers; all these tasks were not peripheral distractions to the composer's main job, they were integral to the role. It was a model Vaughan Williams endeavoured to follow: as music inspired his life, so he hoped life would inspire his music.

In this context the writings of Vaughan Williams become doubly valuable as a source of information. Firstly, we can read the composer's views about the nature of music in passages such as the one quoted above. Secondly, given the interrelationship of life and music advocated in the writings, we can also read Vaughan Williams's own accounts of his social and cultural interactions—in the areas of amateur music making, or folk song collecting, for example—and consider how he expressed the life of the community in his music. These writings contain not only facts of biography and the substance of aesthetic debate; they are reason to return again to the composer's music with fresh ears and explore the relationship of his life to his creative work.

Readers will chart their own paths through the 102 items in this collection, perhaps starting with Chapter 7, discussed above, or focusing on a particular interest of their own in Vaughan Williams's life and music. In order to provide an overarching structure to the collection, the chapters are grouped into six thematic sections and then run chronologically under each of those headings.

Part I is the broadest in scope, embracing the interrelated topics of 'Musical Life and English Music'. It begins with Vaughan Williams's earliest known article, written in response to the death of Brahms in 1897. Some elements of his mature views are already present, including a commitment to evolution as the driving force of musical history, but there is a clear focus on continental music and the nineteenth-century legacy, and no mention of indigenous sources of inspiration. Vaughan Williams does turn to native music in the next chapter, 'A School of English Music', but only to argue against the use of folk music as the basis of a national style. It is curious to find this article in the same issue of *The Vocalist* as Vaughan Williams's 'Linden Lea', subtitled 'A Dorset Folk-Song'.[1]

In later items the focus settles on national music, including a lengthy and idiosyncratic history of British music, originally published in four parts (Chapter 8), and a strongly worded complaint about English musical culture from the early 1930s (Chapter 10). The importance of amateur music making is apparent, especially in items written during World War Two: in Chapter 17, for example, Vaughan Williams illustrates the practical nature of his musical aesthetics, applying his underlying principles to the specific context of making music in the armed forces, as he had done himself during the First World War. This section of the book also illustrates Vaughan Williams's longevity: the preface to *The English Hymnal* from 1906 (Chapter 6), is later followed by the composer's reminiscences on that subject, written in 1956 (Chapter 25).

One item does require special comment at this stage. The Howland Medal Lecture was given by Vaughan Williams at Yale University on 1 December 1954. A summary of this lecture formed the last chapter of Vaughan Williams's book *The Making of Music*, later reprinted in *National Music and Other Essays*.[2] However, that 'summary' leaves out long sections of the original version, and so a transcription of the full lecture is given in Chapter 22 of this book. Here we can read a survey of Vaughan Williams's musical aesthetics, addressing the nature of music, originality, nationalism and the importance of folk song. There are some passages which are

---

[1] The connection of this tune to a folk song source is unclear, as Kennedy implies: 'Vaughan Williams developed a type of song midway between folk song and art song, for 'Linden Lea' owes as much to Schumann's 'Widmung' as to any folk tune.' See Michael Kennedy, *The Works of Ralph Vaughan Williams* (2nd edn, London: Oxford University Press, 1980), 77.

[2] 'Epilogue: Making Your Own Music', in *National Music and Other Essays* (2nd edn, Oxford: Oxford University Press, 1987), 237–42.

not particularly fluent on the page, but they have been retained here in order to try to convey a sense of Vaughan Williams's lecturing style. The occasional minor stumble and its subsequent clarification has been silently edited, but in every other respect the transcription remains faithful to the original. On the whole Vaughan Williams speaks slowly and deliberately, often pausing for breath, and one imagines that he is sticking closely to the script, rustling in his hands. Yet there are points where he apparently departs from what he has prepared, and the rate of speech increases. The question remains unanswered as to how much was omitted from the many other lectures written up in *National Music and Other Essays*. On the basis of the Howland Medal Lecture, it seems that Vaughan Williams was a dogmatic orator, but he did lighten the mood with humour, something which is not necessarily communicated by his published summaries. Such humour is not merely incidental; it too betrays a serious purpose, that of engaging effectively with his listeners in order to make music accessible and enjoyable for a wide audience.

Vaughan Williams's articles on continental composers, in Part II, are drawn from opposite ends of his musical career. The early items (1902–10), like the first chapters in Part I, reveal the composer grappling with the legacy of recent European musical history. The debates of contemporary music critics often centred on rather crude binary oppositions at this time, pitting Brahms's symphonies against Strauss's symphonic poems, neatly creating a distinction of absolute music from programme music. Vaughan Williams pursues a similar comparison between Brahms and Wagner in Chapter 1, although he refuses to favour one at the expense of the other. The status of the symphonic poem as a genre returns as an issue in articles on Strauss's *Ein Heldenleben* and Brahms (Chapters 31 and 32), and here we find Vaughan Williams embroiled in a *fin de siècle* debate of the 'long' nineteenth century. The lengthy article on Wagner, from 1902, is also the product of careful listening and detailed score study, illustrating a composer's concern for matters such as text setting and dramatic pacing.

The late items in Part II, spanning 1951–55, are more reflective in tone. Two of these are taken from articles which comprise contributions of varying length from a number of musicians on a given subject, although Vaughan Williams's single sentence on Schoenberg must rank as one of the shortest offerings to such an endeavour (Chapter 34). It could not contrast more strongly with the subsequent chapter, a nuanced critical assessment of Sibelius, published on the occasion of that composer's ninetieth birthday (Chapters 35).

It seems fitting that a collection of writings by Vaughan Williams should contain a large number of pieces on the subject of folk song. The items in Part III are spread fairly evenly across the composer's professional life, a reminder that although Vaughan Williams's period of active folk-song collecting lasted from 1903–13, the impact of these tunes, and his practical involvement in the folk-song movement, continued until his death. In fact the last item on this subject was first published posthumously, in 1959, co-authored with A. L. Lloyd. One short sentence summed up Vaughan Williams and Lloyd's aim for that publication: 'This is a book to sing from'. Practical, plain speaking, without dwelling on the details, the focus is on providing amateur musicians with the materials they need.

There has been much debate about the methodology of collectors such as Vaughan Williams. Comments such as 'the editorial hand has been used where necessary' (Chapter 59) certainly raise more questions than they answer. But elsewhere it is clear that Vaughan Williams was well aware of the historical context for the folk song movement in England. He notes the European precedents for building a national music on folk song, and makes passing references to the scholarship of Carl Engel and the Grimm brothers, besides the tributes to his colleagues in the English folk song movement: Lucy Broadwood, Frank Kidson, Ella Mary Leather, Cecil Sharp, and Arthur Somervell.

While collecting was an essential task for Vaughan Williams prior to the First World War, lecturing on folk song was of vital importance over a longer period. Chapter 38 provides one account of his teaching, based on a series of lectures given in 1912; it is notable that many of the arguments from this period were equally serviceable in *National Music* (1934), and the Howland Medal Lecture (1954). Indeed, it would seem that there is a core message, expressed countless times in print and in lectures: folk song is a true form of self-expression, and, as such, it provides the germ of inspiration for great art. It is central to music, inspiring the composition of original works, and vital for social life, supporting formal education in schools and social engagement in the wider community. This was an idealist's vision; but through Vaughan Williams's practical involvement in the folk song movement, partially recorded in the writings, we can recognise his attempts to bring this into reality.

Part IV is dominated by Vaughan Williams's tributes to composers who inspired and influenced him. The prominence of Holst is perhaps unsurprising, and there is at times a palpable sense of frustration on Vaughan Williams's part that his friend did not experience the greater public success he surely deserved. The articles on Parry are similarly inspired by his personal experiences, although a rare, and rather obvious, display of diplomacy emerges in the discussions of Stanford, especially when an 'intolerant and narrow-minded' approach is presented as the mark of 'a good teacher' (Chapter 72). But, as Vaughan Williams notes, Stanford did secure the premiere of *A Sea Symphony* at the Leeds Festival in 1910 at a time when the festival committee were extremely resistant to commissioning new works.

Vaughan Williams's programme notes on his own music, collected in Part V, are among some of his most quirky, and occasionally baffling, writings. While, in other contexts, the composer frequently addressed the fundamental questions of music, he was evidently very reluctant to provide a commentary on his own works. As Ursula Vaughan Williams explains, 'he would have liked to print Mendelssohn's saying that "the meaning of music is too precise for words" on every concert programme at which his works were played.' Vaughan Williams particularly disliked receiving praise for his works from members of the public. Ursula explores this further: it 'had nothing to do with modesty or, as was sometimes suggested, humility, a quality which he detested in others and of which he had no trace. Perhaps it was partly shyness but it sprang also from a great dislike of discussing his work except with a very few of his friends.'[3] With this in mind, it is unsurprising that a writer from *The Music Student*, interviewing Vaughan Williams about the meaning of his music in 1920, was unable to discern much about individual works. However, Vaughan Williams's more general remark is still revealing:

> My business is to write music ... not to talk about it. And if my music doesn't make itself understood as music without any tributary explanation— well, it's a failure as music, and there's nothing more to be said. It matters, of course, enormously *to the composer* what he was thinking about when he was writing a particular work; but to no one else in this world does it matter one jot.[4]

In this light the austerity and flippancy of the so-called 'analytical' programme notes is a little easier to understand; however, the fact remains that they helped fuel negative critical reactions, especially at a number of first performances. Vaughan Williams is apparently adhering to a kind of idealist aesthetic which holds that music should speak for itself; it was a source of great frustration that he could not prevent others attempting to speak for him, something that was particu-

---

[3] Ursula Vaughan Williams, *R. V. W.: A Biography of Ralph Vaughan Williams* (Oxford: Oxford University Press, 1984), 283–4. Mendelssohn's remark is made in a letter to Marc André Souchay, 15 October 1842. See Peter le Huray and James Day (eds.), *Music and Aesthetics in the Eighteenth and Early-Nineteenth Centuries* (Cambridge: Cambridge University Press, 1981), 457.

[4] Katharine E. Eggar, 'Ralph Vaughan Williams: Some Reflections on his Work', *The Music Student*, 12/9 (1920), 515–19 at 515.

larly prevalent in the reception of the later symphonies. Vaughan Williams's rejection of Frank Howes's description of the Sixth as a war symphony illustrates this point.[5]

There is a clear contrast when we turn to Vaughan Williams's programme notes on the music of other composers. His enthusiasm and generosity of spirit return in these notes for concerts given by the Bach Choir and at the annual Leith Hill Musical Festival. In the other sections of this book, items have been selected for inclusion so long as they have not been included in *National Music and Other Essays*, and do not create excessive duplications within the volume itself (see the footnote to Chapter 38). However, Vaughan Williams's programme notes are so numerous that it has not been possible or desirable to include them all.[6] The Leith Hill notes reprinted here have been selected on the basis of their intrinsic interest; the excluded items include numerous 'analytical' programme notes for canonical orchestral works that reveal little about Vaughan Williams's music, personality or interests. There are also brief remarks on individual movements from choral works and songs that appear sporadically in these sources. However, when Vaughan Williams did set about placing a work in its historical context the results are often well worth reading, and such items comprise Part VI. It is apparent that Vaughan Williams worked hard to ensure his performers and audiences could enjoy a wide range of works at this annual festival with which his name is indelibly associated.

By reading the items in this collection, and the books and essays collected in *National Music and Other Essays*, we can survey Vaughan Williams's writings on an extremely wide range of topics. Furthermore, the composer's correspondence will become available in due course, in a collection to be edited by Hugh Cobbe for Oxford University Press. In a practical sense reading Vaughan Williams has never been easier; however the question of interpreting the composer's prose is not quite so simple. The frequent and enthusiastic discussion of music in general, coupled with reticence on the subject of his own music, presents a challenge. Can we interpret his writings on music in general to try to deepen our understanding of his music in particular? This enterprise is not without its difficulties, but in some ways it is quite tempting to make such extrapolations. As Michael Kennedy suggests in his foreword to the second edition of *National Music and Other Essays*, Vaughan Williams 'may appear to be writing about folk-song, Beethoven, and hymn-tunes, [but] he is also telling the reader what it was like to be the man who set out

---

[5] Kennedy, *Works*, 301–2.
[6] In addition it has not been possible to locate all of the Bach Choir programme notes.

deliberately, with his friend Gustav Holst, to turn himself into an English composer.' These writings, in Kennedy's view, can be considered as Vaughan Williams's 'musical autobiography...although it is presented in disguise'. However, our interpretations must proceed with care as Vaughan Williams was 'in the mildest and least aggressive way, a revolutionary...[and] like all revolutionaries...he often over-stated or over-coloured a point in order to put it across.'[7] As a case in point, Alain Frogley examines the expression of nationalistic beliefs in *National Music*:

> Although it contains some statements that actively discourage an attitude of narrow insularity, others suggest a hardening of the composer's earlier opinions.... Vaughan Williams was never a jingoistic patriot in political terms, [yet] it is difficult to escape the impression that he was swayed to some degree by the further heightening of nationalistic sentiment around this time.[8]

This raises the possibility that *National Music*, long accepted as the seminal expression of Vaughan Williams's beliefs, may be an atypical representation of the composer's long-held views in certain respects. Interpretation of his writings is indeed a risky business.

If the relationship of life and music remains problematic, Vaughan Williams's attitudes to the nature of music and the vocation of composer are stated unequivocally. He may write on a diversity of topics, but the central themes—originality, folk song, a sense of history, the importance of self-expression—keep returning. Vaughan Williams was a campaigner and so he was bound to repeat himself, but in each iteration the emphasis shifts and the tone is different. While the variety of topics should not be overlooked, an underlying theme emerges time and again in these writings. Put simply, Vaughan Williams was pursuing his chosen task: to build a musical community.

[7] Kennedy, Foreword to *National Music and Other Essays*, p. v.
[8] Alain Frogley, 'Constructing Englishness in Music: National Character and the Reception of Ralph Vaughan Williams', in Alain Frogley (ed.), *Vaughan Williams Studies* (Cambridge: Cambridge University Press, 1996), 1–22 at 17–18.

PART I

MUSICAL LIFE AND ENGLISH MUSIC

CHAPTER 1

The Romantic Movement and Its Results

THE DEATH OF Brahms has revived in all its vigour the old controversy on the subject of classical and romantic music. Several simple-minded people who wished to be considered progressive were shocked to find that, in the opinion of experts, Brahms belonged to the classical school. These conventional radicals had always connected the word 'classical' with pedants and reactionaries, and now they were forced to leave . Brahms—for whom they really had a sneaking admiration—in the cold, as being behind the times, while they pinned their progressive faith on those composers who, for no other reason than that they were not classical, have been dubbed 'romantic'.

It is, of course, true that there is no room for the reactionary in music, and that no movement which is out of the straight line of musical evolution has ever produced any good results; therefore, if Brahms is really lagging behind the age it may well be argued that his music is not likely to stand the test of time. But musical toryism is not necessarily implied in the word 'classical'. The tenets of both schools can be held alike by progressives and reactionaries, and their real cause of conflict can be broadly stated thus: that the classical composers work on a purely musical basis, while the romanticists include some external non-musical factor as the emotional basis of their work.

Source: *The Musician*, 1/23 (1897), 430–1.

However, among the immediate successors of Beethoven, the progressives were all of the romantic persuasion, and this continued to be the case until Brahms appeared and returned to the apparently obsolete methods of Beethoven, producing music which was, as his admirers say, pure music, rather than music eked out by other arts, or, as his detractors have it, the 'mere development of musical themes', without any of the emotional influences which give the dry bones life.

It seems, then, either that it is true that Brahms is born out of due time, and can have nothing to say to this generation, or else that the whole movement which led up to Schumann and Wagner was a river destined to be lost in the sand. However, if we trace the course of the romantic movement we shall find that though its day is over, yet it has not perished in the wilderness, but that it has reached its goal and done its work, and that this work was the creation of the New Art of Richard Wagner.

The beginning of the romantic movement is to be found in the reaction against formal perfection which followed the death of Beethoven.

Beethoven was a classical composer—this does not mean that he was not imaginative, but it does mean that he was a musician and nothing else—that the emotional germ of his music was simply a musical pattern in his mind, which was translated into an analogous musical pattern on paper. With Beethoven, then, abstract form and emotional expression were inseparable, because they both sprang from the same source.

Like so many other new movements, the romantic school owes its origin not to the appearance of some new factor in the composer's scheme, but to the loss of an old one. The power which the early romanticists lacked was the sense of abstract form, which Beethoven had used to elucidate and formulate the emotional side of his music. Of emotions these pioneers had enough and to spare, but there was wanting the distinct decorative pattern on which to weave their emotions into an organized whole.

In this particular, then, their musical organization was incomplete, but art, like nature, abhors a vacuum, and the lack of musical qualities had to be made up from without; thus, instead of the power to organize their ideas through the means of a nice sense of proportion, there came upon the first romantic composers an intense desire to make their music intelligible by connecting it with the outside world: in fact, to make it in some sense a 'criticism of life'.[a]

---

[a] This seems to be an allusion to Matthew Arnold's literary criticism. For example, in an essay on William Wordsworth, Arnold writes: 'It is important, therefore, to hold fast to this: that poetry is at bottom a criticism of life; that the greatness of a poet lies in his powerful and beautiful application of ideas to life,—to the question: How to live.' See *Essays in Criticism: Second Series* (London: Macmillan, 1888), 143–4.

To accomplish this end the musician must, through his music, put himself in imagination into an emotional state foreign to his musical nature. This cannot be done except by the co-operation of one of the other arts, namely, that of the dramatist; and thus an external growth, having in it some of the characteristics of dramatic art, is grafted on to the musical stem.

Schubert and Weber, the founders of the school, were not, of course, aware that they were laying the corner-stone of a new art; they aimed at writing music, just as their predecessors had done before them; but Schubert, on the one hand, found himself most inspired when he guided his emotional utterance by the thoughts of some poet whose words he was setting to music; and Weber, on the other hand, was seldom other than trivial, and even vulgar, except when he was illustrating some situation which particularly appealed to his imagination, such as the weird forest scene in *Der Freischütz*, or the romantic story on which the 'Concertstück' is based.

At first, then, the new dramatic element in musical composition influenced musicians quite unconsciously. The first composer who recognized it was Berlioz. He not only recognized it, but welcomed it and invented elaborate dramatic situations and programmes, which the hearer is to conjure up through the medium of music. Of him, indeed, it may be said that the dramatic element did not inspire his music, but rather that his music illustrated the events which his dramatic nature conceived of. Thus the new factor takes its place side by side with the musical element. However, the romantic movement is not yet full-blown; a further most important development has yet to take place before it is time for the flower to drop and the fruit to appear. The early romanticists had no other means of satisfying their dramatic longings than that of illustrating other people's thoughts; Berlioz, though he invented his own programmes, yet invented them first in his character of dramatist, and illustrated them musically afterwards. It was left to Robert Schumann to take the final step, when, for the first time, the dramatic and musical ideas sprang simultaneously from the same mind. On the whole, the musician was paramount in Schumann's nature, and he was often content to illustrate the work of others; but from the first his music had a dramatic as well as a musical basis—that is to say, not that his music had two germs but that it had one germ of a composite nature.

This is the history of the romantic school—first one art influenced by another; then one art illustrating another, and finally the first glimmerings of a *new art* which combines the dramatic and musical art in one. After Schumann it was for ever impossible to call the new art 'music'; the dramatic element had to be recognized as of equal importance with the musical. To make the new art complete but one step was necessary—to transfer it to its proper home, the theatre—and this was done by Richard Wagner.

Wagner, then, is not a freak of nature standing outside the line of evolution, but he is the logical outcome of the romantic movement in music: in this way he dealt it its death blow, and out of the tentative gropings of Schumann evolved a new art—a subtle blend of music and drama—the whole being entirely distinct from either of its component parts. This is the first result of the romantic movement.

The second result is that no progressive musician can go on writing romantic music; that is over and done for, and the way has been cleared for pure music to resume its sway. The next musical pioneer after Wagner must be a man who will start again on the lines from which the romanticists broke away, and who will write pure music out of a purely musical heart—and who has done this if not Brahms, the first whole-hearted classical composer since Beethoven? True, there has been an interregnum, but that does not make Brahms a reactionary, it only means that he has waited his time.

Thus the problem is solved, and the position of affairs clearly defined. There are now two arts, the musical and the musico-dramatic, either of which a man can take up and be in the forward movement. The real reactionaries are those critics who applaud the performance of an opera in the concert-room as if it were a symphony, or attach a 'meaning' to a symphony as if it were an opera and needed a libretto of theirs; and among composers the real laggards are those who having the brains to write neither a symphony nor an opera are content to sit on the fence, and, under the high-sounding titles of 'symphonic-poem' and the like, to attempt to hide their ignorance both of music and of poetry.

The romantic school has lived its life and done its work, and has died an honourable death; to honour it truly is to let it rest in peace.

CHAPTER 2

A School of English Music

NOT VERY MANY years ago, as is well known, no English musician, as such, had a chance of success; he had either to change his name or his nature; so that all our performers were 'Signors', and all the products of our English composers were, in reality, imported from abroad, and suffered much dilution on the voyage. This state of affairs did not tend to annul the general verdict, that we were an unmusical nation. But of late years an energetic band of pioneers has sprung up, full of the noble idea of reviving the musical prestige which England once enjoyed. To them it seemed impossible that we were at the core unmusical. 'No unmusical nation', says a recent writer, 'could have produced 'Sumer is icumen in....' No unmusical nation could have filled its churches with the strength of Tallis or the sweetness of Farrant.' In fact, English music was not dead, but only dormant, and the question was, how to re-awaken it. Here the pioneers of the English school made a great mistake; they sought a panacea, and sought it abroad. This universal remedy was to be the 'folk-song'; on the continent its exploitation was in full swing. Russia had already exchanged the exotic languor of Field for the fresh exuberance of Glinka, while in Bohemia and Norway, Dvořák and Grieg were introducing to the drawing-room the musical phraseology of the cottage. But in England, there had

Source: *The Vocalist*, I/I (1902), 8.

been no national upheaval of song; the Reform Bill produced no peasant poet, nor did the Repeal of the Corn Laws bring in its train a Marseillaise; even the discovery of gold in Australia produced nothing more stirring than 'Cheer boys, cheer'. Nevertheless, the leaders of the English revival would have it that their remedy was applicable to every case; they did not perceive that to borrow one's scheme of national music from abroad is as bad as to have no national music at all.

We cannot but be grateful for the energy and true love of what is beautiful which has inspired the collectors of English country tunes. If it had not been for their care and labour we should have lost much that is beautiful; but new wine can not be put into old bottles, and it is surely doubtful if any good result will follow the extremely artificial course of setting before a composer music which is entirely foreign to his temperament, and which even the peasantry have long since ceased to sing. In truth, the nature of our national melody has been misunderstood—we are not unmusical, but insincere. A musician who wishes to say anything worth saying must first of all express himself—in fact, his music must be the natural utterance of his own natural emotions. These natural emotions need not necessarily be those of the peasant, for the rural element in national music is only one of many. The 'folk' music of Bohemia and of other countries is the music which is sung and played by the peasantry in those parts of the country which still remain primitive and unsophisticated; and it so happens that Dvořák (for instance) was born among these surroundings, so that 'folk' music was absolutely a part of his musical life, a language in which he speaks, naturally and unpremeditatedly. The list of great composers to whom the country song is the natural basis of expression is, however, extremely small, and if this is to be the test of nationality in music, then Beethoven is not German, Berlioz is not French, and Palestrina is not Italian. Moreover, Beethoven has made much use of Russian tunes, and Brahms has founded many movements entirely on Hungarian phraseology, but Beethoven and Brahms are, none the less, thoroughly German, and they are German for the reason that they use the natural speech of that state of society from which they spring. Now, English composers do not spring from the peasantry. Indeed, in England there are no true peasantry for them to spring from. Why, then, should an English composer attempt to found his style on the music of a class to which he does not belong, and which itself no longer exists?

Experience of the past is a warning to avoid artificiality. In former times, musical England came to grief by trying to be foreign; no less surely shall we now fail through trying to be English. It is useless to invent a style and then model individual utterances upon it. The national English style must be modelled on the personal style of English musicians. Until our composers will be content to write the music that they like best, without an ulterior thought, not till then shall we have a true school of English music.

CHAPTER 3

The Soporific Finale

WHY DOES EVERYONE go to sleep over the last movement? Why does a concert-room present such a spectacle of nodding heads during the finale of a symphony or quartet? It is not the soothing nature of the music, for most last movements are of the most vigorous and rousing kind. No; in truth, the last movement owes its narcotic nature to its position in the musical scheme; it fills no emotional niche, and satisfies no sentimental craving; its place in the symphonic scheme is purely decorative, and though it is an absolutely necessary part of that edifice, it seems not to have the same emotional importance as the other three movements. We have already had the solid, the humorous, and the sentimental—nothing remains but to say 'they lived happily ever after', or, in the words of Abt Vogler, 'My resting-place is found, the C major of this life; so, now I will try to—sleep'. And sleep it is, that comes to everyone, whether the child, to whom it is an intellectual feat to keep two notes in his mind, or the cultivated musician who can see the logic of the most abstruse movement without turning a hair.

The weakness is, in fact, purely physical; it cannot be overcome by any study, nor can a genuine interest in the music lessen it; it is the natural result of tiring the nerves by the repetition of similar sensations; a monotonous voice, the roaring of a

Source: *The Vocalist*, 1/1 (1902), 31.

train, and a surfeit of first-rate music, all produce the same result. Of course, last movements are, very often, failures compared to the rest of the work to which they belong, and this is so for the very reason which makes an audience unwilling to give them wakeful attention, namely, that the drama has already been enacted by the Allegro, Scherzo, and Adagio, leaving to the poor Finale the thankless task of lowering the curtain. Whether this difficult state of things affects the composition intrinsically or not, it certainly does affect the impression of the work on its hearers. So a composer must in his last movement take special pains to avoid monotony and special efforts to reclaim the wandering attention, efforts which in the earlier movements would have been not only unnecessary, but harmful. One may almost say that, unless the decorative scheme of the whole work demand it, the conventional 'steady-run-home' style of finale is an artistic mistake, insomuch as it makes demands on the hearer which he is by this time unfit to comply with.

Sometimes the difficulty may be solved by an undisguised appeal to the sensibilities, as in the Finale of the *Symphonie Pathétique* or by a series of short intellectual exercises, as is the case where the last movement takes the form of variations; but these two solutions only cover a few instances. In almost all cases the complete scheme seems to demand that very kind of movement which, if not carefully manipulated, produces the drowsiness which we wish to avoid, that is to say, the usual vigorous, swinging Allegro. In a movement like this no amount of thematic beauty or structural interest will serve to rivet the jaded attention of the listener; something stimulating, or even sensational, must break its even course. Beethoven understood this when, in the C minor Symphony, he dramatically arrested the vigorous march of the Finale to reintroduce the melody of the Scherzo. But usually this sensational awakening is reserved for that part of the movement where the attention is likely to be most wearied, that is to say, at the end. The ear, which has been deadened by the steady progress of vigorous and unemotional themes, must be suddenly arrested by something now. The most obvious way of doing this is to place a new tune in a new time actually at the end of the movement, as in Beethoven's Quartet, op. 95. However, it seems rather late in the day to introduce entirely new matter in the last twenty bars of a work. To avoid this, a more subtle device may be used, namely, to serve up the old material in a new and startling form, as in Brahms' Pianoforte Quintet, where the first subject of the last movement is introduced in the coda in an entirely new rhythm; or, if a composer would be still more subtle, he can imitate Schumann's Pianoforte Quintet, and reintroduce a subject out of the first movement in conjunction with those of the last.

These are a few of the devices which composers have used to ward off the fatal drowsiness. Those who think that it degrades the nature of musical inspiration to speak of it as a device, should remember that a composer writes what interests and excites himself, and that, therefore, to reduce to rule and line the methods by which an audience may be interested is only one way of guessing at the motives which led the composer to express himself as he did. The art of keeping an audience awake may not be the glory of the musical temple, but it is a foundation without which that temple could not exist.

CHAPTER 4

Good Taste

GOOD TASTE IS, without doubt, the stumbling block in the path of the 'Young English school of composers'. These 'rising young musicians' lack neither good teachers nor good models, nor good concerts, nor good opportunities of bringing their works to a hearing; nevertheless, all their promise seems to be nipped in the bud by the blighting influence of 'good taste'.

What is good taste? Is it a quality ever ascribed to a really great artist? Do we ever say of Beethoven or Mozart that their music is in good taste? And why is this? Because good taste is a purely artificial restriction which a composer imposes on himself when he imagines—rightly or wrongly—that his inspiration is not enough to guide him. A genius has no time to consider the claims of good taste; he is hurried blindly forward by the power of his own invention, and it is only when that fails he feels the absence of that prop on which the weak-kneed habitually stay themselves. What 'minor poet' among musicians would make such a fool of himself as to write the 'Battle of Vittoria'? What well-brought-up composer but would blush for shame to have thought of anything so vulgar as some of Schubert's tunes? Yet how much would they not give to have invented one bar of 'Erlkönig' or the A major Symphony [Beethoven's Seventh]?

Source: *The Vocalist*, 1/2 (1902), 38.

The truth is that the young Englishman is too musicianly. The 'musicianly' composer has studied the whole anatomy of inspiration, and has found out all the mechanical means by which beautiful music is produced. Equipped with this knowledge, he proceeds to build up compositions with yard-measure and plumb-line, quite forgetting that no man can make a living body out of dead clay unless he has first stolen some of the heavenly fire. Many a young composer has stifled his natural impulses in the desire to be musicianly. If he has elected to be 'romantic' he considers himself lost unless he crushes all his power of invention under an entanglement of trombones and bass tubas—and all because Wagner's special inspiration required special expression. If he favours the 'classical' school, he thinks it only becoming to make a show of exercising Brahms's self-restraint, without considering what a storehouse of invention Brahms possessed out of which to deny himself.

It has been said that education is what a man has learnt and forgotten. The musicianly musician is only half educated; he has learnt, but he has not forgotten.

'He that is froward let him be froward still.'

If a composer is naturally vulgar, let him be frank and write vulgar music instead of hedging himself about with an artificial barrier of good taste. If he is naturally trivial, let him not simulate a mock solemnity which is quite foreign to his nature. If every composer will be himself, his music will at all events be genuine. If it is of bad grain, no amount of veneer can alter its nature; if it is good oak it will not be improved by being made to look like mahogany.

Away, then, with good taste. Good taste is the heritage of critics, and a good critic is, proverbially, a bad composer. What we want in England is *real* music, even if it be only a music-hall song. Provided it possess real feeling and real life, it will be worth all the off-scourings of the classics in the world.

CHAPTER 5

A Sermon to Vocalists

A tenor is not a man but a disease.

—HANS VON BÜLOW

HANS VON BÜLOW was for many years an operatic conductor, and therefore suffered particular annoyance from tenors—otherwise he would probably have included every singer, whatever their compass, in his aphorism. Certainly the disease of singing is a very widespread one, and if it is really as dangerous and contagious a malady as many musicians think, then, in the interests of public safety, it is high time to invent some method of vaccination and to erect isolation hospitals. Now, what is the precise nature of the disease from which you, singers, suffer? The author of our text supplies us with the answer: 'When God wanted to create a fool,' writes von Bülow, 'he made him a tenor.'

So *foolishness* is the singer's disease.

Please do not be offended before you understand me. Singers may be, and often are, much cleverer than most people in the ordinary affairs of life; it is only when they come to singing, their especial talent, that they think it necessary to put

Source: *The Vocalist*, 1/8 (1902), 227–9.

off intelligence as a garment. In what other study is it imagined for a moment that brainlessness is a necessary qualification? In music even, in all other music than that of the vocalist, who is there who imagines that thought is not absolutely necessary, both to the performer and the listener? What about chamber concerts or pianoforte recitals—do people attend these in a state of mental quiescence? Or take the 'promenades', which emphatically appeal to the 'man in the street'—he would feel insulted if he were told to leave his mind with his overcoat in the cloak-room before he began to listen to the music. He may prefer light, brilliant, even sensational music; but whatever its nature, it must brace and stimulate his mental capacities, otherwise he will want to demand his money back; he must have fare set before him which is solid enough for him to mentally masticate.

How different is the case at a ballad concert, one of those orgies where the singer reigns supreme. Here the slightest trace of anything but the merely inane is at once ruled out of court. The music and the words provided at these entertainments vie with each other for the first prize in utter lack of meaning; even the lowest form of intelligent appreciation, that of the performer's technical dexterity, is absent here; what the average listener would not tolerate in instrumental music, what he would laugh at if it were recited in a theatre he accepts as an established fact, and applauds as an artistic feat at the hands of the singer.

Our forefathers used to distinguish 'music' from 'singing', and singers have done their best to make the distinction painfully correct. Music (so far as the human voice is concerned) consists of melody and rhythm. Now the typical 'royalty ballad' possesses neither melody nor rhythm. Melody—a real tune, must be vital and in-dividual; and individuality is just what the musical penny-ice-man abhors. He makes his poisonous sweetmeats out of old scraps. Phrases picked up here and there from the successful songs of former times, and hitched on to each other anyhow like the trucks of a goods train. The well-known phrases, so thinks the 'composer', will save the public trouble, and their haphazard arrangement will be all the easier for him. As to rhythm, a perfunctory arrangement of note-values suffices; as much like something else as possible. The accent of the words, which should be a guide to the music, is carefully disregarded—the unimportant words such as 'and' and 'to' are given whole bars to kick their heels in, while important sentences are over-crowded into a few quavers. Not that I blame the composer entirely for this; the singer will make short work of his efforts, good or bad. Minims, crotchets, rests, pauses, time, everything will go to the wall. The long notes will be cut short, short notes stretched to an excruciating length. Long rests will be hurried through, short rests will be made into enormous pauses—in fact, every factor antagonistic to rhythm, melody, sense, or beauty, if not already put in by the composer, will be added by the singer. This is the tribute which the modern ballad pays to melody and rhythm.

The words of these precious productions are worthy companions to the music. Most of them are only saved from blasphemy or indecency by being absolutely meaningless. Often a vicious and mechanical emotion is stirred by some verbal phrase such as 'When the city lights are low', or 'When the children are asleep'; or worse still, the author introduces some tag which he imagines is out of the Roman Liturgy—a device well-calculated to wring the withers of all those unacquainted with Latin.

Here follows a very fair specimen of the results which such tactics lead to:

The vesper hour

I stood in the old cathedral,
When the city lights were low,
And the children all were sleeping,
And my heart was aching so.
    Among the white-robed choir
    There rose a voice so clear;
    But he sang one note of sorrow,
    Which only Love could hear:

[To be sung to a slow valse.]
$\left\{\begin{array}{l}\text{\textit{Pax vobiscum,}}\\\text{\textit{Eheu fugaces,}}\\\text{\textit{Che sara, sara,}}\\\text{\textit{Gloria in excelsis.}}\end{array}\right.$

I solemnly declare that this verse is quite as good, if not better than the ordinary stuff provided by our purveyors of 'lyrics' to the trade. What should we say if our daily paper was a farrago of all the stale scandal of the last twenty years? What should we think if our friends' letters consisted of the mere commonplaces of polite correspondence? And what can we say of the unmusical music and illiterate verbiage of the modern ballad?

Amateur singers! I ask you in all seriousness, why do you sing such songs?

I am not appealing to professional singers, most of them are past praying for, the rest cannot help themselves. But amateur singers need only sing when they like, and what they like; therefore, if they fail to choose the good the guilt is entirely theirs, so again I ask, why do you sing such songs?

Someone may answer, 'I want to show off my voice.' What! is your voice such a wretched thing that it can only be shown off by pronouncing bad poetry to worse music? Surely, if this is the best use that the human voice can be put to, we had better leave off singing altogether. Besides this—what is 'showing off your voice'? Do you imagine that the effect of singing depends merely on the sort of sound you produce? Why, an average steam whistle makes a much greater noise than the best singer alive. The reason why a singer's voice is beautiful and a steam whistle is not, is that the voice can be made the medium of the best and deepest human emotion. The beauty of the singer's art is not a question of mere noise, it is a question of the human effort and human feelings which lie behind that noise. I was once at the rehearsal of some composition in which there were soli for soprano and tenor voices. The tenor soloist had been singing for some time when there was a pause in the rehearsal. When the music started again I happened to have my back to the performers. Suddenly I heard what I thought to be a thin, harsh, weak tenor note— as if the singer had all of a sudden caught a bad cold—but, on looking up, I found that it was the *soprano* singer tackling a note in the lowest part of her compass. At once the note sounded rich and full, coming as it did from a soprano; yet the sound was the same all through. What I had really admired or disliked was not the sound, but something which lay behind the sound. The human voice, as an instrument, is a very poor substitute for the violin or the clarionet—as a vehicle for human feeling it is unique.

Another singer may say: 'This is all very nice and ideal, but my object is to attract a large audience, and get good applause.' Very good; but in that case, why do you sing at all? You would gain much more applause from a far larger audience if you played the concertina with a string.

Or again—'I cannot sing anything difficult; I can only sing what I have heard other people sing.' You cannot? Then why not try? You will, I'll be bound, spare no pains to make yourself perfect at ping-pong; surely, it is at least equally worth while to overcome some of the elementary difficulties of a great art.

Then, perhaps, you always sing what you have heard the so-called 'great' singers sing. Well, in the first place, have these singers, at whose shrine you bow, in any way proved themselves to be really great artists? Perhaps they can sing higher, or lower, or louder than anyone else. In some cases, perhaps, they really have surprising natural beauty of voice. But is this a reason why you should imitate them? Is it not, rather, a reason why you should hiss and hoot at them, when, as is too often the case, they degrade and pervert their talent to gain cheap applause by meretricious trickery? Or worse still, when they betray their powers to the mercenary service of some impostor of a song-writer, or the commercial chicanery of a publisher. Do you really, in your innocence, imagine that 'great' singers always sing what they like best?—or that a 'royalty' ballad is so called because it is patronised by Royalty?

And lastly, we have the time-honoured complaint, 'I like something simple; I like something with a tune in it.' Why, so do I, and so does everyone but a fool! And these are just the qualities which we look for in vain in the lucubrations of our ballad-mongers. There is nothing in their work which can be dignified by the name of a tune, and their emotions are false, artificial, and vulgar, but emphatically not simple. I know that there is a great difficulty in getting good English songs; we seem to come to grief between the pedant and the confectioner. In Germany there are many beautiful and simple songs simply brimming over with tune. What song has a more distinct tune than Schubert's 'Sylvia'? And what can be simpler than Beethoven's 'Kennst du das Land'? The first of these, at all events, can be sung in English; and with regard to other German songs, it is my opinion that any singer ought to be able to make his audience appreciate a song in a foreign language, if a good translation is provided on the programme. But if you want a rich storehouse of national tune why do you not go to our own dazzling treasury of British folk-tunes. Here we find all those qualities which are so painfully absent from the 'ballad-concert' song—sincerity, depth of emotion, simplicity of expression, and, above all, beautiful melody. There is not a vocalist who could not learn to sing 'Barbara Allen', or 'Loch Lomond', or 'The arbutus tree', or 'All through the night', with a great deal more effect than the output of our ballad manufactories. What! Did I hear a sneer about 'old-fashioned' and 'countrified'? Does anyone dare to sneer at our one hope in the slough of despond—the one fact to which we can point and say, 'We are not an unmusical nation'? Let him take care that he has not, like the cock in the fable, kicked away the diamond to bury his beak in the mound of unspeakable refuse which to-day in England passes under the name of song.

Amateur singers! You are in a position of great responsibility. The British public is not unmusical; it is only undiscriminating. When you come on to the platform to sing to an audience you hold them at your mercy. The better your voice, the more telling your delivery, the more surely will you mesmerise your hearers, and rob them of all their critical faculties. You have only to open your mouth wide enough, and they will open theirs, and swallow any stuff you are pleased to hurl at them. But you yourselves are in no such position of suspended animation; you have learnt your songs, you have studied them calmly at home, you have had plenty of opportunity of serenely judging their merits. With you will lie the guilt, if you give your audience milk-and-water instead of wine, or poison instead of stimulating food.

I do not ask you to do anything difficult. I merely want you to ask of every song you propose to sing: Is it sincere or false? Is its tune individual, or is it mere resurrection-pie? Is the song a logical whole, or is it a series of cheap sensations? You may be going to sing an elaborate scena, or a modest ballad, or a comic song. The same test applies to all. What we want in music, as in everything else, is something alive, something genuine; not the shoddy imitation of a bad model.

CHAPTER 6

Preface to *The English Hymnal*

THE MUSIC OF this hymnal is divided into two main sections; the plainsong melodies and the comparatively modern music. The modern music only is dealt with here. The plainsong is discussed separately.

THE CHOICE OF MATERIAL

The music is intended to be essentially congregational in character, and this end has been kept in view both in the choice of tunes and in the manner of setting them out. Fine melody rather than the exploitation of a trained choir has been the criterion of selection: the pitch of each tune has been kept as low as is consistent with the character of the melody.

Where there is congregational singing it is important that familiar melodies should be employed, or at least those which have stood the test of time: therefore the 'specially composed tune'—that bane of many a hymnal—has been avoided as far as possible. There are already many hundreds of fine tunes in existence, so many indeed that it is impossible to include more than a small part of them in any one collection.

Source: (London: Henry Frowde, 1906), pp. x–xix.

The task of providing congregations with familiar tunes is difficult; for, unfortunately, many of the tunes of the present day which have become familiar and, probably merely from association, popular with congregations are quite unsuitable to their purpose. More often than not they are positively harmful to those who sing and hear them. The committee were therefore placed in the hard position of having to decide whether they should risk momentary unpopularity by discarding certain tunes, or whether they should sacrifice the greater ultimate good for the lesser and more immediate advantage. The problem, however, solved itself in a happy and unforeseen manner because the insertion of several of the tunes in question was not allowed by the owners of the copyright. Thus the committee, while regretting that they are not able for a few years to include such beautiful tunes as Dykes' 'Dominus regit me' or Stainer's 'In Memoriam', yet feel that nothing but gain can result from the exclusion of certain other tunes, which are worthy neither of the congregations who sing them, the occasions on which they are sung, nor the composers who wrote them.

The committee believe that many clergymen and organists are now realizing their responsibility in this matter, and will welcome a tune-book in which enervating tunes are reduced to a minimum. The usual argument in favour of bad music is that the fine tunes are doubtless 'musically correct', but that the people want 'something simple'. Now the expression 'musically correct' has no meaning; the only 'correct' music is that which is beautiful and noble. As for simplicity, what could be simpler than 'St Anne' or 'The Old Hundredth', and what could be finer?

It is indeed a moral rather than a musical issue. No doubt it requires a certain effort to tune oneself to the moral atmosphere implied by a fine melody; and it is far easier to dwell in the miasma of the languishing and sentimental hymn tunes which so often disfigure our services. Such poverty of heart may not be uncommon, but at least it should not be encouraged by those who direct the services of the Church; it ought no longer to be true anywhere that the most exalted moments of a churchgoer's week are associated with music that would not be tolerated in any place of secular entertainment.

There are, however, many who recognize this bad state of things, but are timid about removing old favourites. Those who have this fear should remember that most of our 'old favourites' are of very recent growth, dating at the earliest from the year 1861—a very short life for a hymn tune; also that it does not take more than a couple of years to make a tune which congregations like into an 'old favourite', and furthermore that it is not by any means necessarily bad music which is popular. The average congregation likes fine melody when it can get it, but it is apt to be undiscriminating, and will often take to bad melody when good is not forth-coming. Is it not worth while making a vigorous effort today for the sake of estab-lishing a good tradition? Especially should this be the case with children's hymns. Children at all events have no old association with any particular tune, and in-calculable good or harm may be done by the music which they sing in their most impressionable years.

An attempt has been made to set a minimum standard in the music selected for this work. This does not mean that austerity has been unduly sought, or that dif-ficult and colourless music has been preferred to that which is vigorous and bright. A tune has no more right to be dull than to be demoralizing. Indeed, anxiety to ensure the co-operation of the congregation may have caused the boundary to be occasionally overstepped, so that a few tunes have been retained which ought to have been rejected, but on this borderland individual tastes must necessarily differ, and the committee have done their best to select the most suitable tune for each hymn. To make the possibilities of selection wider, numerous cross-references have been given, which should be freely used, and a short appendix is added of alternative tunes to certain hymns for the use of those who do not agree with the choice of the musical editor.

THE MANNER OF PERFORMANCE

(a) Pitch. The pitch of all the tunes has been fixed as low as possible for the sake of mixed congregations. Except in the case of tunes with an extended compass the highest note is not above D or E♭. Some choirmasters may object to this on the ground that it places the hymns in the worst part of the boy-chorister's voice, and that it takes the basses and altos rather low. The obvious answer is that hymns are essentially for the congregation; the choir have their opportunity elsewhere, but in the hymn they must give way to the congregation, and it is a great mistake to suppose that the result will be inartistic. A large body of voices singing together makes a distinctly artistic effect, though that of each individual voice might be the opposite. And it may be added that a desire to parade a trained choir often accom-panies a debased musical taste.

Where a tune occurs twice in the book it is usually given in two different keys, and in one or two cases a higher version of certain well-known tunes is given in the appendix. If this is not sufficient it is always possible to transpose the tunes to a higher key. Where a tune is only given once it is obvious why it should be printed in a lower key. Such a key is particularly suitable for village churches where the organist is rarely able to transpose. On the other hand, in churches where it is desired to give the first consideration to a trained choir, the organist will certainly be competent to transpose at sight into the key desired.

(b) *Unison singing.* Every hymn is so arranged that it can be sung in unison accompanied by the organ. Certain verses are marked as being specially suitable for unison singing, and it is suggested that the first verse of most hymns should be sung in unison as well as all the doxologies. In any case the congregation must *always* sing the melody, and the *melody only.*

In these circumstances it has been thought advisable occasionally to introduce harmonizations (especially those of J. S. Bach) rather more elaborate than usual. These will no doubt add greatly to the beauty and the popularity of the tunes. If some choirs find them difficult the tunes can be sung in unison accompanied by the organ; the organist will find no difficulty in playing them, if they are taken at the proper speed. It is a great mistake to suppose that untrained musicians are insensible to fine harmony. They may not be able to analyse the effect, but there can be no doubt that a well-harmonized tune makes a more powerful appeal than one in which the harmonies are bad or unsuitable. Choirs would be much better occupied in learning these beautiful settings of Bach (which are not hard if practised a little) than in rehearsing vulgar anthems by indifferent composers.

(c) *Choir and people.* There are churches in which the experiment has been successfully tried of making choir and people sing some hymns antiphonally. By this means the people are given a distinct status in the services, and are encouraged to take an intelligent interest in the music they sing, while the eternal war between choir and congregation, each considering the other an unnecessary appendage to the services of the church, is done away with.

The congregation might be encouraged to sing and appreciate the finer melodies if a system of monthly congregational practices were held, at which the less known tunes could be made familiar in some such way as the following: The first two verses might be sung by the choir alone, or some body of singers with good voices who already knew the melody: at the third verse the congregation would be invited to join in, and would finally sing a verse unaided by the trained singers. A *hymn recital*, at which some of the less familiar hymns might be sung by the choir, would also be a pleasant variety from the Sunday evening organ recital.

(d) *Speed.* The present custom in English churches is to sing hymns much too fast. It is distressing to hear 'Nun Danket' or 'St Anne' raced through at about twice the proper speed. Metronome marks are added to each hymn, which, the editor believes, indicate the proper speed in a fairly large building with a congregation of average size. The speed indications should not be judged at the pianoforte.

Another painful experience is to hear an organist trying to play through a C.M. or L.M. tune[a] in absolutely strict time, regardless of the slight pauses which the congregation, with unconscious artistic insight, are inclined to make at the end of every line. Pauses have been marked wherever they should be made, and a sign ⟩ has also been extensively used to designate a very short break, less than the ordinary pause (⌢). Sometimes ⌢ and ⟩ are used together, signifying a pause as well as a complete break in the sound.

Some of the hymns are marked to be sung 'in free rhythm'. This direction is especially applicable to unmeasured tunes, but all hymn tunes should be sung more or less freely; at all events a stiff clock-work rendering should be avoided. If this is borne in mind, and the hymns are not sung too fast, the bad effect will be largely avoided of those false accents which inevitably occur when several verses of a hymn are sung to the same tune.

(e) Expression. Expression marks have been altogether omitted, as it is considered that subtleties of expression are entirely unsuitable for congregational singing. The organist can use his own judgement as to the general dynamics of each verse, and convey his idea to the congregation by his registering. All sudden 'pianos' or small 'crescendos' and 'diminuendos' should be avoided as destroying the broad and massive effect which congregational singing should convey.

(f) Notation. Both minims and crotchets have been employed, the former for the slower and more solemn hymns and the latter for those of a brighter nature. The point of division has been fixed at M. 85 for hymns in duple time, and 100 in triple time in the more ordinary hymns, but special rules have been framed to govern special cases.

Sources of the Melodies

No particular country, period, or school has been exclusively drawn upon to supply material, but an attempt has been made to include the best specimens of every style. In settling the form which each melody shall take, no rules have been made, but each case has been decided on its merits. The object has been to print the finest

---

[a] CM is 'common metre', LM is 'long metre', referring to the number of syllables per line throughout a verse. A verse in CM has the following number of syllables per line: 8,6,8,6; LM follows the pattern 8,8,8,8.

version of every tune, not necessarily the earliest. Thus the later forms of 'Wachet Auf', 'Nun Danket', and 'London New', to give a few examples, have been preferred to the originals. But the old method of mutilating tunes to suit new metres has been as far as possible avoided—only in one or two cases have a composer's rhythms been very slightly adapted, and then for some very special purpose. In cases where such a slight adaptation from a composer's rhythm is made the general outline is never destroyed, so that the original can at any time be restored without disturbing a congregation. But adaptations already made have been occasionally retained when the result is a fine and popular tune: thus 'Dix', 'Narenza', and 'Ravenshaw' have not been discarded, though the fact of their adaptation is duly acknowledged. On the other hand the committee are glad to be able to restore the true metres of such tunes as 'Innsbruck', 'Weimar', or 'Les commandemens', which have been disfigured into dullness in so many hymnals.

The original rhythms of many of the old psalter tunes have also been restored, especially the long initial on the first syllable, which gives such a broad and dignified effect to these tunes. Attempts to adapt them to the procrustean bed of the nineteenth-century hymn tune have merely taken away their character and made them appear dull. For the same reason no attempt has been made to square the irregular times of some tunes. These irregularities are always easy to sing by ear—and this is the way in which a hymn melody should be learnt—so that choirmasters should not let the fear of what may appear to be irregular deter them from using many splendid and essentially congregational melodies.

The following classification shows the chief sources from which the tunes come:

A. GERMAN. (1) Lutheran chorale tunes sixteenth and seventeenth centuries. (2) Tunes from the sixteenth and seventeenth century Catholic song books (chiefly Leisentritt's, 1567, and the Andernach *Gesangbuch*, 1608). (3) Tunes of the eighteenth century, chiefly by Bach and Freylinghausen. (4) Modern German tunes. (5) German traditional melodies.

B. FRENCH AND SWISS. (1) Tunes from the Genevan Psalters of the sixteenth century. (2) Ecclesiastical melodies from the *paroissiens* of various French uses (chiefly those of Rouen and Angers). (3) French and Swiss traditional melodies.

C. ITALIAN, SPANISH, FLEMISH, DUTCH. Ecclesiastical, traditional, and other melodies from these countries are also included.

D. AMERICAN. Among American tunes may be mentioned Lowell Mason's tunes, certain tunes from 'Sacred Songs and Solos', and a few 'Western melodies' in use in America as hymn tunes.

E. BRITISH ISLES.

I. *Ireland.* (1) Irish traditional melodies. (2) Tunes by Irish composers.

II. *Scotland.* (1) Melodies from the Scottish Psalters of the sixteenth and seventeenth centuries. (2) Melodies from the Scottish tune-books of the eighteenth and nineteenth centuries. (3) Scottish traditional melodies.

III. *Wales.* (1) Archdeacon Prys' Psalter, which contains the famous tune 'St. Mary'. (2) Welsh traditional melodies. (3) Tunes by eighteenth and nineteenth century Welsh composers, which partake decidedly of the nature of their traditional melodies.

IV. *England.* (1) Tunes from Day's, Damon's, Este's, Ravenscroft's, and Playford's Psalters of the sixteenth and seventeenth centuries (the original versions of these, with the melody in the tenor, are occasionally included as alternatives to the modern version). (2) Tunes by Tallis, Gibbons, Lawes, etc., from their own collections. (3) Tunes from eighteenth century books—especially those by J. Clark and Dr Croft. (4) English carol, and other traditional melodies. (5) Tunes by nineteenth and twentieth century composers.

CHAPTER 7

Who Wants the English Composer?

Come Muse migrate from Greece and Ionia,
Cross out please those immensely over-paid accounts,
That matter of Troy and Achilles' wrath, and Æneas', Odysseus' wanderings,
Placard 'Removed' and 'To Let' on the rocks of your snowy Parnassus,
Repeat at Jerusalem, place the notice high on Jaffa's gate and on Mount Moriah,
The same on the walls of your German, French and Spanish castles, and
    Italian collections,
For know a better, fresher, busier sphere, a wide untried domain awaits,
    demands you.

—WALT WHITMAN, *'Song of the Exposition', lines 15–21*

IT IS REPORTED that the head of a famous publishing firm once said, 'Why do you young Englishmen go on composing? Nobody wants you.'

Is not this what we all feel in our secret souls at times? Nobody wants the young English composer; he is unappreciated at home and unknown abroad. And, indeed, the composer who is not wanted in England can hardly desire to be known

Source: *Royal College of Music Magazine*, 9/1 (1912), 11–15.

abroad, for though his appeal should be in the long run universal, art, like charity, should begin at home. If it is to be of any value it must grow out of the very life of himself, the community in which he lives, the nation to which he belongs.

Is it perhaps this misunderstanding of the very essence of the vitality of any art which makes the English composer a drug in the market? We are too fond in England of looking on music as a matter of detached appreciation. The English amateur believes with Rossini that there are only two kinds of music—good and bad—and if he can afford it, he prefers to import, together with the best brands of cigars and champagne, the best brands of music also. The connexion between music and every-day life is entirely severed.

Now, in no other art except music is this connexion doubted. No one with any pretence to culture would fail to keep abreast with all that his fellow-countrymen were saying in literature, painting, or drama. Such a man may well say, 'I think Velasquez a greater painter than Augustus John, Goethe a greater poet than Masefield, and Dostoievsky a greater novelist than Arnold Bennett,' yet he would know that unless he had seen and read the pictures, poems, novels, or plays of his contemporaries, he would lose one of the surest means of realizing what he himself was dimly and inarticulately feeling and thinking, and that the temper of the age was in danger of passing over him, leaving him untouched and unready.

And yet music, the subtlest, most sensitive, and purest means of self-expression, is supposed to be on a plane by itself, a thing detached from its sur-roundings, a mere sensation to be enjoyed by the epicure. Thus it comes about that the cultured amateur says to the composer, 'What have you to offer me better than the great Masters? I have my Bach, my Beethoven, my Brahms. They are enough to satisfy me; or can you show me more subtle harmonies than Debussy, more striking orchestral effects than Strauss? If not, why should I bore myself by listening to you or trying to play you?' And the amateur, judged by his own standard, is perfectly right. The English composer is not and for many generations will not be anything like so good as the great Masters, nor can he do such wonderful things as Strauss and Debussy. But is he for this reason of no value to the community? Is it not possible that he has something to say to his own countrymen that no one of any other age and any other country can say? When English people realize this—that the composer is their own voice speaking through his art those things which they can only dimly grope for—then indeed the English composer will be wanted, if only he is ready.

But is the English composer ready? Does he keep his part of the bargain? The composer on his side is much too apt to look on his art from an aloof and detached point of view, to think of composition as a series of clever tricks which can be learnt and imitated. The desire to 'do it too' whenever the newest thing comes over from abroad is very strong with us all. So long then as our composers are content to write operas which only equal Wagner in length, symphonies made up of scraps of Brahms at his dullest, or pianoforte pieces which are merely crumbs from Debussy's table, we can hardly blame the amateur for preferring the genuine article to the shoddy imitation.

We English composers are always saying, 'Here are Wagner, Brahms, Grieg, Tchaikovsky, what fine fellows they are, let us try and do something like this at home,' quite forgetting that the result will not sound at all like 'this' when transplanted from its natural soil. It is all very well to catch at the prophet's robe, but the mantle of Elijah is apt, like all second-hand clothing, to prove the worst of misfits. We must be our own tailors, we must cut out for ourselves, try on for ourselves, and finally wear our own home-made garments, which, even if they are homely and home-spun, will at all events fit our bodies and keep them warm; otherwise, if we pick about among great ideas of foreign composers and try to cover our own nakedness with them, we are in danger of being the musical counterparts of the savage clothed in nothing but a top-hat and a string of beads.

How is the composer to find himself? How is he to stimulate his imagination in a way which will lead to his voicing the sentiments of himself and his fellows? I need hardly at this time of day point to the folk-song as a worthy study to all musicians, the germ from which all musical developments ultimately spring. But are there not other incentives for inspiration, imperfect perhaps and overlaid with dross, but pregnant with meaning to those who have ears to hear? Must not any genuine and unforced musical expression be full of suggestion to the musical inventor?

Our composers are much too fond of going to concerts. There they hear the finished product; what the artist should be concerned with is the raw material. Have not we all about us forms of musical expression which we can take and purify and raise to the level of great art? For instance, the lilt of the chorus at a music-hall joining in a popular song, the children dancing to a barrel organ, the rousing fervour of a Salvation Army hymn, St Paul's and a great choir singing in one of its festivals, the Welshmen striking up one of their own hymns whenever they win a goal at the international football match, the cries of the street pedlars, the factory girls singing their sentimental songs? Have all these nothing to say to us? Have we not in England occasions crying out for music? Do not all our great pageants of human beings, whether they take the form of a coronation or a syndicalist demonstration, require music for their full expression? We must cultivate a sense of musical citizenship; why should not the musician be the servant of the State and build national monuments like the painter, the writer, or the architect?

Art for art's sake has never flourished in England. We are often called inartistic because our art is unconscious. Our drama and poetry, like our laws and our constitution, have evolved by accident while we thought we were doing something else, and so it will be with music. The composer must not shut himself up and think about art, he must live with his fellows and make his art an expression of the whole life of the community—if we seek for art we shall not find it.

Modern music is in a state of ferment. Composers all the world over are trying new paths, new experiments. This you may say will not produce great composers: perhaps not at first. There are hardly any great composers, but there can be many sincere composers. There is nothing in the world worse than sham good music. There is no form of insincerity more subtle than that which is coupled with great earnestness of purpose and determination to do only the best and the highest—this unconscious insincerity which leads us to build up great designs which we cannot fill and to simulate emotions which we can only feel vicariously.

If we look back into the history of music we find a state of things almost exactly parallel to that of our own times: the musical revolution of the seventeenth century. Here we have the same ferment, the same striking out of new paths and new experiments. Here also we find an absence of great names. But this ferment, this age of experiments, made possible in time the advent of Johann Sebastian Bach. It was not his musical ancestry only that made it possible for Bach to be a great composer; the social conditions which immediately preceded him are also partly responsible for him. He was the last of a race of musicians who started humbly enough, but gradually rose to occupy the very highest musical posts amongst their fellow-townsmen. It was the sense of musical citizenship which produced them; they served the community as composers, as organists, as 'town pipers', and it was out of this musical environment that there came at last the greatest of all musicians.

Perhaps the future has another Bach in store for us and perhaps he will be an Englishman, but if that is to be so we must prepare the way for him.

CHAPTER 8

British Music

THE FOUNDATIONS OF A NATIONAL ART

A work of art, if it is to have strength and vitality—in short, if it is to have any value, must grow out of the character of its inventor. It must be the outcome of the desire for self-expression on the part of some person or group of persons, otherwise it means nothing either to those who make it or those who hear, see, or read it.

A nation is made up of individuals bound together by ties of race, of domestic relationships, of common laws, customs, institutions and sympathies; and just as a particular work of art must represent an individual, so the art of a nation as a whole must represent that nation.

If an art is to live it must spring direct from the life and character of the people where it had its origin. No art has any strength or life which is imported from without and planted down on a community from the outside. The strength of German, French, Italian, or Russian music is the result of this close bond between a people and its art; the weakness of English music (where it has been weak) has been caused by a spirit of musical aloofness or divorce between the art of music and the people by whom and for whom it is made. We are too often led away by that

Source: *The Music Student*, 7/1–4 (1914), 5–7, 25–7, 47–8, 63–4. This article is described in the source as 'Course no. 1 of the Home Music Study Union'.

entirely false aphorism of Rossini: 'I know only two kinds of music, good and bad,' forgetting that, for example, the gay-hearted tunes of Schubert are absolutely at one with the valses and coachman's songs of Vienna, that the innocent sentimentalism of Schumann is the exact counterpart of the romanticism of the German student of 1810, and that it is this bond of union which gives these composers their strength—which in fact has enabled them to write 'good music'.

Houses Fit to Live In

The English composer will not make his music good by covering his own art with the shell of Brahms' Teutonism, Tchaikovsky's Slavism, or Debussy's Gallicism, and forgetting about the kernel. A house is meant to be lived in; it must be planned to suit the class of people who are to inhabit it, the climate of the country where it stands, the kind of life that will be lived in it. The great palaces and narrow tall streets of Venice are no more possible among the mountains of Switzerland than is a Swiss chalet on the shores of the Adriatic.

Arnold Bennett has truly pointed out that the real artistic greatness of America lies not in the pseudo-Florentine palaces of its millionaires, filled with pillage from Italian picture galleries, but in her 'sky scrapers' and railway stations. So it should be with English music; it must be built up on the spontaneous expression of our own natures, and that expression will finally evolve a great architectural form in which to enclose itself.

We shall not evolve great music by trying to fit our home-made ideas to foreign forms. The nobility of Beethoven, the passionate utterance of Verdi, grew out of their own nationality. We have to build houses which inside and outside are houses fit for us to live in.

How are we to find the national character? What is its simplest, most spontaneous and most undoubted manifestation?

Before we can answer this we must put ourselves a wider question—What is the ultimate sanction of all music? On what foundation does our musical edifice stand? What reason can we give for our artistic canons? Is music a mere set of tricks, devices, rules, or is it something inborn in human nature? This, surely, is a question which everyone who is at all inclined to music must settle in his own mind before he begins to consider it seriously.

Innate Music

And the answer seems to me to be this: If we can find a man naturally and spontaneously expressing himself musically, and if that expression contains the seeds of what we believe to be musical beauty, whether of form or expression, then we can feel sure that music as we have developed it is something which is necessary to our being, that it is a serious factor in our life. It will be necessary for this supposed man to be removed by circumstances from all extraneous and factitious influences, so that we can be sure that his self-expression is genuine and spontaneous. To achieve this he must be unlettered (this is not the same as illiterate), un-travelled; he must live among those to whom his expression would be intelligible—that is to say, he must live in a homogeneous community.

If we had no evidence that this kind of music ever had existed, we should still have to presuppose it before we could account for the existence of music at all; just as astronomers have imagined a planet which they could not see to account for the movements of those which they already knew; and, just as astronomers have been justified by time, and the telescope eventually discovers in fact the planet which had before only existed in theory. So in music, fact agrees with theory, and in the folk-song we find our ultimate justification.

In studying the musical development of our own country we must start with its simplest and most undoubtedly genuine manifestation—our own folk-songs. Have we any folk-songs? If so are they beautiful? Do they provide a groundwork which makes it likely that we can build up a musical edifice of our own?

In the face of recent discoveries in folk-songs it seems absurd to ask such questions, but there are still people who answer them in the negative. These people should remember that it is not a question lightly to be dismissed. If we have no folk-songs, or if they have none of the qualities which I have mentioned, it must mean that music is to us not a natural means of expression, in which case we had much better stick to football and let music in England remain an expensive exotic.

Songs of the People

But we have in our folk-songs conclusive evidence to most thinking people that this is not so. The importance of folk-song from the musical point of view is almost universally misunderstood. How often is a lecture or article on folk-songs referred to as being about 'old songs', or worse still 'folk-lore songs', as if their only value was their 'quaintness' or supposed antiquity.

Our folk-song, like our language, is neither new nor old. They are both of communal, not individual origin—they are both of immemorial antiquity and both are means of expression today just as they were 500 years ago. In our native song just as in our native speech the form gradually changes with the changing needs of the community. Our language and our song are like an old tree, continually putting out new leaves.

We often hear it said of a folk-song, 'That cannot be an old tune, it sounds like the eighteenth or nineteenth century.' But why should not a folk-song spring into being in the eighteenth, the nineteenth, or even the twentieth century? And a folk-song which appears to have marks of the eighteenth or nineteenth century about it may always be a development from a much older source.

It does not follow that because we have evidence that a tune was being sung in mediæval times that it is 'older' than some other which the collector only found yesterday; both tunes are equally old or equally new. The *Agincourt Song*, for example, was sung in the 15th century, but *Died for Love*, which is obviously a variant of the same theme was sung in Lincolnshire only five or six years ago, and has been found capable of being fitted with very modern and very appropriate harmonies by Percy Grainger.

I am far from suggesting that a 'national style' can be mechanically made by sandwiching in scraps of English folk-song between slices of Brahms, Debussy, or Scriabine, according to taste; but to most English musicians the recent discoveries in their native folk-song have come as a revelation and an inspiration; they have taken to them as to a well-known but long-forgotten friend.

Our music, then, if it is to live, must represent the people; folk-song is not the only people's music, though it is the most perfect and the most beautiful form. Besides the music made by the people there is also the music made for the people— our music-hall tunes, our popular revivalist hymns; they are often vulgar or silly, but they do represent a form of unadulterated musical expression, and this desire for expression might be satisfied in a greater and nobler way by some musician who could purge away the dross and discover the fine gold underneath.

In the great periods of English music it has been part of the nation's life. The centuries which produced John Dunstable, acknowledged by his contemporaries to be the greatest musician of his time, was also the time when the English were pre-eminent by their partiality for 'carolling'. In the golden age of the English madrigalists it was possible for Morley to picture the musical amateur who was ashamed because he could not read his music at sight when the part-books were given round after supper. The age of Purcell was also the time of the innumerable editions of *The Dancing Master*.

Classical VERSUS Popular

And the reason why 'English Music' is nowadays considered negligible by so many writers is that we have separated our music from our nationality. 'Classical' music is considered to be a foreign luxury imported from abroad with our champagne and our cigars for those who have the money to afford it and the taste to appreciate it. We must break down the distinction between 'classical' and 'popular'—all music should be classical and all music should be popular. If we can give up that nervous apprehension about what other people are thinking of us and can be content to make our own music for our own people, then we shall earn for our music the respect of others and regain the proud position we held in the days of John Dunstable.

British Music in the Tudor Period

Only once in its musical history has England had a school of composers. It has had great men who appeared and disappeared like meteors and left no trace behind (Dunstable, Purcell, Wesley), but a great composer may appear in a barren land as a sport of Nature: a *school* of composers implies a nation saturated through and through with music. Such schools have been the great Bach family, the Viennese school of Haydn, Mozart, Beethoven, and Schubert, and perhaps the most striking as a group of kindred minds all united in one purpose—as undistinguishable as a school of early Italian painters or Elizabethan poets—is the modern school of Russian 'Nationalists'. These schools do not necessarily contain any very great names (the great composers are often meteoric) and it is to be noticed that when a great man appears as the member of a school (in music at all events) he ends it, he does not start it. No great composer has started a school—'Wagnerites', 'Brahmsites', 'Debussyites', are mere hangers on. The great men sum up all that has gone before and leave the field clear for a fresh start.

Only once then has England boasted a 'school' of composers (unless indeed one is forming now)—in the Tudor Period. No name stands out pre-eminently in the Tudor group. We think rather of the names, Byrd, Tallis, Wilbye, Weelkes, Farrant, Morley, Dowland, Gibbons, as forming one great personality, a sign that music was part of the national life.

In any age the type of people to whom music appeals largely settles the kind of music which composers will write. The age of great and powerful patrons produced great symphonies, colossal masses, and elaborate sonatas. If music is the exclusive privilege of a wealthy class who can pay to have it composed and performed, then there will be a period of insipid and gorgeously mounted operas, difficult concertos, and a general show-off for the virtuoso. But when music is a national possession, when people want music for their churches, for their homes, when they want to produce their own art and not to pay others to make it for them, then is the age (as it was in Tudor times) of the anthem, the madrigal, music for choral singing on a small scale, music for the lute or the virginals.

There are three causes to which may be assigned the sudden flowering of music in England in the sixteenth century:

(1) The new religious spirit, of which the official recognition was the reformed church, and which shows itself in a more spiritual fashion in our treasury of Tudor church music.

(2) The belated effects of the Renaissance, of which we see the results in the secular madrigal.

(3) The gradual approximation of the music of the learned scholars and the music of the people, of which we have evidence in the delight that the virginal composers of that time evidently took in their national folk-songs.

Church Music—Tudor and Present Day

It is a commonplace of English musical history to call the Tudor the 'great' period of English church music; and having paid that necessary homage we are usually content to let the matter drop. We treat our great church composers just as we treat our great poets or dramatists, as a just cause for patriotic pride, otherwise to be laid on the shelf and left to foreigners to keep alive. We talk glibly of Byrd, Tallis, Farrant and Gibbons, but what do we know of their work? Even Tallis's wonderful responses we know only in a bowdlerised four-part version, and as to his litany I do not know of a single cathedral or church where it is sung.[1]

Byrd we know by one anthem, *Bow thine ear*, and a few masses and motets by him have been made accessible through the efforts of Dr Terry, Mr Barclay Squire, and others; but the large bulk lies buried in the British Museum and our cathedral libraries. Of our other great church musicians much the same may be said; and what have we to replace them? Tawdry anthems and melodramatic Te Deums by indifferent modern composers—music which we would not tolerate anywhere but in church.

Our church music gives us a good example of our attitude of detachment toward the art as a whole: do musical people never go to church? Or do they think it fitting that what, presumably, they consider their most exalted moments, should be associated with music which they would not stand from a third-rate pier band? Or do they fail altogether to realise that music if it means anything to them at all is intimately bound up with their whole life?

It is, of course, possible that the present state of religious feeling is really adequately represented by the trash which we usually hear in church; that the great

[1] I hope that such exist, and that this is only my ignorance.

art of Tallis and Byrd connotes an exaltation of mind of which we are not capable: but surely this is hardly a plea which can be put forward by those who are responsible for our church services!

It is sometimes urged that our church music should be brought 'up-to-date'. Well, most of our so-called modern church music is not 'up-to-date' (whatever advantage there may be in that), but lags along about thirty years behind the times. It may be possible to represent the religious spirit in the musical style of the moment, but this is quite a different thing from giving us belated imitations of Gounod's *Messe Solenelle*.

Have we, however, brought our liturgy or our cathedrals 'up-to-date'? Have we re-written the Bible and the Prayer Book in the style of the *Daily Mail* or rebuilt Westminster Abbey to look like a public-house? We realise that our liturgy demands something removed from our everyday goings-on: we realise it in everything except our music.

A form of church music which sprang into being with reformed religion was the metrical psalm and hymn-tune. It was necessary that a popular form of religion should be accompanied by a popular form of musical expression. Needless to say most of the beautiful psalm tunes of the period are now utterly neglected. Of Tallis's ten hymn tunes only two of the least interesting are known; of those by Orlando Gibbons only two are found in most modern hymnals, and those mutilated almost beyond recognition. Other collections have been more fortunate, some of the beautiful tunes, *Cheshire, Windsor* and others, first made their appearance in Day's, Este's, Damon's, and Ravenscroft's 'psalters'.

Madrigal Writers

It is in the work of the English madrigalists that we first find a sense of style in music. The secular and church music of most of the older Flemish and Italian composers is undistinguishable; but no one could possibly mistake Morley's *Ballets* or Dowland's *Ayres* for church music. The English madrigal writers have always a great sense of tune; even such a purely contrapuntal madrigal as *The Silver Swan* has a distinct melodic outline which admirably suits the intimacy of the madrigal, but would be quite out of place in the aloof grandeur of ecclesiastical music.

It is one of those fallacies which die hard that a choral harmonised melody is a modern degradation—something beneath the dignity of the great madrigal writers. It is enough to look at Morley's *Ballets* (*My Bonny Lass*, for example) to disprove this; and as to Dowland's *Ayres*, he wrote them deliberately in two ways, either as choral music or for a solo voice accompanied by the lute. The truth is that the influence of the 'Monodic' school was already making itself felt in England even while the madrigal was at its zenith. Indeed the Tudor period, musically speaking, lasted well into what, dynastically, are Stuart times, and long after Italy had lost the glories of her choral art, and was making crude experiments in opera, the English madrigal school was in the height of its glory, its last great representative, Orlando Gibbons, combining in his art the melodic expressiveness of the new with the contrapuntal fervour of the old.

Folk Influence

There is a theory extant that in Elizabethan times there was a 'folk' revival (or rather evolution) similar to that which is taking place in England now. It is certain that at this time such purely popular pastimes as the morris dance and May Day festival obtained aristocratic and even royal patronage; doubtless, as in our day, the 'move- ment' was perverted by the sentimental rich (who probably talked glibly about bringing Life and Joy to the working classes); at all events this Elizabethan revival has left to us an entirely false tradition as to the real nature of these festivities.

However this may have been, it is evident that Elizabethan composers and their public were well acquainted with English folk-song. The lute and virginal compositions of the time are full of arrangements of folk-songs, chiefly in the form of variations. The most important of these is the *Fitzwilliam* virginal book, in which we find arrangements of such tunes as *John, come kiss me now, My Robin is to the green wood gone, Walsingham*, and *Go from my window*, by John Bull, Dowland, Farnaby, Byrd and other composers. It should be noticed, however, that the folk- tune most generally connected with Elizabethan tunes, *Greensleeves*, is known to us through an arrangement in Ballet's *Lute Book*.

THE AGE OF PURCELL

Our judgments vary with the course of years. The giants of one age become the pigmies of the next. Wagner, once described as a dangerous revolutionary, later on became a popular hero, and is now, so it is whispered, looked upon by the very youngest generation as slightly 'passé'.

As our judgments of contemporary composers change with time so do our ideas about the music and musicians of past generations. The early and middle seventeenth century used a few years ago to be officially pronounced nothing more than a period of preparation for Handel and Bach—an age of interesting but crude experiments, of great value to the historian but intrinsically of little musical value. Schütz, Monteverde, and Lully were looked upon as fit subjects for the study, but not for the concert room. A few bars from one or another composer in a musical dictionary or historical lecture was sufficient just to show the curious that there was nothing new under the sun, and that Berlioz or Wagner had been anticipated in one of their pet inventions. These seventeenth-century musicians were the Cabots, the Wallaces, the Daguerres of music—pioneers but nothing more.

A Tardy Appreciation

Our own Henry Purcell was among those to whom the nineteenth century extended their patronising encouragement, 'Very good for one so young.' He, like his contemporaries, was called an anachronism, he was before his time, he made interesting experiments and all the rest of it; but it was always believed that he was not a musician whose works we need nowadays seriously consider from the point of view of performance.

Of late years, however, a change has come over musical opinion. For one thing musicians have become rather less ignorant of Purcell's music; they have something more to judge him by than a couple of bars in a musical dictionary. During the last twenty years *Dido and Aeneas* has had several stage performances. The *Masque of Love* has been played on the stage more than once (the most notable production being that by Mr Gordon Craig about ten years ago). *King Arthur* is becoming a favourite with choral societies, and now, at last, Purcell's most beautiful work, *The Fairy Queen*, has been rescued from the recesses of a library, has already been given in concert form, and will receive its first stage production (since Purcell's own day) at Cambridge next December.

The Purcell Society has now almost completed its labours of printing the whole work of our great national composer, so we have at last an opportunity of really discovering what he was. Surely there can be no doubt that the composer of Dido's Lament, the anthem *My beloved spake*, or the masque of the seasons from *The Fairy Queen*, is not only our greatest English composer, but one of the greatest composers the world has ever seen. True, his resources were more limited than those of Bach, as Bach's were than those of Beethoven, or those of Beethoven than those of Wagner. But the greatness of music does not depend, like the efficiency of a motor car, on the number of mechanical appliances at its command; if that were so the latest student at the newest conservatoire would be the greatest composer of all. The great composer finds an exact mean between his inspiration and the means at his disposal. Some composers have had more means than ideas, some more ideas than means; Purcell, unlike either of these, was complete master of his means, a true representative of his own age and his own country.

Co-operation of the Verbal and Musical

Purcell cannot be said to have founded or completed a school of composers, yet we find around him a small group of musicians all inspired by the same ideas.

First in point of time comes Henry Lawes, who on no less an authority than Milton was the first to be musically inspired directly by the rise and fall of English prosody.

Nationality in music, it need hardly be said, shows itself most strongly in the musical setting of words. Verbal and musical forms must run exactly parallel if the musical setting is to have any value. If a German or Italian phrase is set with due regard to accent, stress and expression, the music can hardly fail to be of a German or Italian character.

It is one of the evil results of the foreign domination of English music that our composers have got into the habit of trying to screw English words on to foreign music-forms instead of letting the words suggest their own inevitable music. For this the carelessness of our audiences is partly to blame; their ears have been dulled by the hopeless jumble of words, by the carefully misplaced accents and stresses of the English translations of such works as *The Creation, The Seasons, The Spectre's Bride*, and other choral society compositions. To take one example (and by no means the worst). Anyone who has tried to teach a country choral society Haydn's *Spring* knows the difficulty they have in catching the rhythm at the words 'God of light' in the last chorus; all credit to them that it should be so. The original German word here is *Mächtiger* a word which it would be hard to sing in any *other* rhythm than that which Haydn has given it. But it is against human nature to sing the heavily stressed word 'light' on the last beat of the bar.

It is one of the causes which made Purcell so essentially an English composer that he (having learnt well the lesson of Henry Lawes) made such a happy marriage of words and music, both as regards accent, stress, rhythm and feeling. In this art of what Mr Forsyth so aptly calls 'song-speech'[2] Purcell is supreme, and so far as England is concerned we have to look far ahead to a composer of a very different calibre for a parallel. It is found in the light operas of Arthur Sullivan.

A National and Individual Art

Next in our little group come three composers, the immediate predecessors, almost the conporaries of Purcell—Pelham Humfrey, John Blow, and Michael Wise. We all know the passage in Pepys in which he describes Humfrey's return from France 'an

[2] Cecil Forsyth, *Music and Nationalism* ([London:] Macmillan, [1911]).

absolute Monsieur',[a] and we must recognise how much these composers and after them Purcell, our most distinctively English composer, learnt from the French. From this we too can learn a lesson. Our nationalism must be positive, not negative. We shall not make our music individual by refusing to learn what the great musicians of any age or country have to teach us. We all know the type of music which is 'un-Wagnerian' or 'un-Brahmsy' only in so far that having started with Brahms or Wagner it collapses half way. Music to be individual must be so from its first impulse. That granted, the composer can take as many hints as he likes from the outside without impairing his originality. We must be the masters of our art, not its slaves.

Other Stuart Composers

Three more names complete our group of Stuart musicians of note.

One is Jeremiah Clarke, who wrote some of our finest hymn tunes (notably *St. Magnus* and *Uffingham*).

The second is Matthew Locke, the composer of the delightful music to *Macbeth*.

And the third is not a composer at all, but a publisher, John Playford! He published books on music, collections of songs, a psalter, and above all *The Dancing Master*.

It is difficult to classify the tunes in the *Dancing Master;* some of them (*Newcastle* and *The Irish Trot* for example) are doubtless folk-tunes; some (such as *The 29th of May*) are popular tunes of the day arranged for dancing purposes; some of them may well have been composed by Purcell himself or his contemporaries.

An Age of Music and Dancing

Whoever composed these tunes, it is they which give us the clue to Purcell, for they prove that Purcell lived in a country and age which was, artistically speaking, given over to dancing delightful dances to delightful music. We all know the story of how Haydn recognised one of his own minuets being played in a tavern in Vienna; the same might easily have happened to Purcell—witness the *Harvest Home* song in *King Arthur*, the sailors' chorus in *Dido and Aeneas*, or the haymaking duet in *The Fairy Queen*. Could the same thing happen nowadays? And is it the fault of the frequenters of our public-houses? Not altogether; they have been rebuffed by the

---

[a] Pepys returns home to find 'Mr Cæsar and little Pellam Humphrys, lately returned from France and is an absolute Monsieur, as full of form and confidence and vanity, and disparages everything and everybody's skill but his own.' Robert Latham and William Matthews (eds.), *The Diary of Samuel Pepys*, viii: *1667* (London: G. Bell, 1974), 529.

artistic snobbery of our 'serious' musicians. There was no musical snobbery about Purcell.

British Music in the Eighteenth and Early Nineteenth Centuries

The period from 1700–1850 is usually looked upon as the blackest of English musical history. It began with the tyranny of Handel and ended with the tyranny of Mendelssohn; and between these periods come that of fashionable Italian Opera, fashionable foreign fiddlers, and the 'something-aean singers' of Dickens, 'of whom three howled while the fourth grunted'.[b]

A Few Natural Musicians

And, indeed, if we consider the achievements of the accredited leading musicians of this period there is cause for despondency. But look for a moment behind the surface. What of the beautiful tune by the parish clerk of Wareham, which bears the name of his native place? Or of John Wainwright, who wrote *Christians Awake?* What of Dibdin and Bishop? Have we not here a storehouse of really national music? Small, perhaps, in quantity and exiguous in its scope, but of a real beauty and character of its own.

It is the old story; the 'serious' composers despise the duty at their doors, and try to reproduce at second-hand the 'grand style' of their greater foreign contemporaries; while it is left to the smaller fry to carry on the torch for future generations. We talk much nowadays of the 'rennaissance' of English music, and we all hope and believe that it is coming. But who is sowing the seed and setting the plant growing? Not perhaps the well-known names (the 'serious' composers of today), but possibly some quite insignificant writer of music-hall tunes or dance music, in whom the germ of a great national style of the future has begun to fructify.

Two English Art Forms

The eighteenth century, undistinguished as it undoubtedly was in the annals of music—oppressed as it was by the foreign fashionable domination of Italian operas and singers, was yet responsible for two exclusively English art forms—forces small in scope, and not of heroic build, but it was just in such forms as these that

[b] *The Pickwick Papers*, Chapter 15.

the English character found its true utterance; directly it went further it began to lose itself. These two art forms are the Anglican chant and the glee.

There is a movement afoot among church musicians of today to get rid of the Anglican chant, especially the double-chant, which for some reason which is never explained, is held to be extremely inartistic. It is an open question whether the plain-song, which is to be substituted for this, is really suitable to the English language, the English liturgy or English ecclesiastical architecture. Whatever may be the theoretic objection to the double-chant, there is no doubt that many eighteenth-century English composers managed to concentrate their inspiration on this small surface, with the result that in this small and unconsidered space we find some of the noblest scraps of English melody. It is enough to point to the two chants by Mornington, Boyce's Chant in D, or Woodward's in the same key in proof of this; and in the same category come such noble eighteenth-century melodies as the hymn tunes *Hanover, St Anne, St Bride* or *Rockingham*.

The glee is another purely English invention. It differs from the madrigal in that it moves in blocks of harmony rather than contrapuntally, and, rather like the 'verse' anthem, consists of several short movements. A glee is written for solo voices, usually those of men, the top voice being almost invariably an alto. It is this alto voice which largely helps to give a special character to the glee, and to distinguish it honourably from the flood of music for tenor and bass chorus, which swept over Germany a little later. The heyday of the English glee is comprised in the career of its greatest exponent, Samuel Webbe, who was born in 1740, and died in 1816. Such glees as his *Thy voice, O harmony*, Spofforth's *Health to my dear*, or Stevens' *Cloud Cap't Towers*, give a good view of this very characteristic form of art, and one which could have flourished nowhere but in England.

English Opera

The history of English music has been one continual struggle between the natural musical proclivities of the English people and the social and artistic conditions which have prevented the national tendencies from pursuing their natural course.

There could be no more striking example of this than the history of English opera from 1720 to 1860. For it is a fact that all through this period of Italian opera, fashionable Italian singers, of Handel and Buononcini, of Cuzzoni and Faustina, and all the fashionable taste, there flowed a thin but very distinguishable stream of English opera. We can date this period of English opera at the year 1727, when the *Beggar's Opera* was produced. *The Beggar's Opera* was what we should nowadays call a 'musical comedy', and what the Germans call 'sing-spiel'. That is a spoken comedy interspersed with songs. The peculiarity of *The Beggar's Opera* was that the music of the songs was not specially composed for them, but was adapted from the popular tunes of the day; many of them folk-tunes (though in rather degraded forms), some by well-known composers, one song of Purcell's even being drawn on. The great success of the *Beggar's Opera* led to a host of others being produced, and they gained the generic title of 'ballad operas'. The ballad opera has given the clue to all successful English opera of later date; even when the music was original and not adapted, the principle remains the same—the slight texture and almost invariable spoken dialogue instead of recitative.

The ballad opera naturally led to another school of opera, in which the music was original, and choruses and ensembles were introduced; but otherwise the plan remained the same. These operas, as a whole, have fallen into oblivion, but the names of their composers, Dibdin, Hook, Shield, Braham and Bishop, call at once to our minds songs and choruses which are eminently characteristic of their composers, and most of which originally appeared in these operas.

A later school of English opera comprises the names of Balfe, Wallace and Barnett. Some of these operas, especially the famous *Bohemian Girl* are still popular, while many more ambitious works of the same period have died a well-deserved death.

And though it does not belong to our period, it is impossible, in this connection, to omit a series of operas which are in the direct line of the English tradition, the famous comic operas of Arthur Sullivan.

Now that the Wagnerian boom is dying down it is not impossible that English composers will once again take up the thread and develop to a much higher and nobler degree the tradition which has been handed down to them by the English opera composers from the time of Purcell.

CHAPTER 9

Gervase Elwes

'The bells of Paradise, I heard them ring.'

Old Carol

THAT GERVASE ELWES heard those bells continually ringing in his heart was clear to anyone who knew him, or had conversation with him, and more especially to all those who heard him sing. How easily he might have been content with the half-hearted dilettantism of his early surroundings! What a struggle to rise superior to the insincere ideals and ephemeral judgments of the world in which he lived! But, indeed, though Elwes was in that life he was not of it; his art and his faith kept him unspotted from the world.

His nature was that of the 'perfect gentle knight', and it was these qualities in him which were at once the strength and the limitations of his art. He had not the wide gamut of musical expression at his command, and it is due to the very fineness of his nature that this was so. The grosser aspects of passion and feeling were repugnant to him, and the transparent sincerity and honesty of his nature made it

Source: *Musical News and Herald*, 60/1504 (1921), 107–8.

impossible for him to simulate those emotions. The strength of his art lay in his power of making the candour and uprightness of his character an actual part of his singing. In *Gerontius*, for example, he could not (and would not if he could) harp on the aspects of bodily agony and mental prostration, which have tempted other singers differently gifted; but who else could give that sense of vision to such lines as:

Jesu, Maria, I am near to death
And Thou art calling me?

To him the part of 'Gerontius' was not a role to be acted, but an expression of what, to him, was a living faith. It is honourably characteristic of him that he steadily refused to sing Cardinal Newman's poem in the garbled version demanded by the authorities at some of our provincial festivals. This, then, is the key to Elwes' greatness as a singer, the indivisible connection of his life and his art; it was not necessary for him to put on singing like a garment; he sang as he spoke, from the heart. For him to sing as he spoke was easier than for some singers, because Elwes did not have to learn correct English as a foreign language. Not the least of his claims to our grateful remembrance will be that he was one of the band of pioneers in the fight against 'singers' English; he realised what a wonderful vehicle for musical sound our noble language is and refused to degrade it into a kind of bastard Italian.

It was the personal quality which told in the actual quality of his singing voice. In one way it was not a great voice; it was not very powerful, although it had a peculiar carrying quality, and judged as a mere instrument it may not have been of outstanding beauty, but it was Elwes' own voice, it had a beauty which was more precious than that of vocal sound; that golden tone could only come from a golden heart.

Elwes' singing was distinguished by that indefinable quality which we call style. No one can say what style is, but one knows at once whether a musician possesses it or not; one had only to hear Elwes sing two bars to realise that his style was perfect; perhaps occasionally too perfect; his care not to overstep by one inch the limits of good style took away from the spontaneity of the whole effect. This was, I believe, largely due to excess of modesty. His attitude towards a new song was not: 'How will this song suit me?' but 'How can I best do justice to this song?' He was too anxious to sink his own personality in the music, not realising that the more he gave us of himself in his singing the better we should be pleased.

To those who heard it, Elwes' singing of the narrator's part in the St Matthew Passion will be a lasting memory. We all know how intolerable this part may become at the hands of a bad performer. One wonders what sort of a tenor Bach had to sing the part for him, whether tenors in his day had the same evil reputation which they have since achieved. At all events, Elwes has silenced once for all those cheap gibes which it has been the fashion to level at those who possess this beautiful but perilous voice; those who have heard Elwes know now that it is possible for a tenor to be a great musician and a true man. Surely Bach must have imagined such a singer as this when he wrote his narrator's part. It is in music like this that all Elwes' gifts came into play. His beautiful diction made every word tell; his sense of proportion caused him to differentiate between mere narrative and passages of dramatic or emotional import; his feeling for phrase gave its full value to passages of melodic beauty; his ease of production triumphed without sense of strain over Bach's cruel high notes; above all, his steadfast faith gave to his whole conception a sense of reality and conviction.

Other performances like those of the 'Benedictus' in the B minor Mass, or some of Brahms's songs, come to mind when thinking of Elwes' singing, but it was not only in religious music or in the great classics that his powers had play; his qualities also found their outlet in music where grace and lightness were required. He was an indefatigable searcher after new songs; many composers have him to thank for first performances of their music at his recitals and concerts; and in one case, at all events, his researches in unfamiliar fields met with signal success. If it be true that singers found their style on some particular composer, the converse is equally true, and there can be no doubt that the graceful and refined music of Roger Quilter owes its inspiration largely to the exquisite style and perfect phrasing of Gervase Elwes.

It is sometimes thought that when a singer ceases to sing his art dies with him. This is not so. A great singer leaves a tradition behind him which carries on from generation to generation, long after the sound of his own voice is silent:

> *Bright is the ring of words*
> *When the right man rings them:*
> *Fair the fall of songs*
> *When the singer sings them;*
> *Still they are carolled and said,*
> *On wings they are carried,*
> *After the singer is dead*
> *And the maker buried.*[a]

[a] Robert Louis Stevenson, 'Bright is the Ring of Words', lines 1–8, from *Songs of Travel*. Vaughan Williams set these words in his song cycle of the same title.

CHAPTER **10**

Introduction to *English Music*

CAN WE CLAIM music as part of our national heritage? Are we not the 'land without music'?[a] Did not Charles Lamb refuse to music the title of a liberal art? Do not our friends abroad and our enemies at home insist that music is outside our sphere? Only the other day a writer in one of our important London papers, in lamenting the end of the German opera season and the reign of the cheaper form of Italian opera, said that all the musicians among the audience had departed and that only the British remained. It is curious, by the way, that the 'British' who watched these operas from the stalls all had guttural voices, while the 'British' from the gallery shouted 'bravo' and 'brava' with a very correct accent, and smelt strongly of Soho. Nevertheless they were obviously deaf to the higher implications of music, therefore they must be 'British'. It is the old story, our own country can do nothing right. It was so in the eighteenth century. Professor Trevelyan in his *Blenheim* writes: 'Nothing is more striking than the inability of the English to stand by their native traditions in art.'[b] Have we any native traditions? for surely without them our art is meaningless. If our music is of any value it must strike roots down into its native

Source: W. H. Hadow, *English Music* (London: Longmans, Green, 1931), pp. vii–xiii.
[a] Oscar Schmitz, *The Land Without Music*, trans. H. Herzl (London: Jarrolds, 1926; first published as *Das Land ohne Musik*, München, 1914; rev. edn, 1918).
[b] *England Under Queen Anne*, i: *Blenheim* (London: Longmans, Green, 1930), 87.

soil. Miss Margaret Kennedy entirely misunderstands the mind of the musician in the scene which she imagines between Sanger and the workman.[c] Any musician who is worth his salt realizes that his ultimate sanction rests with the *en masse*. Possibly Miss Kennedy was misled by the analogy of painters, for painters, at all events in Chelsea, inherit from Whistler a snobbery which has not yet disappeared.

If we are the 'land without music' then this lack of music must go down to the very foundations of our life. But is this so? Do not recent discoveries show at the basis of our musical life a power of musical invention and a poetical impulse unsurpassed anywhere? Can the primitive music of any nation show anything to compare with the grim fantasy of 'The trees they do grow high', or the delicate beauty of 'Searching for lambs'. But here our snobbery comes into play again. That an English countryman can invent beautiful tunes must be nonsense. Those delightful Austrian peasants perhaps, or those wild wicked Russians, or those dear picturesque Italian contadini; even the Hebrides are just within the pale, but 'Hodge'! I use this name advisedly because it has been actually used in a sneering reference to our English folk-songs, not at a suburban debating society of the 'eighties', but by the accredited musical critic of a cultivated journal of the present day.

Nevertheless, our foreign critics sometimes understand us better than we do ourselves—and the one artistic activity which foreign students and teachers come to England to learn from us is the study of our own national folk-songs and dances.

Now let us look at the matter from another point of view. Are these occasional displays of brilliance which mark the musical history of England mere accidents? These accidents, these freaks, do not occur except in the minds of sentimental novelists. The genius who springs from nowhere and does something that no one has thought of before is contrary to the facts of artistic history. The great man closes a period, he does not inaugurate it. It is the small men, the Monteverdes, the Emmanuel Bachs, the Liszts and the Stravinskis who are the innovators, forerunners who prepare the way for those who are to sum up the work of a musical generation. And so our great men, Byrd, Purcell, Sullivan, Parry, Elgar, could not have existed without the crowd of small fry who preceded them.

English music is like the tree which flowers once in a hundred years; but unless the tree were alive there would be no flower and its life depends, not only on its intrinsic vitality but on the soil on which it grows, the rain that falls on it and the

[c] A reference to Margaret Kennedy, *The Constant Nymph* (London: Heinemann, 1924). This novel was a best-seller in the 1920s; the first of three film versions, released in 1928, also predates the publication of this essay.

sun which shines on it, the care with which the soil is dug and turned and weeds are got rid of and pestiferous insects warded off. The plant of English musical culture is a small and tender growth, for the very reason that those whose business it was to nurture it have failed to do so. Instead they have done their best to stifle it, not necessarily from malice but because they did not realize its existence. They were looking for flaunting hydrangeas and exotic mimosa and finding none they declared there were no flowers to be seen, having failed to notice the modest violets and daisies that were hidden in the grass.

If we want to find the groundwork of our English culture we must look below the surface—not to the grand events chronicled in the newspapers but to the un-obtrusive quartet parties which meet week after week to play or sing in their own houses, to the village choral societies whose members trudge miles through rain and snow to work steadily for a concert or competition in some ghastly parish room with a cracked piano and a smelly oil lamp where one week there is no tenor because at the best there are only two, and one has a cold and the other being the village doctor is always called out at the critical moment; and there they sit setting their teeth so as to wrench the heart out of this mysterious piece of music which they are starting to learn for the coming competition.

'Competition,' you will say, 'that is just the sporting spirit, nothing to do with art.' Well, unless we have learnt that art comes to the Englishman unconsciously we have yet to learn the first thing about that spirit which has produced our great poetry, our great drama and our great pictures.

The average Englishman does not care to parade his bravery, his patriotism, his artistic ideals or his spiritual longings—but they are there all the same. Professor Dent told me that he was much shocked because while the young composers in Germany and Italy were never tired of talking about art, their contemporaries in England preferred to discuss football matches. Quite so, in England we don't talk about these things, we just do them.

It is said that England has never produced a virtuoso. Of executants this is possibly true, though surely Elgar and Holst are virtuosi among composers.

The virtuoso performer is the foaming crest of the wave, very delightful to look at, but the real power of the wave lies below the surface. We can get on very well without the virtuoso executant; he always has a touch of the showman about him and the English are not good showmen. We want to do honest work without fuss and, if necessary, without recognition, and if we would be true to ourselves we must produce music which will represent that side of our national character. Why ask for more? If we cannot produce diamonds let us not waste our time manufacturing paste.

It is in such surroundings as these and such only that our Byrds, our Purcells, our Sullivans, our Parrys and our Elgars will find their congenial soil. We are so afraid of being parochial. The truth is we are nothing like parochial enough. We are always judging ourselves by foreign standards and wondering what foreigners will think of us. What does it matter? Is art to be standardized as if it were an electric fitting or a safety razor? What will it profit the Englishman if he tries to pose as a Parisian or a Berliner? Will he not be the laughing-stock both of the country which he has deserted and of that whose outward characteristics he vainly tries to adopt? Cosmopolitanism in art means loss of vitality. It is the stream pressing against its narrow banks which will turn the mill wheel. In every nation except ours the power of nationalism in art is recognized. It is this very advocacy of a colourless cosmopolitanism which makes one occasionally despair of England as a musical nation. A few years ago someone invented the very foolish phrase, 'A good European'. The best European is the most convinced nationalist, not the chauvinist but he who believes that all countries should be different and friendly rather than all alike and at enmity. I cannot sum this up better than by quoting the noble words of Stresemann in 1926: 'The man who serves humanity best is he who, rooted in his own nation, develops his spiritual and moral endowments to their highest capacity, so that growing beyond the limits of his own nation, he is able to give something to the whole of humanity, as the great ones of all nations have done.'[d]

Our English heritage of music goes quietly on, ignored, stamped on, untended and uncared for; a very Cinderella of the family of arts, but unobtrusively pursuing its way; occasionally when the moment is ripe showing a timid flower, none the less lovely for being unnoticed by those whose eyes are everywhere but on the ground at their feet. Did not our language go through the same phase? Let me again quote Professor Trevelyan, who, for a self-styled Philistine, has an extraordinary quantity of pregnant things to say about the arts: 'There is no more romantic episode in the history of man than this underground growth and unconscious self-preparation of a despised island *patois*, destined ere long to burst forth into sudden blaze, to be spoken in every quarter of the globe, and to produce a literature with which only that of ancient Hellas is comparable.'[e]

Music is the youngest of the arts, just as I suppose poetry is the oldest. Will a future historian be able to use words like these of our music? It is not impossible.

---

[d] Germany was granted membership of the League of Nations in 1926. These words are from the speech given by Stresemann, as German Foreign Minister, on that occasion. See George Scott, *The Rise and Fall of the League of Nations* (London: Hutchinson, 1973), 155.
[e] *History of England* (London: Longmans, Green, 1926), 132.

The great composer of the twentieth century is yet to come. By all the historic precedents he should be born in 1985 just as John Sebastian Bach was born in 1685, and he will be born in that country which is the best prepared for him. The artistic surroundings into which Bach was born were distinctly 'parochial'. His predecessors knew nothing of 'world movements' in art, but worked quietly and conscientiously as local organists and music directors to provide the artistic expression of the simple-minded people among whom they lived. Thus quietly and unostentatiously they built up the great tradition which made possible the advent of the greatest musician of all times.

Is there not a moral for us English here?

CHAPTER 11

Elizabethan Music and the Modern World

WE OF TODAY are the immediate heirs of a great musical revival which started about twenty years ago. In that revival certain names will stand out when its history comes to be written—Cecil Sharp, who restored to us our own natural melody, and Edmund Fellowes, who rediscovered the great choral works of the past and showed us that deep down in the consciousness of our country there exists a beautiful and characteristic art, which has defied the indifference of our fashionable audiences, the snobbery of our intelligentsia, and the neglect of those in high places.

I believe that the great work of our musical revivalists is not only that they have brought to our notice some very beautiful music of a past age, revolutionized our ideas of choral and of solo singing, and freed composers from certain technical inhibitions, but that, whether in chorus, song or dance, they have given us a national consciousness in our music without which art is uncreative and therefore lifeless. A colourless cosmopolitanism may produce a crowd of dilettante gourmets, but it will never produce a creative artist. This is not jingoism. Jingoism tends to a flat standardization of the things of the spirit, coupled with a fierce antagonism in everything material. Artistic nationalism goes hand in hand with international unity and

Source: *Monthly Musical Record*, 63/752 (1933), 217–8. A footnote to the title in the source describes this as: 'the substance of a speech delivered at the dinner of the Tudor Singers and the Madrigal Summer School on October 28 [1933].'

brotherhood between the nations, where every nation and every community will bring to the common fund that which they, and they only, can create. The great artists are only international and universal in so far as they are also intensely national.

If Elizabethan music were nothing more than a museum piece—a survival, interesting only to scholars and antiquarians, I venture to think we should not meet to do honour to this music, its preservers, and its performers. We do so because Elizabethan music is still a living force both for today and tomorrow, because it means something to us still, both for its own sake and for what it presages for us both for the present and for the future.

Our present musical situation seems to me in many respects parallel with Elizabethan times. Our country is seething with musical inventiveness, now as then. The Elizabethan golden age, after a short period of unexampled activity, suddenly faded out. Are we going to allow our golden age to do the same? These young minds and hearts, still young and tender growths, can either be nurtured and fostered or they can be starved by indifference and neglect.

We are at present stifling this youthful creativeness. There are now in London four important series of orchestral concerts. Have our young unknown composers the right of entry, even for ten minutes, into a single one of these? We are told that the box office rules supreme, and that the public are supposed not to be interested. Does it not occur to the promoters of these concerts that these young people represent their own generation, that they are expressing in music what their audiences are trying inarticulately to feel, that, even if they are not so slick, so self-assured, so showmanlike as some of their continental contemporaries, they still have something to say to their own people that no one else can express?

Glinka, the first of the Russian nationalists, used to say that he wanted to make his own people feel at home. Apparently an English audience does not want to be made to feel at home. They have been sedulously taught, either that, in the words of the little schoolgirl, 'all composers are dead', or that music to be of any value must be something apart from our real life and therefore either old or exotic; that good art and good form cannot go together and that therefore an Englishman, though he may tolerate music, cannot possibly be expected to be capable of making it; that music is a slightly suspect drug which is all very well for damned foreigners but cannot possibly grow in our native soil.

It has been left to the young unknown adventurers to try to discover whether our new composers have the heart of the matter in them, and they get very little recognition for their trouble. When a new composer appears on the horizon there is always the chance that here is the great man come at last; but apparently half a dozen lines of small print is enough to discuss this possibility. It is after all so much easier to write half a column of fine thoughts about Beethoven and Wagner—one does not have to make up one's mind about their quality.

Or if those, in whose hands the fate of these young composers lies, really believe that no good thing can come out of our country, then let them openly declare that we cannot create. But let us remember that an art that is not creative is no art; if we have no composers we are in truth the land without music. In that case let us wipe out all our paraphernalia of concerts and lectures, of colleges and academies of aural training and musical appreciation. Let us beat our fiddles into cricket bats and our bows into golf clubs and once for all drop all this nonsense about art.

In reality we know better than this. What we have done before we can do again. We feel we have the heart of the matter in us. It may not express itself in the same way as in other nations, it may produce a kind of art which other nations cannot appreciate and which will not be reducible to their standards. In the present circumstances, we must not expect to find it in the great places of the world or in the front page of the daily paper, but if we look behind the scenes at the local competition festival, the village choral society, our schools and universities, who will dare to say that music is not with us a living art?

We probably all believe this to be true, but we have got to prove it to the unwilling world. I admit that the composer himself is partly to blame. If the people are to believe in him he must speak the language of the people. I fear that composers are in some ways the worst snobs of all. The composer has two duties, first to himself, secondly to those whose mouthpiece he is. We are too apt to neglect both of these while trying to convince our fellow-craftsmen that we are up to all the latest tricks.

Here it is that we can learn from the Elizabethans. They knew nothing of international celebrities or of world movements in art, but wherever four or five people were gathered together they wished to make music on those instruments which heaven had provided for them—their own natural voices. And who was to invent that music for them? They did not search Europe for the latest thing in novelty. They knew better than that; they knew they only had to go into the next street and call in Mr Byrd or Mr Weelkes or Mr Wilbye, who could set our own incomparable poetry to their own incomparable music—incomparable indeed, for it ventured into regions undreamt of by our continental contemporaries. Italy might condemn it, because it had not the classical purity of Palestrina, Belgium might disapprove because it ignored the scholastic devices of Lasso, but it had something better than all this, something common to all English literature and art—the spirit of gay and careless adventure, bound by no academic restrictions and ignorant of all binding traditions. The Elizabethan composers wanted just to express themselves and the words which they set for their neighbours to sing, with no thought of what the world would say or posterity might think, so that their works remained for years, forgotten and neglected, imprisoned in the dusty shelves of remote libraries, only to be rescued for our lasting delight by the untiring labours of a modern knight errant.

CHAPTER 12

Sir Donald Tovey

THE FOLLOWING STORY is told, and I for one believe it to be true. A string quartet party met to rehearse. The viola player failed to appear, neither was there any full score to be found. At the critical moment in walked Donald Tovey and played the viola part on the pianoforte by heart.

Here indeed was the quintessence of Tovey—unfailing memory, encyclopædic knowledge and unerring artistic insight.

Add to this a delightful literary style and a rare sense of humour and we can understand why the Reid professor has put the town of Edinburgh on the musical map. The programmes of the Reid concerts alone are enough to prove this.

Therefore we all rush to buy, beg, borrow or steal each of his volumes of essays as fast as they come out. That on the ninth symphony of Beethoven reaches the summit of artistic analysis.

Tovey's playing is said sometimes to be 'unpianistic'. Thank heaven for that! All I know is that when he plays, the music seems almost to take visual shape.

As a composer his love and knowledge of the classics has led him along the great lines of musical thought by the narrow way right up the hill and not along the way of destruction, to stumble, fall and rise no more.

Source: William Rothenstein, *Contemporaries: Portrait Drawings by Sir William Rothenstein, with Appreciations by Various Hands* (London: Faber, 1937), 102–4.

Perhaps his intense love of the classics has caused him to be too diffident about his own initiative. There are two pieces of music by Tovey that I particularly love; one is an early chamber work in two movements for which scheme there is no precedent in the classics and the other is a great choral movement from *The Bride of Dionysus* for which again there is no precedent in earlier music drama.

He sometimes sings 'The Owl and the Pussy Cat' in private to his friends. This is a memorable experience.

CHAPTER 13

A. H. Fox Strangways, AET. LXXX

WHEN FOX STRANGWAYS first entered into the world of musical journalism he was like the child in 'The Emperor's New Clothes'. He had knowledge, insight and a well-stored mind, but he was disconcertingly without prejudice and was blissfully unaware of the conventions that ruled in the world of music. So he began in all innocence to strip the supposed clothes off our musical emperors and showed them up in all their nakedness. Thus, when he told the famous soprano, Mme. Squallina, that she sang out of tune, or the well-known conductor, Herr Auftakt, that a circular beat was not the best way of getting unanimity from an orchestra, the dovecotes began to flutter.

Daily musical journalism must be an unsatisfactory business. It was this feeling, I suppose, that unconsciously prompted the inception of a magazine devoted to music in which the literary style should be leisured and well considered, which was not tied to any publishing house and whose opinions were not fettered by the tyranny of the advertisement page. In *Music & Letters* the contributor is free to express any opinion he chooses, provided he has knowledge, vision and an educated pen. In his first number the Editor prophesied for his literary infant a short life and a merry one. *Music & Letters* can be merry when the occasion demands, but its

Source: *Music & Letters*, 20/4 (1939), 349–50.

life has not been short: it is now approaching its majority, yet there are no signs of the deadly smugness of middle age in its features in spite of its successful career, successful that is in the artistic sense. True, no one is materially much the richer for it (its promoters are probably poorer) but the spiritual riches which lie stored up in its pages will stand for great wealth when the eternal accounts are made up.

To read Fox Strangway's writings is like following the flight of the kingfisher, often darting out into the sunlight, blue and vivid, and then as suddenly disappearing into the shadow so that we cannot track his course; often we are compelled to say 'that is the truth, that is what we have all been wanting to say but lacked the words to say it.' But sometimes the actual richness of his mind seems to obscure his message. Allusions, first principles, analyses, classical quotations, come tumbling out, often just hinted at, so that the ordinary reader, who knows no classics and dreads first principles, cannot follow up an allusion and finds it difficult to grasp his intention.

Occasionally, it must be confessed, his intense honesty and fair-mindedness cause him to all appearance to be blaming what he most admires and praising what he most dislikes, and his desire to reach the bottom of things leads him to discover first principles where none exist or to trace causes and resemblances that are purely accidental.

But perhaps these very obscurities are only part of a well-conceived chiaroscuro. Anyhow, who would not give these and more as a price for those flashes of revealing insight, those sudden gleams of irrefutable truth to which they are the background?

CHAPTER 14

Making Your Own Music

I AM GOING to speak to you tonight about making your own music.

In olden times we *had* to make our own music. When there was no writing or printing or wireless or gramophones or celebrity concerts, if people wanted music they just had to make it for themselves.

And that is the real test even now of how much you really care for music, whether you are willing and able to try to make it for yourselves. If you are not willing, then you are not worthy of it when someone else makes it for you.

Perhaps you may wonder what this self-made music of our forefathers was like. (Music starts softly.) Remember that they probably could not read or write— certainly could not write down music—that they had nothing to guide them but their own intuition—no one to please but themselves—only that mysterious impulse to self-expression which is latent in us all if we do not deliberately stifle it. (Music swells out. Two verses.) That is one of our English folk-songs. (Music fades out slowly.) One of those tunes which our forefathers made by themselves and for themselves. One of those tunes which prove conclusively that we unmusical English are capable of creating beauty.

Perhaps you will say this is all ancient history—nowadays there is no necessity to make our own music—it is made *for* us with no trouble to ourselves except to

Source: BBC Home Service, 3 December 1939. From script held in BBC archives.

press a button—To which I answer that unless you yourselves lay the foundation, you will find in time that the supply of expert music on which you depend will fail you because there will be no groundwork on which to build it. I will explain this later.

In modern times we have come to differentiate between highly skilled professional music which is made for the benefit of others by experts and amateur homemade music which we make for ourselves to satisfy our innate need of self expression.

In a healthy musical commonwealth we want both—the professional and the amateur, not as rivals but as partners; the expert helping and guiding the amateur by example and precept, and the amateur guided by the expert both in listening and doing.

In one way of course we are all amateurs. If a musician does not love his art he is no artist and the difference is not only that the professional plays or sings or composes better than the amateur though this is usually though not universally true—Both amateur and professional must see their vision and try to translate it into sound but the professional must have acquired sufficient skill and knowledge to convey his message to others while the amateur may possibly rest content if he can convey it to himself.

However, the expert cannot reach the heart of others till he has persuaded his own heart; and the amateur, on the other hand, is often able to give his message to others as well as to himself.

So you see we want both these elements in our musical life.

If we, in these times of crisis, neglect the professional he will perforce have to cease from the practice of his art and when happier times come back and we want him again he will no longer be there.

If we neglect the amateur side of music and become a nation of mere passive listeners all the life will go out of our art—Art must be creative if it is to be vital. When I say creative I do not mean only putting black dots on pieces of paper— Anyone who plays or sings a phrase beautifully or even taps a drum with a live and compelling rhythm has done his creative share and all these little bits of creation joined together will produce an atmosphere of living art in which alone the great leaders of music can survive.

Flowers cannot grow on a barren soil—we are inclined to think of the great singers and players on our concert programmes as permanent and immortal but we have to face the fact that one day they will disappear and by some means, others must be found to take their places.

How shall we secure that when the time comes? The private shall step out of the ranks with the Field Marshal's baton in his knapsack. For this we must look to our competition Festivals, our local choral societies, our school orchestras, our piper guilds, in fact all those who have discovered the necessity of making music for themselves.

Now I do not want to deal only in generalities, and it has been suggested to me by Sir Walford Davies that I should tell you a little of how we are keeping music going in my own district of Dorking.

For years now we have had a flourishing yearly Festival in Dorking at which over twenty choirs from towns and villages around spend the day singing in competition and we have a concert, in the evening, at which all the choirs join and sing in one body.

Last September the blow fell—First, the black-out, then the commandeering of our only large hall and then the petrol ration. Everyone, of course, said we could not carry on—but we held a conference and decided that we would carry on. Every town and village society has now started its weekly practices—There will indeed be no competition but we do not need that to stimulate our enthusiasm. Only we have decided that the attendance rule shall be relaxed and that the meetings shall be more of a drop-in-and-sing affair. All who can will come, and when they can't we will do our best. Nor, of course, can we have our grand final concert, but we hope to arrange several small concerts in our village halls where those villages that are within walking or cycling distance of each other can meet and perform.

In choosing the music we have avoided anything outrageously difficult or extremely experimental. The towns and larger villages will sing as much of *Elijah* as they can learn in time—the smaller villages are tackling some of the choruses from *Judas Maccabeus*—we shall also sing some madrigals and part songs, and to make the practises less formal we shall occassionally relieve the tension by singing for our own pleasure some well known unison songs.

Besides this many of the choirs, on their own iniative are singing carols at Christmas. Nor, I hope, shall we forget the professional artist—the amateur can no more exist without the professional than the professional without the amateur.

So, as far as funds permit, we shall, I hope, engage professional help for our solos, and instrumental accompaniments.

There remains the question of the children—Again we cannot have a competition, but we shall hope to be able to send round judges to each school separately to hear them sing and to criticise them, and I see no reason why we should not collect the children like the grown-ups in small parties to give concerts of their music in the village halls or when spring comes, in the open air—And in this joint singing we hope that our evacuee guests will be able to join in with us.

And this raises another problem—are the evacuees to go without music? In the case of grown-ups we hope the problem will be solved by all those singers who are temporarily with us as school teachers or members of evacuated office staffs joining the nearest choral society—They will indeed be a great asset—I know of one case in which a well known conductor of an urban choral society has offered his services either to train a choir or even to sing in one.

And I know of another case of a school teacher recently settled here who belongs to a well known choral ensemble and has been eagerly snapped up by one of our local choirs.

But to return to the children—they are in a way the most important because if they lose the habit of making music in their most impressionable years they will never pick it up again.

The children of today will become the mature performers of tomorrow.

Think of Dvořák trying out his earliest compositions with his father's amateur band in his native village—Think of Verdi as a boy writing his little marches for the local musicians of Busseto—Who knows that among the children who are now running musically wild for the want of a little instruction there may not be a mute inglorious Dvořák or Verdi. We cannot indeed ensure that he shall be glorious, but we can prevent him being mute—Even a percussion band or a sing-song on Saturday afternoons may set the musical seed germinating.

I know at all events of one case in which an accomplished musician is devoting her small leisure to this very purpose among evacuated children.

Music is the one thing that neither bombs nor blockades can take away from us—We can always sing and we can always make a pipe and play on it.

I should like to think of our musical Commonwealth as a great pyramid with its apex in the clouds among the great names of the art and its base firmly fixed on the groundwork of our amateur music-making. (Music starts softly.) And below that again the sure foundation of those melodies which our forefathers made and which still live for us to hear, to love and above all to sing. (Music swells out.)

CHAPTER **15**

Local Musicians

IT IS SAID that in the parlour of the average Englishman you will usually find *The Soul's Awakening* hanging on the wall, *The Way of an Eagle* in the bookshelf and a volume of Bach on the pianoforte.'[a]

We unmusical English have taken John Sebastian Bach to our hearts.

A young exquisite once said to me, 'I don't like Bach, he is so bourgeois', to which I probably answered that being bourgeois myself I considered Bach the greatest of all composers.

It is Bach's intense humanity which endears him to me and my fellow bourgeois. The proletarians (if there were any in this country) would be too much occupied with their wrongs, and the 'governing classes' (if indeed they existed outside the imagination of the *New Statesman*) would be too much occupied in preserving their rights to have time to be human.

The warm human sentiments are reserved for the bourgeois; therefore of all Bach's works it is those great choral expressions of his personal and anthropomorphic religion which appeal most to us country and small-towns folk.

Source: *The Abinger Chronicle*, 1/1 (1939), 1–3.
[a] Vaughan Williams is highlighting the continuing popularity of romantic art and fiction in this reference to Ethel M. Dell, *The Way of an Eagle* (London: T. Fisher Unwin, 1912), and James Sant (1820–1916), *The Soul's Awakening*.

It is my privilege once a year to conduct our local choirs in concerts of great music and of all that great music it is Bach, his Matthew Passion, his B minor Mass, his church cantatas which seem to come most naturally to our minds and our hearts.

My business on these occasions, is to come in at the last minute, wave a stick about and say 'very good', but I know well that the real hard work has been done elsewhere, namely at those weekly winter evenings with their devoted leaders and enthusiastic singers who for the sake of music will after a hard day's work endure arduous toil and drudgery for an end which only gradually appears in view.

Week by week these dedicated hierophants trudge miles through mud and snow to a cold but stuffy village schoolroom lit by one smelly oil lamp which usually goes out half-way through.

The only accompaniment is a strange array of broken keys and snapped wires which was once a pianoforte. They are but a small body, there are probably only two tenors and one of these being the village doctor, is invariably called out in the middle to officiate at one of those happy events which are so frequent in our prolific neighbourhood, leaving Mr Smith of Kosikot to struggle with the cruelly high tenor part alone.

However, nothing daunts us (if I may for the moment identify myself with this glorious company of apostles). There we sit, week after week, wrestling with this strange mystery of music and saying in our hearts, 'I will not let thee go unless thou bless me'.

We are not experts, many of us have at first but the vaguest idea of what sounds are represented by these curious little black blobs and straight stems at which we stare, but this weakness is also our strength; until we have made these sounds bone of our bone and flesh of our flesh, we cannot attempt to sing them. The expert can pass from one musical experience to another, lightly, easily and forgetfully, but we, when once great music has burnt into our minds and souls, have it for an ever-lasting possession.

For a while we work by faith alone, then one day suddenly revelation comes to us, the notes we are singing are, all at once, not mere sounds, but symbols of a new world, something beyond mundane experience. We have looked through the 'magic casements, opening on the foam of perilous seas, in faery lands forlorn'.[b]

But the end is not yet. On a certain day in spring we shall meet all the other small bands of singers who like us have been struggling alone.

[b] John Keats, 'Ode to a Nightingale', lines 69–70.

Then we shall realize the profound mathematical formula of all choral singing: $2 + 2 = 40$. By the very force of numbers we have each magnified our own power and imagination tenfold. Not that we have lost our own individuality, but that we have merged it in harmonious concord with the other devotees who like us have been working for this same end. (Is this not perhaps a microcosm of what we all wish for the whole world?)

By faith, hope and love we have achieved that, compared with which the achievements of the greatest virtuoso, if he be not also informed by these three, is but as sounding brass and tinkling cymbal. We have unlocked the heart of music's mystery, we have found our faith and have proclaimed it to all such as have ears to hear.

Some indeed have not such ears—we are not 'news' nor do we wish to be. The 'intelligentsia' ignore us, the clever young men who 'do' the music for 'advanced' journals have (thank God!) never heard of us. The most we ever achieve is a patronizing paragraph in one of the daily papers. We are in fact local musicians and are content to remain so.

I believe that it is better to be vitally parochial than to be an emasculate cosmopolitan. The great names in music were at first local and the greatest of all, John Sebastian Bach remained a local musician all his life.

History emanates from the parish pump. We musicians of hundreds of Abingers all over the country are making history because we are laying well and truly those foundations from which alone the great artist can spring.

CHAPTER 16

The Composer in Wartime

WHAT IS THE composer to do in wartime? There are three possible answers. Some lucky devils are, I believe, able to go on with their art as if nothing had happened. To them the war is merely an irritating intrusion on their spiritual and therefore their true life. I have known young composers refer with annoyance to this 'boring war'. Such a phrase as this, I confess, shocks me, but it set me wondering what their point of view was and whether it was a possible one.

Whatever this war is, it is not boring. It may have been unnecessary, it may be wrong, but it cannot be ignored: it will affect our lives and those of generations to come. Is it then not worthwhile even for the most aloof artist to take some stock of the situation, to ensure at least that if and when the war ends he will be able to continue composing, to consider whether the new regime which will inevitably follow the war will be good for his art or bad and to bestir himself, even at the risk of losing a few hours from his manuscripts to help forward a desirable end?

How much does the artist owe to himself and how much to the community? Or, to put it in another way, how far is it true that the artist in serving himself ultimately serves the community? This is possibly the case in normal times; unless the artist is true to himself he cannot but be false to any man. But times at present

Source: *The Listener*, 23/592 (1940), 989.

are not normal. I suppose that even the most self-absorbed composer would hardly go on writing music if his house was on fire; at all events he would gather up his manuscript sheets and take them to a place of safety. The artist must condition his inspiration by the nature of his material. What will be the musical material on which the composer of the future can count? It will be no use writing elaborate orchestral pieces if there are no orchestras left to play them, or subtle string quartets if there are no subtle instrumentalists available.

One thing, I think, we can be sure of, no bombs or blockades can rob us of our vocal chords; there will always remain for us the oldest and greatest of musical instruments, the human voice. Is it not possible that the quality of our inspiration and the nature of our material will meet here? Surely the most other-worldly composer must take thought for these things.

At the other end of the scale are those composers who feel that music in wartime is just an impossibility, either because the present unrest inhibits for them that serenity of mind which is essential for artistic invention, or because they are obsessed with the idea that they must do something 'useful' and that composing music is not 'useful'. It is to me, a doubtful point whether this salving of one's conscience by 'doing one's bit' is not a form of cowardice, but if the necessary calmness of mind can be obtained in no other way let the artist by all means drive an ambulance or sit in a telephone box for a sufficient number of hours to enable him to return with an untroubled mind to the things of the spirit.

I have up to now taken it for granted that music is not 'useful'. How far is this true? It is certainly, to my mind, one of the glories of the art of music that it can be put to no practical use. Poets can be used for propaganda, painters for camouflage, architects for machine-gun posts, but music is purely of the spirit and seems to have no place in the world of alarms and excursions. Would it not indeed be better for music to keep out of the struggle and reserve for us a place where sanity can again find a home when she returns to her own?

Nevertheless, the composer feels that he would like to be able to serve the community directly through his craft if not through his art. Before a man can become a good artist he must have become a good craftsman. Are there not ways in which the composer without derogating from his art, without being untrue to himself, but still without that entire disregard for his fellows which characterizes the artist in his supreme moments, use his skill, his knowledge, his sense of beauty in the service of his fellow men?

Composers are, perhaps, too apt to think only in terms of the very highly skilled executant, but cannot they in present circumstances think of the needs of the modest amateur, the parties of ARP [Air Raid Precaution] workers who have to spend long hours waiting for an ambulance call that never comes, the group of nurses eating their hearts out in an empty hospital, the businessman and his family forced by the blackout and the petrol ration to spend their leisure hours at home. Would it not be a worthy object of the composer's skill to provide for these modest executants music worthy of their artistic imagination, but not beyond their technical skill? These very limitations may be the salvation of the composer.

It is right even to learn from the enemy. There has been in Germany of late years a 'Home Music' movement. Some of the best-known composers have occupied their time and their talents in arranging and composing music for the amateur to play in his own home. I should like to see this idea developed here—music for every fortuitous combination of instruments which may happen to be assembled in a parlour or a dug-out, with a part for anyone who happens to drop in. Why should we confine ourselves to the stereotyped string quartet or pianoforte trio? Why should the voice be always accompanied by the pianoforte? There seem to me great possibilities in voices and instruments in combination. Our old madrigalists marked their works 'Apt for voices or viols', we could develop this; that rare bird the tenor could be replaced by a viola or clarinet, a weak soprano could be doubled by a flute and—(I hardly dare to breathe it)—the contralto part might be played on a saxophone. New material stimulates new ideas. Might not all these possibilities be a source of inspiration?

Art is a compromise between what we want to achieve and what circumstances allow us to achieve. It is out of these very compromises that the supreme art often springs; the highest comes when you least expect it. There is a delightful phantasy by Maurice Baring in which he imagines Shakespeare and his Company rehearsing *Macbeth*. The principal actor complains there is not enough 'fat' in his part, whereupon Shakespeare goes into a corner and hurriedly scribbles a dozen more lines for him beginning 'Tomorrow and tomorrow and tomorrow'. That is how great art often grows, by accident, while we think we are doing something else—often as a supply to meet a demand.

The great English madrigal school grew up because singing round the supper table was fashionable and people demanded something to sing. Nowadays with our War limitations upon us, with concerts few and far between, with the BBC ration of one symphony a week, home music will again come into its own. Is it altogether beneath the dignity of the young composer to meet that demand? These young composers are having a bad time now, no one seems to want them—there seems to be no midway between Beethoven and Sandy Macpherson. This may be true as far as public music is concerned, but how about the musician in the house? To write for the amateur may limit the scope, but it need not dim the inspiration of the composers. The amateur player, also, has his duty toward the young composer. Let him welcome and encourage him. In so doing, who knows that he may not entertain an angel unawares?

CHAPTER 17

Introduction to *News Chronicle Musical Competition Festival for HM Forces*

MUSICAL EXPERIENCE IS of two kinds, active and passive. We can listen to others making music for us or we can make it for ourselves. To listen to fine music beautifully played is a great spiritual experience, so, also, is that of making our own music. Both are necessary for a full musical life.

We are all grateful for the wonderful opportunities of listening to music which the gramophone and the wireless give us; but these benefits have their accompanying danger—that of causing us to become a nation of passive listeners instead of active doers.

Vital art must be creative; by creative I do not mean only writing black dots on ruled paper. The humblest second violin or side-drummer, so far as he adds to the sum total of beauty, is creative.

But anyone who is content to listen only is not being creative. In primitive times if anyone wanted music he had to make it for himself, there was no one to do it for him—no gramophone, no wireless, no cheap editions of cheap music. The

Source: *News Chronicle Musical Competition Festival for HM Forces in Association with National Service Entertainments Board* (London: News Chronicle, 1942). This publication contains test pieces for the solo singing competition.

result was those beautiful folk-songs which we have ceased to create, but which are still a joy both to the learned and the simple.

Where there is no vision the people perish. Unless everyone takes his share in building the temple of beauty it will fall like a building with no foundations, however magnificent the architectural superstructure may be.

Does this mean that we have no use for the professional expert, those who have given their whole lives to perfecting their art? By no means; the expert is an absolutely necessary part of our musical commonwealth, and for three reasons: He can delight our souls by the practice of his art; he can set a standard for the amateur to aim at, however humbly; he can join with us as guide and leader in our music makings.

The glory of English music lies in this working together of professional and amateur—the amateur quartet coached by an expert, the amateur orchestra strengthened the professional leaders and trained by a professional conductor, the amateur choral society led by professional soloists and accompanied by a professional orchestra. In this way the greatest and the least can join, not in rivalry, but in cooperation, to build the great edifice of musical art.

One more thing. This Musical Competition Festival is for members of HM Forces. I understand that some military authorities consider that music is 'softening' for the soldier. I would remind them that Socrates held that certain kinds of music put courage to the heart of the soldier, that David was an expert harpist but managed to slay Goliath, that Mr Valiant-for-Truth carried his marks and scars with him across the river and that when he passed over all the trumpets sounded for him on the other side. Who shall dare who say that music is not an essential part of the soldier's equipment?

When Victory is won we shall need all those soldiers' qualities of courage, endurance, and hope as much as we do now; perhaps even more, when the stimulus to active endeavour no longer upholds us. Then, even more than now, we shall need to turn from the things temporal to the things eternal.

But how can we make sure of this if during these years of stress and toil we lose touch with those ultimate realities to which music points the way?

CHAPTER 18

First Performances

WE HEAR MUCH, and rightly, of the noble work which Henry Wood did for the young British composer—the list of 'first performances' at the 'Promenade Concerts' by British composers, usually young and unknown, occupies several pages.

It behoves us, however, to ask ourselves what did the young British composer do for Henry Wood? How far did he justify the trust which Wood placed in him? Facts speak for themselves—very few of these new works survived their first performance; indeed many of them died of inanition before their last bar was played.

How can we account for these numerous failures to stay the course? Did Wood fail to spot the winners, or were there no winners to spot? If that is the case where does the British Renaissance come in? No, the winners were there sure enough and Henry Wood went about the only way to find them; he went out into the highways and hedges and invited all and sundry to the banquet, in the hopes that occasionally a guest would appear wearing the wedding garment—then the Woodian policy was justified.

A scheme that was responsible for the first appearance of such works as Elgar's *Pomp and Circumstance* marches, Bax's *In the Faery Hills*, Quilter's *Children's Overture*, and in England of Balfour Gardiner's *Shepherd Fennel's Dance* would

Source: Preface to Henry Wood Promenade Concerts prospectus (London: BBC, 1949), 3–4.

justify itself even if all the other novelties had been still-born. But of course this list is by no means complete. A publisher who had to show a balance sheet would, I believe, be quite satisfied if he had as many good sellers on his catalogue as appear in the list of 'Prom Premières'.

It is said that it takes a thousand bad composers to make one good one and the Promenade audience had to endure the thousand failures so as to be sure not to miss the thousand and first—the man who had the heart of the matter in him.

What was wrong with the rest? Not necessarily want of technique or industry, often not lack of invention of a kind, but it just was that the composer had not at the moment the irresistible urge to create which is essential to vital art: such art may be very bad as in *The Holy City* or it may be supreme as in the B minor Mass, but neither the very bad nor very good can be the result of any lesser impulse, which will inevitably be damned as mediocre.

How many of these young aspirants to Parnassus experienced that irresistible urge before they offered their wares to Henry Wood? If not, then they were unworthy of his trust in them.

The greatest composers have always wanted to be understood. 'It will please one day,' said Beethoven. But did these young composers want to be understood? Were they not rather thinking how they could astonish their fellow composers and (they hoped) shock their audience by thinking out some strange device of harmony, tone or technique which the other fellow had not thought of—they were for ever trying to go 'one better' than the 'Modernists' of France, Italy, and mid-Europe. Truly they had their reward, their fellow composers were not even jealous and the public was not even shocked.

The pinchbeck is happily forgotten—the metal which rang true still rings for us to the lasting honour of him who believed in our art and justified his faith by works.

CHAPTER 19

Art and Organisation

WHAT IS ALL this talk about 'co-operating' and 'contacting', about planning, policy and administrative machinery? What has this got to do with art? Is not art a matter of fine, careless rapture; will not this rapture be destroyed if it is encompassed and guided by executive committees and standing conferences?

However, we know on the best authority that the wise thrush sings every song through twice, and this cannot be done without some amount of organisation.

Or take the case of the solitary reaper. She does not require a committee to help her sing her melancholy strain. But the reaper, we must remember, was solitary. Supposing twenty reapers all wished to sing together of old, unhappy, far-off things. Would they not have to invoke the aid of the paraphernalia of organisation with all its dreary but, I suppose, necessary jargon of local authorities, questionnaires and the like?

I suppose that even anything so primitive as one cuckoo answering another involves some arrangement. Indeed, I fear that the cuckoos even have to 'contact' each other; and are not the birds which sing in our gardens probably taking part in a competition with a committee all complete and probably bitter controversies as to whether to offer worm prizes?

Organisation is not art, but art cannot flourish without it.

Source: *Music and the Amateur: A Report*, Standing Conference of County Music Committees (London: National Council of Social Service Incorporated, 1951), 3.

CHAPTER 20

Choral Singing

THE PHILOSOPHY OF choral singing is comprised in the mathematical formula $2 + 2 = 40$.

We find this fact strongly emphasized in our village choral festivals, where each choir singing by itself sounds feeble and tentative, but when combined in one big choir suddenly has, by some miracle, found its powers increased tenfold.

I shall never forget the astonishment of the basses at one of our early Leith Hill Festivals in the opening passages of Charles Wood's 'Full Fathom Five' where the rather poor efforts of six shy singers by themselves were converted, as if by magic, into a sonorous confident crowd.

If this is true of a village choir, how much more true of the Royal Choral and Huddersfield Societies, where every voice is hand-picked and severely tested? When hundreds of these get together the effect is overwhelming.

A friend of mine used to say that choral singing is not an art but a game. Cannot it be both? Choral singing is a great art, but to become so it has to imbibe some of the qualities of a great game, and it is those very characteristics which go to

Source: Concert programme for performance of Vaughan Williams's *A Sea Symphony* and Walton's *Belshazzar's Feast*. Huddersfield Choral Society, Royal Choral Society and London Symphony Orchestra, conducted by Sir Malcolm Sargent. Royal Albert Hall, 9 June 1951.

make a good footballer or a good cricketer (but not a good golfer, which is not a game under the terms of the act).

A good footballer requires to sink himself in the whole, to co-ordinate carefully with his opposite number, to desire not personal glory but the success of the whole. So it is with a good choral singer. These qualities it is true refer more to the craftsman than to the artist, but if craft without art is dead, art without craft is impotent.

So my choral friend who thought he was playing in a game was really practising a great art. This is how we do things in this country.

Like Mr By-Ends' father, we look one way and row the other. Bunyan himself wrote his great epic under the impression that he was saving men's souls. Reynolds practised his wonderful art for material reward. Shelley thought his poems were important only insofar as they promoted social reform. So we choralists think we play a game and lo! we have achieved a great art.

Are we a musical nation? Not because we pay large fees to grasping foreigners to make our music for us, but by making our own music for ourselves.

The expert is the foam on the top of the wave, but the force of the water must come from our own effort. This is where football and music make contact, or at all events used to, but alas! even in our games we are beginning to stand aside and watch others whom we have paid to play for us, and the victory rests with those who can pay the largest amount to their professional gladiators. Heaven forfend that the same thing should happen to our choral singing! Fancy if the Royal Choral Society tried to entice a tenor from Huddersfield by a large salary, or Huddersfield tried to bribe a Royal Choral soprano with much gold! No, our ideal, and especially today, is not rivalry but co-operation.

A great many years ago I had the privilege of being a pupil of that great master, Hubert Parry. He once said to me, 'Write choral music as befits an Englishman and a democrat'. This ideal the Royal Choral and Huddersfield Societies have nobly enabled us English composers to realize.

CHAPTER 21

Carthusian Music in the Eighties

I SUPPOSE THAT it behoves me as one of the oldest of Old Carthusians, and one who has devoted most of his life to music, to tell you how that art was regarded in my school days, between 1884 and 1890.

It is a mistake to suppose that the public schools of that period were entirely philistine and ignored the arts; probably this false idea arose from the equally false legend that in the sixties an Etonian who was caught practising a musical instrument was subjected to the extreme penalty. However, by the eighties, at all events at Charterhouse, the arts, even the art of music, were mildly encouraged.

There were in my time two presiding authorities over Carthusian music, Mr G. H. Robinson, the organist, and Mr Becker who taught the pianoforte and also played the horn. Robinson was a sensitive musician and a kind-hearted man and gave me, and others, leave to practise on the chapel organ. There was in my time at least one competent organist among the boys, H. C. Erskine, who was able to give a very good performance of Bach's 'St Anne's' Fugue. Mr Becker was a very remarkable man and a fine teacher, I am sorry I never came directly under his influence. He was brother to the well-known Miss Lydia Becker, one of the forerunners of the suffragist movement. Among the pianoforte pupils were several

Source: *The Carthusian*, 21/1 (1952), 1–2.

remarkable performers, H. V. Hamilton, N. G. Smith (later Swainson), who both became well known in the professional world, and Ramsbotham who later made his name as a musicologist. And I also ought to mention a boy whose name later became vicariously famous, Gordon Woodhouse. One cannot write of Carthusian music without mentioning 'Duck' Girdlestone, he was a keen amateur musician and conducted the weekly practices of the school orchestra. I was one of the two violas, the other being the famous Mr Stewart ('Stewfug') whose chief business in life was to preside with complete inefficiency at 'extra school', however he was a good viola player and great help in the orchestra. One of my first practical lessons in orchestration came from playing the viola part in the slow movement of Beethoven's First Symphony, when I was excited to find that my repeated notes on the viola were enriched by a long holding note from Mr Becker's horn.

Then there was, of course, the school choir which practised once a week in the time otherwise devoted to 'extra French' and was therefore very popular. Choir and orchestra used to meet once a year for a grand concert at the end of the summer, and occasionally for an oratorio: I remember taking part in Handel's *Judas Maccabaeus*.

Girdlestone also lives in my affectionate remembrance because in the winter months he used to invite some of us to his house on Sunday afternoons and there we played through many of the Italian concerti grossi from the old band parts. The performances were pretty rough ('Duck' was himself an execrable violoncellist) but I learned much from the experience.

One of the most astounding events of my school musical life took place when Hamilton and I decided to give a concert of our own compositions. It was my task to approach Dr Haig Brown, the Headmaster, for leave to use the school hall. Dr Haig Brown was a formidable man, and in later life I should never have dared to make the request, but leave was obtained, and we gave the concert, and it was attended by several of the masters and their wives, and even some of the boys. I was complimented after the concert by Mr Noon, the mathematical master, who said in his well-known sepulchral voice, 'You must go on'. That is one of the few words of encouragement I have ever received.

Partly as a result of this concert, Girdlestone, who organized the Saturday evening 'Entertas', decided to devote four of them to national programmes and I was ordered to provide a Welsh concert. This was my first introduction to the beautiful melodies of the Principality. Another vivid reminiscence is the annual concert given by the Misses Haig Brown, two of them played the pianoforte and they invited six of us boys to join them in music for sixteen hands on four piano-fortes. As I was one of the performers I never appreciated the full horror of the result.

In my list of Carthusian musicians I have not mentioned composers, but we had our seed-bed for these also. About a year after I left school I came down for a visit, and found that one of the boys was deputising for the organist who was ill, at the Chapel services, and playing remarkably well. His name was Balfour Gardiner.

Now, one last word about the 'Carmen Carthusianum'; it is my definite artistic opinion, not at all tinged with school chauvinism, that the 'Carmen' is the finest of the school songs. In my time we all knew it and used to sing it on all big occasions. Later on it was apparently allowed to lapse, and it is a cause of great pride to me that I was partly instrumental in its resurrection at the recent Charterhouse masque. May it flourish for ever with the 'Domus' which it celebrates.

CHAPTER 22

Howland Medal Lecture

MR PRESIDENT, LADIES and gentlemen, I need hardly say what an honour I feel it to be presented, by you Sir, as representative of this famous university, with the Howland Medal. And especially I feel the honour because, as the President has told you, it has already been presented to two distinguished musicians: Paul Hindemith, and another name of an equally distinguished but still more precious name to me, that of Gustav Holst. Because I had the privilege of having Gustav Holst as a close friend, and though he was never nominally my teacher, I think I've learnt from him more about art, and also about life more generally, than from anybody else. And I feel that had it not been for Gustav Holst's instruction and example and advice, I would probably not have been here today receiving this honour. Now, Gustav Holst, though professional of the professionals in his own work, as a composer he was one of the virtuosi. But yet he had great sympathy and understanding of the

Source: Audio recording of lecture held in Yale University Library and the British Library Sound Archive. The lecture was given at Yale University on 1 December 1954. As one of the two speakers introducing Vaughan Williams explains, 'the Henry Elias Howland Prize, established in 1915, is awarded to the citizen of any country in recognition of some distinguished achievement in the field of literature, the fine arts, and the theory of government or politics.' See introduction for further discussion of this lecture, and compare with 'Epilogue: Making Your Own Music' in *National Music and Other Essays* (2nd edn, Oxford: Oxford University Press, 1987), 237–42, Vaughan Williams's published version of this talk.

amateur. And it is about the amateur that I wish to say a word or two this afternoon; those who are making their own music.

But before I start, I want to say one thing. I think, of course, that lectures on music are dreary things at the best. I never go to one myself if I can possibly help it. But a lecture on music, merely talking about music, would be quite implausible. Therefore Mr Keith Faulkner, the well-known baritone, has kindly consented to come, and at the end of my lecture, to sing you some examples of what I can only haltingly describe. Well, what I want to talk about for a short time this afternoon is making your own music.

All vital art is creative art; and musical appreciation especially demands active participation rather than passive acceptance on the part of the hearer. When we listen to a symphony as we should do, we are actually taking part in it, together with the composer and the performers. We are taking part in the creation of that symphony. Shakespeare wrote some very beautiful lines about letting soft music steal in our ears,[a] but this is not a true picture of real, creative listening which cannot exist except as the counterpart of active participation by the hearer. Therefore, before we can truly listen, we must be able also to create.

Now when I talk about the creation of a piece of music I don't really mean putting down black dots on a piece of paper. The humblest member of a choral society, the shy beginner who takes his place in the back desk of the second violins in an amateur orchestra, the child who plays the triangle in a percussion band, if they sing or play with understanding and purpose, they are all creators. Now I yield, I'm hoping, to no-one in my admiration of the wonderful revolution in the status of music which has been achieved in our time by the radio and the phonograph. These inventions have given to millions the opportunity to hear, for the first time, great music, greatly played or sung. They have also set a standard for many amateurs and students of music of what to imitate, and occasionally, one must confess, of what to avoid—if only they will profit by it.

But will they so profit? Will not all this listening to superb, expert performances bring on a counsel of despair in the mind of the humble amateur who plays, perhaps, the flute or the violin a little for his own amusement? Will he not feel inclined to say 'With my limited capacities, my small opportunities for practice, I cannot hope to approach this perfection. Better to give up the struggle and become a merely passive listener.' If the amateur thinks this, then he will have lost one of

[a] 'Here will we sit and let the sounds of music / Creep in our ears: soft stillness and the night / Become the touches of sweet harmony.' *Merchant of Venice*, V. i. 64–66. Vaughan Williams set this text in his *Serenade to Music*.

the greatest assets of his spiritual life, that vision of the ultimate realities through the making of music for himself.

I'm glad to be able to quote my old friend Gustav Holst again, and he is reported to have said that 'if a thing was worth doing at all, it was worth doing badly.' Now I entirely agree, with this proviso—that this 'doing' must be a sincere attempt towards self-expression. Superficiality, half-heartedness, sham and swagger must have no part in the scheme. Guard it in, this sincerity of purpose. You may well say, with that delightful comedy poet, Calverley, 'Play, play, your sonatas in A / heedless of what your next neighbour may say!'[b]

But remember, say, you may always hitch your wagon to the star, however far behind your wagon may lag behind its leader. Music, then, is first and foremost self-expression; without that it is a falsehood. I believe that a man who was marooned for life by himself on a desert island would all the same continue to make music for his own spiritual exaltation even though there was no-one to hear him. But sometimes these self-expressive, spiritual exercises spread beyond the individuals; the neighbours may, after all, like the result. And so we go on and on till we come to the famous expert, whose music spreads all over the world. But first expert though he be, he must be to his own self true, and he cannot then be false to any man. Wordsworth's Solitary Reaper sang for herself alone, little thinking that she would be indirectly responsible for one of the world's greatest poems.

Now supposing we did all become passive listeners—who then would there be left to listen to? For a time, of course, we would have with us the great virtuosi who are still alive and they would satisfy our needs. But voices fail, fingers grow stiff, vision grows dim, even in the greatest of us. And our loved art will die of inanition unless there are young men and women to seize the torch from the faltering hands of their elders. But where are these young men and women to be found? Would it not be from among those who are attempting to make music for themselves? And how are we to discover these? How are we to find out which private soldier, in that crowd, bears the marshal's baton in his knapsack? We can only do it by trial and error.

So, I believe, that music must be offered to all, though it may not be accepted by all. It is only by speaking the password to everyone that we can find out who will respond. The many must be called in order that the few may be chosen. In Virginia Woolf's delightful book, *A Room of One's Own*, she writes: 'Masterpieces are not single and solitary births; they are the outcome of many years [of] thinking in common, of thinking by the body of the people, so that the experience of the mass

---

[b] Charles Stuart Calverley, 'Play', lines 22–3, from *Fly Leaves*.

is behind the single voice."[c] That was all I was trying to say, so really, in a nutshell, I'd better read it to you again. . . .

Now, I don't want you to think that I'm trying to exalt the dilettante at the expense of the expert. The virtuoso is absolutely essential to our musical life; both to give us the exaltation of beautiful music, beautifully performed, and also to set a standard by which we lesser folk can measure our own efforts. The world famous musician is like a pinnacle shining for everyone to see; but unless the pinnacle rests on a solid foundation it will totter and fall. I sometimes like to imagine our polity of music, the musical life of our community, to a pyramid, at whose apex are the great and the famous; and below this, in rank after rank, stand the general practitioners of our art, competent and enthusiastic, and often endowed with a musical insight which their more famous but more specialised brothers and sisters do not possess. These hard working and unassuming men and women are the musical salt of the earth. They wish for neither fame nor fortune; their one desire is to spread the gospel of music both by precept and practice; and, just as Chaucer's Poor Parson pushed the gospel of goodness, but for first he followed it himself. And finally we come to the great army of humble music makers. These are the foundations of the pyramid, depending for guidance on those above them in the hierarchy of art. So, by laying stone on stone, we build up a great structure of music, reaching higher and higher into the empyrean, but with foundations firmly set on the great traditions of our art. Thus the humblest and the highest can join in the service of music.

Well, that is one side of the question, but there is another. As the preacher discovered, years ago, it is the business of some men to find out musical tunes. Nowadays, we call them composers. Now before we get any further, I think I'd like to digress for a little bit and try and find out what we mean when we talk about composing music.

A musician, or any artist for that matter, has a vision. At first it is vague and cannot be accurately expressed. Well, that is the same with all arts. It has to be crystallised into some definite form. And in the case of music the man who has to have had this vision, has to crystallise it into definite musical sounds. And that is so especially if he wants others to share the vision with him. But how are these musical sounds to be explained to people? Well, of course, the obvious way is to sing it or to play it. Whether the singing or playing came first is a moot point, which I hope I shall have a word to say about later on. But supposing he wants to reach people who are out of earshot, or wants somebody else to take his musical sounds which

[c] (London: Hogarth Press, 1929), 98.

he invented and spread them broadcast. Well then, he must do something about it, mustn't he? And as you know musicians have invented what is I must confess, a very incomplete and clumsy system of symbols, dots, dashes, circles, and so on, to indicate what sounds he wishes to be made, so that his vision may be realized. In fact, he is saying, by means of these symbols to anybody who knows, 'If you blow or scratch or hit, in the way indicated by these dots and dashes, you will (I hope) achieve, ultimately, the vision which I have in mind.'

Now, another point, having got so far—which came first? I ought to say first perhaps that before the performer, as we call him, can set to work on translating the composer's vision, he has to learn some means of doing it, a violin or flute or double bass or whatever it is—now the question comes, which came first, the means or the end? Did somebody invent an instrument, and then music grew out of that; or did he think of some music and invent an instrument to perform it? I think both are to a certain extent true. Let us for a moment imagine ourselves in Arcadia. And Amaryllis has a nice little voice and she invents little tunes which she sings, and then Strephon blows on a pipe, and plays them according to the holes he has pierced in his pipe. Now one of two things may then happen. Either Amaryllis may now say, 'There's this new tune I've invented with a note that's not on your pipe, you must pierce a new hole'; or Strephon may say, 'Well I've pierced a new hole in my pipe, and you must invent a new tune to fit it.' And that's gone all through music. [inaudible] . . . once he realised what a beautiful instrument it was and wrote his clarinet quintet and concerto for it. On the other hand, Wagner, when he wanted to suggest the Valhalla in his *Der Ring des Nibelungen*, couldn't find the right kind of instrument to make the sound he wanted, and so he set to work with an instrument maker, and they invented a thing called a Wagner tuba which could do what he wanted. And so it goes on, all the way through. Well then, we'll imagine that done. The instrument has been invented and the player has learnt how to play it; he must have the skill to play the exact notes indicated; he must have the artistic insight to realise the connection between one note and another, and he must have the poetic vision to be able to see the ultimate vision behind that. That done, he can play this music to anybody he likes, and from there you get back to the original vision. So it's backwards and forwards, vision-notes-performance, performance-notes-vision, and that's all about it. Well that was all by way of a digression.

Now one would have thought that this was making music for oneself—something personal, if ever anything was—and yet, a foolish fellow once labelled music as the universal language. And equally foolish was Whistler when he wrote that it was as wrong to talk about national art as about national chemistry. And as a climax we have Rossini's famous epigram 'I know only two types of music, good and bad'. Now let us think about these three remarks for a moment. It is true that music has a universal vocabulary, but each composer uses that vocabulary as his own nature and the circumstances of his own surroundings, his own community where he lives, his own tradition, dictate. No-one could possibly mistake Verdi for Wagner, though their vocabulary is superficially the same. And we must say to Whistler that chemistry, being a science, its business is to discover and co-ordinate facts, while art is the means by which one man communicates spiritually with another. And as for Rossini, let me quote an example which I hope you all know: Verdi's Requiem. Now here is a work which defies all the canons of good taste; it is melodramatic, sentimental, sometimes almost cheap; it employs without shame such well-worn means to excitement as a diminished seventh and a chromatic scale. And in spite, or perhaps because of this, it is one of the greatest of works of art, and gained the reluctant admiration of a composer with such a different artistic philosophy as Brahms. Well you can ask Mr Rossini, is that good music or bad?

Having got to the question of the composer and his personal attitude towards music, let's go a little bit further into the question. Emerson once said that the most original genius is the most indebted man; and Professor Gilbert Murray has really put his own gloss on that when he writes 'that the most original genius is at once a child of tradition and a rebel against it.'[d] All young artists are rebels, and very right and proper too; but when they plunge into unknown waters let them hold fast to the lifeline of our own national tradition, otherwise the siren voices from foreign shores will lure them to destruction. It has been said that musical invention is an individual flowering on the common stem. Now may I say to young composers do not try to be original. If you're going to be original I assure you it will come of itself. However individual your flowering may be, unless it is firmly grafted onto the common stem, it will wither and die. I have all honour for those adventurous spirits who explore unknown regions; I confess that I cannot always follow them, but that is probably my fault. At all odds I admire their courage, but sometimes, you know, I ask myself whether those composers have not even more courage who find new and unheard of beauties along the beaten track. And always, I do beseech you to try the beaten track first; and then if an irresistible impulse leads you into the jungle, make sure you know the way back.

America has a great cultural tradition behind her; why not add to this a great musical tradition? You will find it in unexpected corners of this country, but do not

[d] 'Shakespeare; Or, the Poet' in *The Complete Works of Ralph Waldo Emerson* (London: George Bell, 1876), 352–65 at 352. Gilbert Murray, *Euripides and his Age* (London: Oxford University Press, 1965; first published London: Williams and Norgate, 1918), 4–5.

rest until you have found it, and when you have done this, do not deny your birth-right. I think that I am going to tread on rather dangerous ground now, but I am going to venture all the same. I'll say this much, which is that what I am saying about America applies almost equally to England; so when I'm saying anything at all blameworthy to you, I'm saying it about England as well. I think in the nine-teenth century, both our countries suffered from an inferiority complex as far as artistic things were concerned. If you wanted a mansion, it must be an imitation of a Florentine palace; if you wanted a church it must be sham gothic; if you wanted a bit of music for a ceremony, it must be composed by a German composer who evidently was rather bored with the thing, and I think, in the particular case I'm thinking of, got someone else to write it for him. You forgot Walt Whitman's advice, all those years ago, to the American poet:

> Come Muse migrate from Greece and Ionia,
> Cross out please those immensely overpaid accounts,
> That matter of Troy and Achilles' wrath, and Æneas', Odysseus' wanderings,
> Placard 'Removed' and 'To Let' on the rocks of your snowy Parnassus,
> Repeat at Jerusalem, place the notice high on Jaffa's gate and on Mount
>   Moriah,
> The same on the walls of your German, French and Spanish castles,
>   and Italian collections,
> For know a better, fresher, busier sphere, a wide, untried domain awaits,
>   demands you.[e]

That is a fine motto for any musician. Now I see time is getting on and I want to say a word that really is the most important part of making one's own music. The primitive music, which was made by unlettered, untravelled, in our sense of the word uncultured people, to satisfy their own needs; the people who Hubert Parry said 'who made what they liked, and liked what they made';[f] that is, after all, the foundation on which all our art is built up, and unless music is a natural expression of feeling, it is worthless. And if it is a natural expression it must surely come from people without any special training. I'm not speaking against special training—it is

---

[e] Whitman, 'Song of the Exposition', lines 15–21, from *Leaves of Grass*.

[f] See Parry's address to the inaugural general meeting of the Folk Song Society: 'The old folk-music is among the purest product of the human mind...In the old days they produced music because it pleased them to make it, and because what they made pleased them mightily, and that is the only way in which good music is ever made.' From 'A Folk-Song Function', *The Musical Times*, no. 673 (1899), 168–9 at 168.

necessary—but without that natural desire, it's useless. But we can find out whether that natural desire is there by listening to songs which unlettered, uncultured, primitive people have sung, and seeing if they have artistic value; or at all events, see if they have something which is going to lead to artistic greatness.

I'm afraid I can't go into the question of how these songs arose. There is one theory that merely attributed music came first from making a hole in a pipe and blowing through it. Other people think that it came from excited speech. Well as I say I'm not learned enough and it would talk a long time to discuss those two attitudes of mind. But after all, an ounce of practice is worth a pound of theory, and I want to give you an example from a personal experience I had of excited speech growing into song.

I was once years ago in the isles of Skye where they all talk Gaelic, and I was at an open-air service and there was a preacher who preached in Gaelic. Well, I don't understand the language, therefore I was unable to understand the words, and I could concentrate on the tones of the preacher's voice. Now remember it was out of doors and he was in a highly emotional state, and his voice gradually grew from a speaking voice to a definite singing voice on particular steady notes. First of course, just a monotone, and then as he got excited he went up one (F-G-F); and then he gradually went up three (F-G-Ab-G-F); and gradually sometimes he dropped (F-G-Ab-G-F-Eb-F); and then finally at that very low point of his emotion he dropped to the fifth (F-C); and so you had that formula with variations; either (F-G-F-Eb-F) or (F-G-Ab-G-F-Eb-F-C). Now that is a formula that we find in many English, Scottish and Irish folksongs for the start. For the initial opening of so many folksongs you find variants of those actual notes.

Now you'll be very glad to hear that I'm not going to talk for very long more, but I'm going to ask Mr Keith Faulkner to sing two songs for you. The first is the song 'Bushes and Briars' which was sung to me by an old shepherd in Essex about fifty years ago and incidentally he told me, it's rather interesting, I asked him how he got the tune. And he said well he had learnt the words, but when you get the words the Almighty will send you a tune.[g] And I think in this case I think he was right. You judge for yourselves. Well first comes 'Bushes and Briars' and then a song that was sung to Mr Sharp in Somerset especially for lambs.

[Performance of 'Bushes and Briars' and 'As I went out one May morning']

[g] This encounter inspired Vaughan Williams to begin his own work as a folk song collector. See Ursula Vaughan Williams, *R. V. W.: A Biography of Ralph Vaughan Williams* (Oxford: Oxford University Press, 1984), 66.

I want to say a little word more about this question of folksongs. I dare say you may have noticed, those songs—those of you who are interested in these things—were in the Aeolian mode, and another was in 5/4 time. Now I once heard a very distinguished musical critic said he could not understand how an uneducated English countryman could possibly sing in the Dorian mode. He didn't realise of course that these words—modes, 5/4, and so on—are only explanations by scientists, of what is really happening naturally. [inaudible] . . . Do you remember, Monsieur Jourdain? He was so delighted to find that he was speaking prose, he had no idea.[h] And this is the same with country singers; if they were told they were singing in the Dorian mode, they wouldn't know what it meant; but it is something that is natural to a human being.

Now there is one song I am going to ask Mr Keith Faulkner to sing— a song called 'I am seventeen come Sunday'—which is in the Dorian mode. Some people say the fact that these songs are in the same mode, the same scale of tones as a church plainsong, that they must be developed from that. Well you'll hear a song in a minute, and I think you'll agree there's no possibility of that song being anything to do with church plainsong, either in the words or music. The other song, that Mr Faulkner will sing first, is a delightful little song which was sung by children in Northern England on All Souls' Day when they run round begging for what they call 'soul cakes' and a little money to add to it. The interesting part of that song really is that it's all on three notes; and you know, some of Beethoven's most sublime efforts are founded on three notes; for instance, well it has five but it's just going up the scale [plays the Trio theme from Beethoven's Ninth Symphony]. So you could say anyone could do that, couldn't they? Like the boy who said 'I'd have written all of Shakespeare myself if I'd only thought of it'; but he hadn't thought of it; and nobody had thought of that little tune by Beethoven; and nobody but these children up in the north of England has sung such a delightful little tune for a soul-ing song. Well I'm going to ask Mr Keith Faulkner first to sing the soul-ing song and then 'Seventeen come Sunday'. And if you're inclined to laugh during 'Seventeen come Sunday', remember please it's in the Dorian mode!

[Performance of 'A Soul Cake' and 'I am seventeen come Sunday']

I'd like to end the afternoon with that delightful song, but I don't think that would be quite correct in academic circles! So instead I want to not tell you anything of my

[h] Jean-Baptiste Poquelin de Molière, *Le bourgeois gentilhomme*, III. iii.

own, but to quote you a wonderful passage on the English language from George Treveylan's great *History of England*:

> One outcome of the Norman Conquest was the making of the English language. As a result of Hastings, the Anglo-Saxon tongue, the speech of Alfred and Bede, was exiled from hall and bower, from court and cloister, and was despised as a peasants' jargon, the talk of ignorant serfs. It ceased almost, though not quite, to be a written language. The learned and the pedantic lost all interest in its forms, for the clergy talked Latin and the gentry talked French. Now when a language is seldom written and is not an object of interest to scholars, it quickly adapts itself in the mouths of plain people to the needs and uses of life. This may be either good or evil, according to circumstances. If the grammar is clumsy and ungraceful, it can be altered much more easily when there are no grammarians to protest. And so it fell out in England. During the three centuries when our native language was a peasants' dialect, it lost its clumsy inflections and elaborate genders, and acquired the grace, suppleness and adaptability which are among its chief merits. At the same time it was enriched by many French words and ideas. . . . Thus improved, our native tongue re-entered polite and learned society as the English of Chaucer's Tales and Wycliffe's Bible, to be still further enriched into the English of Shakespeare and of Milton. There is no more romantic episode in the history of man than this underground growth and unconscious self-preparation of the despised island *patois*, destined ere long to 'burst forth into sudden blaze', to be spoken in every quarter of the globe, and to produce a literature with which only that of ancient Hellas is comparable.[i]

That's a magnificent passage, and it seems to me that this fable is also told of you and me, and our music. I will not weary you with our sins against light in England. But you here in America have not been blameless. What did you know of the music germinating in underground growth while the so-called educated classes, if they considered music at all, thought of it in terms of Wagner and the world's worst Festival March, or highly-paid European [inaudible],[j] while the real foundations of your art were neglected, with the result that for years, American music, as well as

[i] (London: Longmans, Green, 1926), 131–2.
[j] Vaughan Williams writes 'performers showing off their fine feathers' at the parallel point in *National Music and Other Essays*, 242, although it is unclear whether he also says this in the lecture.

English music, in the nineteenth century, consisted of watered-down European models. Even that American of all Americans, Walt Whitman seemed to think that music, for him, existed of nothing but Italian coloratura and cornet solos by Verdi.

But I believe that now both our countries are returning to the true path. Now the last thing that I want to do is to advocate a back-to-folk-song policy. Chaucer, Shakespeare and Milton have enriched the English language with cullings from France, Italy, Rome and Greece. In the same way we must, in America and England, enrich our music from foreign models, but it must be an enrichment of our native impulse, not a swamping of it. The truth is that on both sides of the Atlantic we have suffered from an inferiority complex. We have always imagined that the foreigner must necessarily be better than us in questions of art; and further, that if we imitate these tricks of diction, we shall achieve the same inspiration, forgetting that these tricks of diction are often nothing more than the outward and visible sign of a deep inspiration founded on an age-old tradition. Of course I am not speaking now to mature composers, either in this country or mine. I will not be guilty of such impertinence. They will find their own way, which is germane to their own country. But I think that the young people are still rather apt to be dazzled by the array of shop-finished goods displayed to their wondering eyes by distinguished foreign composers who have made their home here. By all means learn all that you can from these mighty examples, but be sure that before you learn from them, you know what it is you want to learn. Then, their example will be an addition to your inspiration and not a substitute for it.

Well, ladies and gentleman, I have only now once more to thank you, Sir, as representative of this famous university, for giving me this great honour; you, Mr Dean, for your kind-hearted hospitality to my wife and myself; and to you, Mr Faulkner, for a beautiful sing; and finally to you, ladies and gentlemen, for your patient listening. Thank you.

CHAPTER 23

Preface to *London Symphony*

I AM OLD enough to remember the London Symphony Orchestra from its very inception. It seems to us old people now that there were giants in those days whose names are household words. There was the famous horn quartet, led by Adolf Borsdorf. There was John Solomon, the infallible trumpeter. One has to confess that he was fully aware of his infallibility. Once, when I was quite young, I had the honour to conduct the LSO in a composition of my own. It was almost my first experience of conducting. To the novice, music, from the conductor's desk, sounds absolute chaos. I thought however I detected a wrong note from the first trumpet. Of course I was too frightened to say anything at the moment, but after the rehearsal I shyly approached Mr Solomon and said to him 'Did you play B♭ or B♮ at letter A?' 'What was written in the part?' 'B♭.' 'If B♭ was written in the part, B♭ was what I played.' So that was that!

The timpanist was that superb player Henderson. He gave me my first and my best conducting lesson. I had had the audacity to conduct the first performance of my *Sea Symphony* at Leeds. I happened to come into the orchestra room together with Henderson before the concert, and the following conversation took place:

'You look pale and nervous.'

Source: Hubert J. Foss and Noël Goodwin, *London Symphony: Portrait of an Orchestra* (London: Naldrett Press, 1954), pp. iii–iv.

'Well, you see I have never conducted a large-scale work before.'

'Don't you worry, give us a good square four in the bar and we'll do the rest.'

These are only a few of the famous men who 'found out musical tunes' fifty years ago. I am not sure whether Billy Reed was a member of the orchestra right from the beginning, but by the time I was in a position to have frequent association with the orchestra he was the leader, and a wonderful leader he was. Many a time has he helped a conductor out of a difficulty. He had a marvellous ear, and could detect at once where a wrong note came from. I can remember being completely flummoxed by a strange sound in the orchestra at rehearsal. Reed whispered to me, 'It's the second oboe, but don't stop yet, go on for a few bars, and then try the passage again.' I remember, on another occasion, I had to conduct a piece in quick 6/8 in the middle of which there was a quick bar of 9/8. Just before he went on to play, I said to Reed, 'I know you'll help me out if I miss that 9/8 bar.' 'My dear fellow,' he answered, 'we shan't be looking at you!'

There are players in the orchestra today whose names will be equally famous, fifty years hence, with those of the great men of old. But the LSO know well that an orchestra does not depend entirely on the artistic insight and skilled craftsmanship of individual players. There is a story by Kipling of the maiden voyage of a new ship. For the first few days the timbers and the metal work and the sails and the ropes each sang a different tune, till one day the tune was all merged into one and the ship had achieved unity. The members of this orchestra know then that all their art and all their skill are valueless without that corporate imagination which distinguishes an orchestra from a fortuitous collection of players.

Long may the LSO continue over and over to renew that song, and keep in tune with Heaven.

CHAPTER 24

Introduction to *The Art of Singing*

IT IS REPORTED of the eighteenth-century Italian singing teachers that they used no method or theory, but merely sang to their pupils and said 'make a noise like that'. And the pupil had simply to go on till he did make a noise approximately like 'that'. If singing consisted in no more than making a nice noise no book could impart the singer's art to a pupil. But Arthur Cranmer's singing means much more than this. It is the presence of that emotional insight which informs his singing which makes its real beauty, lovely though his velvety tone is. And this integrity of purpose he can impart to the reader.

Brahms used to say to young composers 'you may not be able to write as well as Mozart, but at all events you can write as cleanly'. It will be given to few to sing as well as Cranmer, but this book will help the student to sing with that sureness of purpose and artistic conscience which has made Cranmer's 'Christus' such a great musical experience to all that heard it.

Source: Arthur Cranmer, *The Art of Singing* (London: Dennis Dobson, 1957), 5.

CHAPTER 25

Some Reminiscences of the English Hymnal

IT MUST HAVE been in 1904 that I was sitting in my study in Barton Street, Westminster, when a cab drove up to the door and 'Mr Dearmer' was announced. I just knew his name vaguely as a parson who invited tramps to sleep in his drawing-room; but he had not come to me about tramps. He went straight to the point and asked me to edit the music of a hymn book. I protested that I knew very little about hymns, but he explained to me that Cecil Sharp had suggested my name, and I found out afterwards that Canon Scott-Holland had also suggested me as a possible editor, and the final clench was given when I understood that if I did not do the job it would be offered to a well-known church musician with whose musical ideas I was very much out of sympathy. At this opening interview Dearmer told me that the new book was being sponsored by a committee of eight clerics who were dissatisfied with the new *Hymns Ancient and Modern*, which they considered unsatisfactory. He told me that these eight founders had put down £5 each for expenses, and that my part of the work would probably take about two months.

I thought it over for twenty-four hours and then decided to accept, but I found that the work occupied me two years and that my bill for clerical expenses alone

Source: *The First Fifty Years: A Brief Account of the English Hymnal from 1906 to 1956* (London: Oxford University Press, 1956), 2–5.

came to about £250. The truth is that I determined to do the work thoroughly, and that, besides being a compendium of all the tunes of worth which were already in use, the book should, in addition, be a thesaurus of all the finest hymn tunes in the world—at all events all such as were compatible with the metres of the words for which I had to find tunes. Sometimes I went further, and when I found a tune for which no English words were available, I took it to Dearmer, as literary editor, and told him that he must either write, or get someone else to write, suitable words. This was the origin of Athelstan Riley's fine hymn 'Ye watchers and ye holy ones'. Perhaps I may tell an amusing tale about the birth of these words. At the time they were written the bishops were making trouble over the unorthodox nature of some of the hymns included, especially such as suggested worship of the Blessed Virgin Mary. At one of our committee meetings Riley pointed out, with the delight of a schoolboy who has outwitted his master, that though the objectionable ideas were present in the hymn, they would not be recognized except by those in the know.

Another fine hymn is Dearmer's 'Holy God, we offer here' which was written to carry the *Choral* tune from Wagner's *Die Meistersinger*.

While trying to include all the good tunes, I did my best to eliminate the bad ones. This was difficult, because I was not entirely my own master. My committee insisted that certain very popular tunes should be retained. The climax came when my masters declared that I must myself write a fulsome letter to a prominent ecclesiastic asking for leave to print his horrible little tune. My committee and I finally settled our quarrel with a compromise by which the worst offenders were confined in an appendix at the end of the book which we nicknamed the 'Chamber of Horrors'.

In many hymnals the first idea of the musical editors seems to have been to include as many new tunes by the editor himself and his friends as possible. I avoided the specially composed tune so far as I could; of course, in the case of a very peculiar metre this was impossible; I then had to have recourse to well-known contemporary composers, for choice not church composers, and the result was some excellent tunes by W. H. Bell, Thomas Dunhill, Nicholas Gatty, and Gustav Holst, among others. I also, contrary to my principles, contributed a few tunes of my own, but with becoming modesty I attributed them to my old friend, Mr Anon.

The new book was also to contain a large proportion of plainsong: on this subject I really was ignorant, so I refused to touch it. This task was undertaken by one of the committee, Mr W. J. Birkbeck. His accompaniments were remade in the 1933 edition according to more modern, and, I think, more sensible ideas by Dr J. H. Arnold.

In preparing the book I employed the help of various friends, especially Gatty and Holst, in finding neglected tunes and the true versions of others which had been 'disfigured' into dullness in modern hymnals: I was much indebted to Robert Bridges's *Yattendon Hymnal* and Woodward's *Songs of Syon*.

I determined that my collection should contain the finest version of each tune, not necessarily the earliest, but if the earliest version were not used the fact should be duly noted; in the case of an altered version of the tune, that alteration should also be recorded. I was also careful to attribute tunes to their right authors, and I determined that I would not follow the careless, slipshod methods of earlier hymnal editors. I admit that in the first edition a few mistakes crept into the text, but with successive reprints these have been gradually corrected.

Percy Dearmer was the literary editor, but he also had a good understanding of music, and when I demanded words for a peculiar metre he was almost always ready to supply words himself or to find some poet who would do it for him. It must be confessed that some of these poets had only the vaguest notions about musical metre and accent, and I admit I was much puzzled by some of the translations of Latin which occurred in the Office hymns. On one occasion a proof of one of these was sent to me which contained the line: 'Dear Lord Jesus, bring us thistles.' I am sorry to say I took this seriously, and I wrote to Dearmer suggesting that though the imagery of thistles might be archaeologically correct it might be misunderstood by the public. No wonder Dearmer answered rather testily that I ought to have realized that thistles was a misprint for 'thither'.

Our committee used to meet and spend hours going through various hymn tunes. On one occasion, in the middle of one of these meetings, Athelstan Riley suddenly asked me if I would play something to act as a musical olive to clear our artistic palates! Riley had a large knowledge of ecclesiastical music, and used to come round often to my house to go through proofs, or suggest new tunes. He arrived on a beautiful white horse which he deputed a young relative of mine, a boy of about ten, to hold while he discussed hymns with me.

I have been blamed for using adaptations of folk tunes for hymn purposes, but this is, surely, an age-old custom. Tierssot has proved, to my mind conclusively, that certain church melodies of the Middle Ages were adapted from secular tunes, for example, the 'Tonus Peregrinus'. In Germany also, is not 'Innsbruck' adapted from a popular tune? And we know that the words of 'Jesu meine Freude' were originally a love song, 'Flora meine freude'. The well-known German tune which we sing as 'Glory, laud and honour' is certainly first cousin to 'Sellinger's Round'. The magnificently solemn tune for which Wesley wrote 'Lo, he comes', is an adaptation from a popular song of the day.

A new edition of *The English Hymnal* was brought out in 1933. In this edition I had the invaluable advice and help of Martin Shaw, and was able to introduce some of his fine tunes which were not extant in 1906. Owing to contract difficulties with certain holders of copyrights we were not able to omit any tunes, but we managed to introduce many fresh ones by substituting them for duplicates.

CHAPTER 26

Hands off the Third

WE HAVE BEEN called the land without music: this is not true, and never has been true; there is behind us a great tradition of music. We have in our midst melodies of classical beauty which can vie with any in the world.

Are we then unmusical? The authorities used to think so, and drove music underground, like the proceedings of a secret society. Music as a revelation and as an education was frowned upon, and was only to be used as an accompaniment to conversation. Indeed, I understand that the official use of military music is to drown the cries of the wounded!

However, in the last fifty years there has been a great change. Young students with artistic aspirations are as likely to write a sonata as a sonnet, or to take up the violin bow in preference to the paint brush.

We are gradually realising that music is not just a tickling of the ear, but an expression of a vision through magic casements of the eternal verities.[a]

More and more people are demanding that their musical needs shall be satisfied. The answer came ten years ago, a direction and guide to all this ferment, to satisfy those aspirations that lie beyond daily life, in the Third Programme.

Source: *Music and Musicians,* 6/2 (1957), 15
[a] The 'Charm'd magic casements, opening on the foam / Of perilous seas, in faery lands forlorn.'
John Keats, 'Ode to a Nightingale', lines 69–70.

Envy and Admiration

This is perhaps the greatest musical event that has happened in this country: wherever I have travelled in America or Europe I find the same story—our Third Programme is at once the envy and the admiration of all.

We are at last coming into our own and can stand as the leading spirits in the great hierarchy of art. Music is now taught in elementary schools, not as a substitute for wool-work, as Emma Woodhouse imagined,[b] but as part of a liberal education, developing the emotional, as well as the intellectual side of life.

If this education is to be of any value it must go on after school days are over, and how better than through the wireless? What a glorious moment it will be when all this potential music is realised, when everyone, from the highest to the lowest, whether as performer or listener, can help to make great music.

Now, when our hopes are highest, suddenly the blow falls; the Third Programme is to be emasculated into impotence, and it seems that the Home Service is to follow suit.

Perhaps the BBC governors imagine that the 'people' want 'popular' music, and must be given it. Has it ever occurred to them that they have a moral responsibility to make the best music popular?

Torrents of Applause

Some years ago I was at a Promenade Concert one Saturday evening, among a very 'popular' audience. Henry Wood had the courage to play one of the Beethoven *Leonora* overtures to this audience. Some of them glanced at the programme, and went out into the bar, many remained unwillingly and continue their conversations, but gradually, silence fell on them, their attention was riveted, and at the end there were torrents of applause.

Here, indeed, was music which was both great and popular—Beethoven had this element of popularity in him; when a friend complained that his latest quartets did not please, he did not answer that he did not want them to please, or that he did not consider the public, but said 'It will please one day.'

---

[b] Jane Austen, *Emma* (Cambridge: Cambridge University Press, 2005) Vol. I, Chapter 10, p. 92. 'If I know myself, Harriet, mine is an active, busy mind, with a great many independent resources; and I do not perceive why I should be more in want of employment at forty or fifty than one-and-twenty. Woman's usual occupations of hand and mind will be as open to me then as they are now; or with no important variation. If I draw less, I shall read more; if I give up music, I shall take to carpet-work.'

Is this new policy a question of expense? How can we, who as a nation willingly spend astronomical millions of pounds on killing the bodies of our enemies, dare to grudge a few paltry thousands on saving our musical souls?

We are told that broadcast music must pay its way—but does St Paul's Cathedral pay its way? Do the courts of justice and our council schools pay their way?

Music is a symbol of spiritual experience, fully equal to that of St Paul's. Must it be fettered to a balance sheet? Anyway, will this new scheme be any less expensive? For the hours, I think, are to be the same, and it costs more to hire a jazz trumpeter from the United States than to engage a second violin in a symphony orchestra.

Up to now I have chiefly considered audiences, but what of the performers and the composers? They have been looking largely to the BBC for their livelihood. Their chief desire is to perfect their art, but those that serve the altar must live of the altar.

The BBC Governors will perhaps say that it is not their business to support young musicians. But is it not their business? Old artists die off, or become beyond work, and who is to take their place if there are not young people trained for that purpose? May not the Marshal's baton be often hidden in the Private's knapsack? Let the Governors see to it that in rejecting one they do not lose the other.

Violins into Cricket Bats?

Well, the blow threatens to fall. Would it not therefore be better to beat our violins into cricket bats, and our bows into golf clubs, and give up all this humbug about being musical?

No, we are not unmusical, and we shall go on being musical, either with or without the BBC.

May I, however, give one warning to the BBC Governors? If they persist in giving the public what it is supposed to want, that same public may one day turn on the Governors and demand something better, and the Governors will not be able to supply it. Then, indeed, BBC music will die a well-deserved death.

To all of us, audiences and performers alike, the Third Programme has been of inestimable benefit. Let me repeat, it has been the envy of the world. Is something worthy, something splendid, something which we should be proud to claim as unique in the world, to be sacrificed for the sake of the kind of standardised entertainment which is already being mass-produced in every country?

Surely we can do better than that; surely we should defend to the last this service which maintains the highest standard of art and scholarship in our midst.

PART II

CONTINENTAL COMPOSERS

CHAPTER 27

Palestrina and Beethoven

IT IS ALWAYS a good plan to revise ones stock of opinions and ideas, and consider whether they are really correct. Special care should be taken with those that take the form of some epithet, which, by reflex action rather than by brain exertion, one applies to certain well-known objects in the mental landscape. Thus, it is always customary to speak of Palestrina as 'unemotional', and so engrafted is this idea on to the minds of most musical essayists, that they take it as an axiom and found many elaborate theories of musical evolution and the like on the assumption.

But is Palestrina really unemotional, and if he is not emotional, is Beethoven also unemotional, or is there some radical difference between them?

Let us first see what we mean by the word 'emotional'. All music, strictly speaking, is emotional, because every impression produced by music is an emotion; but when we talk of emotional music, we mean music which produces a very high degree of excitement in the sensibilities. This narrowing of the term emotion has proved a stumbling-block to many writers on music. The author of *Musical Morals*[a] describes a wonderful diagram of curves and angles which are supposed to represent the various emotions of a thirsty camel. As the camel finds himself fuller of emotion

Source: *The Vocalist*, 1/2 (1902), 36–7.
[a] H. R. Haweis, *Music and Morals* (London: W. H. Allen, 1871).

the curves rise higher, and from this it is argued that music becomes more emotional as it goes up and less as it goes down, so that a tune which is continually hopping is more emotional than one which remains comparatively still—let us say 'The soldiers in the Park' is more emotional than the Variations in Beethoven's B flat Trio! Evidently the problem cannot be settled in so rough and ready a manner; for our present purpose it is enough that there is some music which everyone agrees to call emotional; such are the love duet from *Die Walküre*, Chopin's D flat Prelude, and the Adagio from the Choral Symphony; and when we ask the question, 'Is Palestrina emotional?' we simply mean, 'Does his music have the same kind of effect on the hearer as those works which we have all agreed to call emotional?'

There can, of course, be only one true way of answering such a question, let everyone hear Palestrina sung and settle the matter to his own satisfaction. However, there still remains to see on what grounds Palestrina and the other composers of the sixteenth century are habitually denied emotional qualities; and before proceeding further, one doubtful point ought to be made clear—it must not be thought that unemotional music means bad music. Bach's Prelude and Fugue in B flat[1] is unemotional, and there is no doubt about its beauty; so our present business is not to defend Palestrina on an indictment, but merely to correct a misconception.

What are the chief reasons why Palestrina and his contemporaries should be considered 'unemotional'? One reason may be that they represent a *calm mood;* this is perfectly true—but it is not hard to find instances of music which represents the composer in a calm mood, and yet has a highly emotional effect on the hearer; what stirs the feelings more deeply than Bach's Fugue in E,[2] or the slow movement of Brahms' Pianoforte Quintet; but what *calmer* music can be found?

Again it is true that, though the great choral composers always wrote music for words, yet they paid no attention, in detail at least, to the signification of those words; this is in truth an indirect proof that their music is really emotional, for it means that they wrote for voices, and this in itself gives their music that human character which is found in all highly intense music. Everyone is familiar with the acute tension which is engendered when voices hold a prolonged sound, or the feeling of excitement when voices rise to a high note—true, the emotion is only felt when the sense of human effort is present, and the works of the sixteenth-century composers lose most of their effect when they are transferred to the passionless viols for which they were supposed to be 'apt'—but what would become of the emotion

[1] *Das Wohltemperierte Klavier*, I, No. 21.
[2] *Das Wohltemperierte Klavier*, II, No. 9.

in *Tristan* if it were played on viols? and how halting would be the rush of the 'Appassionata' Sonata if it were performed on a virginal?

It may be contended that the very texture of a mass or motet by Palestrina or Lasso or Vittoria, makes it unemotional, a style which from its very nature seems incapable of climax, since each part goes on its way regardless of the others, and one voice reaches its highest pitch of excitement while another is at its lowest ebb. At first it would appear that such a style as this was the reverse of exciting, and yet it is this very principle of divided climax which produces such a stirring effect in the most emotional music in existence—the Prelude to *Tristan*. Let anyone look at the fifty-fifth and following bars of that Prelude, and notice how the woodwind and first violins alternate their emotional crises, and a few bars later how the first and second violins rise to a climax and sink again, not together but in alternation;[3] let him compare with this the last four bars of Lasso's motet 'Tristis est Anima',— whether the modern or ancient instance produces a more emotional effect it is hard to say.

But it may be objected, 'All this is, possibly, quite true, but it remains un-deniable that Palestrina and Beethoven are as distinct as the two poles, and it seems an abuse of language to call the musical feeling of each composer by the same name.' It is no good pretending that this feeling does not exist. Palestrina and Beethoven certainly looked on their art from quite different standpoints. The musical emotion of the former, if it exists, is purely aesthetic. He was possessed by an intense and self-conscious love of beauty, and nothing else. Beethoven, on the other hand, seems to have throughout much more of strength of expression than of beauty of the sounds he was inventing. His music was the outcome of his life and thoughts. He wrote, not because he wanted to do something beautiful, but because his mind could only find relief in musical expression.

It would seem impossible for the two composers to have anything in common; if the emotion of Beethoven is the true emotion, then surely the textbooks must be right, and the 'aesthetic emotion' of Palestrina is no emotion at all, or else Bee-thoven's emotion is not musical emotion, and his art is not a pure art, but a hotch-potch of scraps, gathered together to hide his lack of true beauty.

The true solution of this dilemma lies in the double emotions which surround a work of art, namely, that emotion which impels the composer to write the music, and that which the hearer experiences when it is performed. These have no nec-essary connection. It is a great mistake to suppose, as many people do, that music is

[3] Full score, page 6.

a sort of phonograph into which the composer speaks his emotions, and that these are in their turn reproduced in the hearer.

The emotion felt by anyone listening to music is *purely aesthetic*, that is to say, the emotion is purely that of pleasure in the perception of beauty. To say that some music is sad and some merry is only tempering the same emotion with our intellectual perception of the composer's emotion in producing the music; but with our emotions in listening to the music the composer's intention has nothing to do. Art is to be judged not by intention but by the results.

For instance, there must be many people who know nothing about Beethoven except as the machine which produced, let us say, the *Eroica* Symphony; is their emotion any less, or, indeed, in any way different from that of those who have read up the whole story about Napoleon in their analytical programmes? There is but one really musical emotion, and it is produced by the music composed, and not by the agency which composed the music.

This does not mean, however, that the composer's aim and ideas are of no importance—they are, indeed, of supreme importance, for without them the music would not be written. But the composer's intention can only affect the listener by the *beauty* of the music which is the result of such intention; the function of music is to be beautiful and nothing less—it cannot be more.

Beethoven is a greater composer than Palestrina, simply and solely in so far as he is more beautiful, not because he composed with a different aim, or because his emotions as a man were stronger. It may be very much to Beethoven's credit if, as Mr Dannreuther says: 'He passes beyond the horizon of a mere poet and singer, and touches on the domain of the seer and prophet'; but it is as a 'mere' singer that he affects us in his music. If he was also a prophet, we will be grateful to him, and, moreover, be extremely annoyed with Palestrina for not also being a prophet— provided always that these prophetic qualities increase the *beauty* of their music.

Therefore we see that his music of Palestrina is emotional, and that of Beethoven is also emotional; and that, to the hearer, the emotion produced by the music of each is the same, namely, that which arises from pure delight in beauty; that is the only true musical emotion. The feelings which lead different people to write music may be as the stars in number, but the artist, like the alchemist, can take every feeling calm or wild, happy or miserable, and turn it into the precious metal of music. We are not called on to peep into the mysteries of the laboratory; it is enough for us to delight in the lustre of the pure gold.

CHAPTER 28

Bach and Schumann

BACH AND JEAN Paul Richter', what a contrast! Jean Paul the humourous senti-
mentalist, and Bach, 'the man who wrote fugues', considered a pedant by the
ignorant and ignorant by the pedants; and yet the writer, who first connected these
two names in one sentence, did so, not for the purpose of violent contrast, but with
a clear feeling of their affinity—'Bach and Jean Paul', writes Schumann, 'had the
greatest influence on me.'

There are at the present time very few musicians who think that Bach is merely
learned, or that learning and emotion cannot go hand in hand. Nevertheless, even
now the whole nature of Bach's work is often misunderstood, and even a well-
known writer can write of the 'old-world sweetness of the *Wohltemperierte Klavier*,'
and considers that 'the spirit of Bach is far enough removed from romance.' But it
cannot be mere coincidence that Bach's music, which had so long lain dormant,
underwent such a revival in the time of Schumann; nor can the famous performance of the 'St Matthew' Passion music under Mendelssohn be dismissed as the
unearthing of a fine but forgotten work. It was, in truth, at once the symbol and
the proof of the close bond of unity which existed between the Leipzig schools of
the seventeenth and nineteenth centuries—a unity not of form only, but of spirit

Source: *The Vocalist*, 1/3 (1902), 72.

also; so that when Schumann acknowledged his indebtedness to Bach he was not simply naming his counterpoint master, but was indicating the true founder of the romantic school.

It would be a poor argument to claim Bach as the inventor of musical romanticism, merely on the grounds that Schumann admired him; even the fact that Schumann was confessedly influenced by him is at best a circuitous course to adopt; but there is no need to use these unconvincing proofs when we have the master's own works to show us of what quality he is. If Bach has anything to do with the writers of musical romance, we can discover the resemblance by examining his compositions and judging if the same forces had weight with him which afterwards influenced the composers whom we call 'romantic'.

The surest means of finding out the nature of a writer's bent is to notice what medium of expression comes most naturally to him. What, then, was Bach's favourite means of expression? And is this medium a romantic one or not? To the first of these questions the answer is not doubtful. Bach's name is indissolubly connected with the fugue, not the fugue of the pedant with its triple counterpoint and its 'Stretto Maestrale', but the fugue in its living and artistic aspect, expanded so as to include all musical forms in which the different phases of one idea are brought one after another under review amidst conditions of ever-increasing excitement.

Surprising as it may seem, it is nevertheless the fact that the fugue as exemplified by Bach is a most perfect romantic medium. The essential difference between a fugue and a movement in 'sonata form', is that the fugue consists of the repetition of one musical phrase on different planes, and in different surroundings, while the sonata-movement consists of several musical subjects which are set off against one another so as to form a decorative pattern. In the fugue there is one idea, in the sonata-movement several; and from this it follows that in a fugue there is one *mood,* and in a sonata-movement several.

Now this is just the distinction which exists between the classical and romantic in music. In literature the classical writers may be said, broadly speaking, to give more attention to beauty of style, while the romantic devote themselves to beauty of subject and of sentiment; the subject or mood of any piece must be homogeneous, but style pure and simple depends for its effect on contrast and variety. Now in 'absolute' music there is no distinction between subject and style; indeed, abstract music may be said to be all style; in this art only is it possible to attain that simple delight in beauty for its own sake which makes an united whole out of a decorative scheme of contrast and repetition; thus the 'sonata' form is the most natural means of purely musical expression, but immediately any extraneous 'thought' or 'subject' is added to absolute music it becomes necessary to consider unity of *mood;* this is the problem which faced Schumann and the other writers of romantic music. For them the purely musical scheme in which equal importance is given to several themes in co-ordination was unsuitable; the form which was suitable was that in which one idea dominates a whole work—in fact, the fugue, in the most romantic of all his compositions, the Fantasia in C, Schumann preserves the unity of mood by means of a poetical idea which recurs again and again in varied surroundings. To what other origin can this scheme be traced than the Bach fugue, and what better superscription could be written over a Bach fugue than Schumann's very motto:

Durch alle Töne tönet	*Through all the notes*
Im bunten Erdentraum	*In earth's many-coloured dream*
Ein leiser Ton gezogen	*There sounds one soft long-drawn note*
Für den, der Heimlich lauschet.[a]	*For the one who listens in secret.*

Bach and Schumann stand on common ground in the way in which they regarded musical form; musical form is essentially decorative, and a composer who looks on the decorative side of music merely as a means will not be likely to add much to the development of music from the constructive point of view. Bach was no inventor in the matter of form; he did not, like Schumann, experience any difficulty in manipulating any form which he chose to employ, but he was content to use the forms ready to hand, such as the aria, from which he did not even eliminate the da capo—not that Bach was no innovator, but his very innovations show the romantic bent of his mind. His amazing harmonic progressions, which sound new and strange even now, are not the result of any conscious constructive aim, but are the direct outcome of the emotional intensity of the moment. This highly coloured polyphony is what Schumann inherited from Bach, as the most direct and personal expression of the moods inspired by Jean Paul, and this personal factor in their music unites under one banner the composers of 'Widmung' and 'Erbarme Dich'. There can be no doubt as to this personal element; music can be absolutely sublime and universal, or absolutely human and personal. Both ways of regarding the art have produced glorious results, but the glory of the one can never be the glory of the other.

One small but not unimportant romantic factor, which appears both in Bach and in Schumann, is musical symbolism. We have only to compare the 'Lettres

---

[a] This quotation prefaces the score of Schumann's *Fantasie*, Op. 17. The source is Schlegel's 'Die Gebüsche' from his poem cycle *Abendröte*. English translation from Nicholas Marston, *Schumann:* Fantasie, *Op. 17* (Cambridge: Cambridge University Press, 1992), 10.

dansantes' of the *Carnaval* with the 'Lass ihn kreuzigen' of the St Matthew Passion to be aware that the same impulse acted on each composer. This symbolism is not a mere mechanical device, nor is it claimed for Bach and Schumann that they invented it. Many composers before Schumann had made musical phrases out of their friend's names. Bach only adopted a device made common by his predecessors, but in the hands of a master it ceases to be a mere trick and represents a real emotion. Bach expresses the poignancy of 'Let him be crucified', in the cross-shaped subject which he uses; and Schumann, in his musical acrostics, has a much deeper purpose than a mere coincidence of letters and notes.

There are, of course, other composers than Schumann who are called 'romantic'. These, it is true, have little in common with Bach. Schubert and Weber were influenced by Beethoven and the Italians, if by anyone; and no one has ever accused Berlioz of being under the spell of a fugue writer. Indeed, Bach had little to do with the material, and often superficial romanticism of storms and wild huntsmen, and processions to the scaffold. But there is a truer and deeper romance, that of the heart, which deals not with external events, but with the minds and souls of human beings. This is the romance which Bach shares with his great apostle, Schumann—the romance which, by making the ideal art subservient to the intimacies of human emotions, finally raises human emotions to the level of ideal art. If it is true that Beethoven and Brahms have caught the 'divine Cecilia's' mantle, and can 'draw an angel down' from heaven, no less is it true that Bach and Schumann have inherited the gift of old Timotheus, and 'raise a mortal to the skies'.

CHAPTER **29**

The Words of Wagner's Music Dramas

IT MAY APPEAR to be a work of supererogation to write about Wagner now that we are well into the twentieth century. Surely, everything for and against Wagner that there is to write has been written down by this time fifty times over. Nevertheless, there are so many sides to the enormous Wagner question that I may, perhaps, be forgiven for adding another atom to the vast mass of literature on the subject.

I have no intention of writing at large about Wagner, this has already been too much done; but I intend to confine myself to one question: What is the relation between words and music in Wagner's musical dramas?—how intimately are they connected?

It is the general custom to describe Wagner's art as 'complex'. Now, complexity implies the joining together of two or more factors. If Wagner's art is complex, what are the factors of which it is made up? What are the various qualities which Wagner has heaped one on the other? If we look for the opinion of the Wagner Society (and surely they ought to know), we come to the conclusion that he is a sort of 'Jack of all trades and master of none', being at once a poet, a philosopher, a religious teacher, and an anti-vivisectionist, besides being, by the way, quite a good

Source: *The Vocalist*, 1/3 and 1/5 (1902), 94–6, 156–9.

composer; surely such a hotch-potch of qualities as these could never be the characteristics of a great artist.[1]

The more general opinion, however—the safe, journalistic opinion—is that Wagner is a 'poet-composer', that is, a poet and composer in equal quantities.

This is the theory; now let us turn to the facts. When Mr Robert Newman wishes to fill the Queen's Hall, what does he do? Does he engage Mrs Beerbohm Tree to recite a speech or two out of *Der Ring des Nibelungen*? No, he engages the Queen's Hall Orchestra to play the 'Walkürenritt', and why is this? Because everyone wishes to hear Wagner's music, but no one in his senses has ever wished to read the words of his dramas, except as a preparation for a complete performance with the music. How, then, about the 'complex art'? There was a famous epigram current in the early days of the Wagner controversy to the effect that he was 'a better poet than Beethoven and a better composer than Goethe'; this was, of course, intended for a sneer, but it represents the conclusion to which many writers on Wagner find themselves driven, namely—that if Wagner's art consists of music and poetry in equal doses, then his music alone is no more bearable than his poetry alone. Here is a specimen of this line of argument from the writings of a most intelligent musician and a professed admirer of Wagner: 'Tried by the standard of *Faust* the verse is not great verse. . . . Tried by the standard of *Fidelio* the music is often lacking in purity and expression. . . . But with all its imperfections it is still sufficiently wonderful that a single man should have combined in his own person so many diverse gifts and capacities.' Surely if Wagner's art consists in uniting bad poetry to bad music, no stretch of imagination can conceive of the result as otherwise than doubly bad.

The whole theory which lands us in this dilemma is a false one. Wagner's art is not complex at all—it is simple, as all great art is simple. Wagner is not of the family of Blake or Rossetti—a double artist. As M. Lavignac says: 'We must not regard him as a poet who knew how to set his verse to music, nor as a composer who writes his own poems.'[2] He does not dabble in two arts, but he is the exponent of a single art—and that is the musical drama.

When we feel that it is Wagner's music which we care for—that without the music there is nothing—we have arrived at the root of the matter. Just as Shake-

---

[1] This is not an empty statement. A lecture, given in the early days of the Wagner Society, has for its title: 'Richard [sic] as a Religious Teacher', and in a footnote to Mr Ellis' translation of Wagner's prose works, he solemnly quotes a line from *Tristan* as an argument against vivisection.
[2] [Albert] Lavignac, *The Music Dramas of R. Wagner*, trans. E. Singleton [(New York: Dodd, Mead & Co, 1898)].

speare wrote dramas in terms of speech, so Wagner wrote dramas in terms of song; and as a poetical drama grows out of a poetical view of life, so a musical drama must, in Wagner's own words, 'generate in the music'. Everyone recognizes poetical justice. Why should there not also be musical justice?[3]

The idea of the *musical drama* may become clearer if I trace, very shortly, the history of Wagner's musical ancestry. This is emphatically not to be found in the history of the opera. It is a mere coincidence that Wagner and Meyerbeer both wrote for the stage—they have nothing further in common. Wagner's real musical pedigree is found in the annals of the so-called 'Romantic Movement'. Romantic music is a reaction from the absolute music of Beethoven's symphonies. The pioneers of the Romantic school had little of that purely musical sense which is the inner strength of Beethoven. Lacking this inner strength, they had to seek support from the outside, and introduced an external factor into their music borrowed from another art, that of the drama. It is the dramatic element which is prominent in Schubert's songs, in Berlioz's programme music and in Weber's operas. There is yet another romantic composer who points the way still more directly to Wagner. In Schumann's music we find, for the first time, a dramatic and a musical idea springing simultaneously from the same inspiration. Thus the dramatic element grew, until at last a composer appeared who could only find his musical inspiration by connecting with it an actual drama, visibly and audibly enacted on a stage. This was the new art of Richard Wagner—the drama in terms of music.

Wagner's early impulses were not musical but dramatic. His first achievement as a boy was not a symphony but a tragedy. He describes in his autobiography how, soon after this tragedy was finished, he was taken by his parents to hear Beethoven's incidental music to *Egmont*. 'I at once determined', he writes, 'that my tragedy must also have music, but thought it better first to study the principles of thorough bass. The study fascinated me, and I resolved to become a musician.'[a] This last sentence puts the matter in a nutshell. What Wagner was at the age of fourteen he remained all his life—a musician, through his dramatic impulses.

Thus the music is paramount in Wagner's dramas—without the music there would be no play; but it is equally true that without the play there would be no music.

---

[3] It is also worth notice that Wagner never contemplated giving the scene painter a third equal share in the proceedings, as is sometimes imagined. The scene painter, like the theatre architect or the stage dressmaker, is a very important factor in aiding the representation; but it is never suggested that he is part author of the play, any more than it is suggested that the dramatist should paint his own scenery or make his own costumes.

[a] 'Autobiographic Sketch' in *The Artwork of the Future and Other Works*, trans. William Ashton Ellis (Lincoln: University of Nebraska Press, 1993), 5.

A musical drama must, of course, deal with such subjects as come within the scope of music. Now, the nature of music is that it can express emotion, but cannot touch reason and fact. Words, on the other hand, cannot express emotion, but can only indicate emotion through the medium of fact. Wagner himself argues thus: 'All music springs originally from the utterances of the human voice.' The primitive man may be supposed to have conveyed all his impressions by means of vocal sounds. Gradually, however, this simple mode of expression divided itself into two—the musical tone to express emotion, and the articulate word which can only express what appeals to the intellect. Now, it is obvious that the musical drama should deal, so far as possible, with musical sounds rather than with articulate words—with song rather than with speech. However, there must be facts in a play, and facts necessitate words. Let us try to imagine such a thing as a play without words.[4] We go into an opera-house; the curtain rises, and we see two women on a ship. (If we are at the Royal Opera, Covent Garden, there will be some difficulty in recognizing even the ship.) Where is the ship coming from? Where is it going to? Who are these women? Why are they on a ship at all? And why is one of them screaming? The music of the most emotional play in existence may traverse the whole range of sensibility without our being any wiser 'as to who they were, and why they were there, and what this is all about.' Nor can we take a real interest in the music until these 'harmless, necessary' facts have been explained to us in words. Through words alone can we find out that the two women are called Isolde and Brangaene, that they come from Ireland and are going to Cornwall, and it is only when we have found this out, that the music can take up its tale, and explain in unmistakable language that the real end of that journey is not Cornwall, 'King Mark's land', but the country beyond the world (Ex. 29.1).

So the drama must have words as well as music, since it must, to a certain degree, appeal to the understanding; the words will, so to speak, locate and crystallize the emotions of the music; but these words, it is to be remembered, must be sung, not spoken. Their business is to express a fact, but this fact must, as often as possible, be capable of an emotional interpretation, in order that it may be expressed in music. In short, the ideas in a musical drama must be such as a man can feel, and not such as he can only intellectually perceive. To make this possible, the plot of a musical drama must be very little dependent on facts. The action must be

---

[4] A 'ballet d'action' or 'pantomime' is sometimes described as a play without words, but in these cases the actors use a series of purely conventional gestures, which are substitutes for audible speech, and which have to be learnt by the audience as a new language; they are in no sense, really, plays without words.

Ex. 29.1. *Tristan und Isolde*, I. 3.

founded on the axioms of life, and not on the accidents of circumstances; for, as soon as reason and fact become part of the scheme, then song must abdicate in favour of speech. In Wagner's own words, 'The subject must be purely human and free from all conventions.'[5] It is a frequent complaint against Wagner that the characters in his plays are not individual people, but 'personified natural forces'. This is perfectly true. Alberich is not any particular dwarf, but an impersonation of the power of wealth. Fricka is not a character sketch of a goddess, but a dramatised idea—the idea of law as opposed to expediency; but his vagueness is not a sign of weakness, but a proof of the absolutely musical nature of Wagner's plots. A musical drama cannot be made out of those subjects which are generally considered dramatic, such as historical plays, comedies of manners, or elaborate analyses of character; as an English critic of the early eighties said with unconscious eloquence, 'Herr Wagner's subjects are not such as would have been chosen by our greater opera composers.'

It is this musical core which distinguishes the true 'musik-drama' from the ordinary grand opera.[6] The grand opera is a play which should be spoken and is sung; the musical drama is a play regarded entirely through the medium of music. In the grand opera the words are written by the 'librettist', presumably according to the canons of the spoken play; they are then handed over to the composer, who 'sets' them according to the canons of absolute music. In the musical drama, which Wagner invented, the dramatic and the musical idea spring from the same mind. To this new art neither the principles of the spoken play, nor those of absolute music can be applied. The musical drama has canons of its own which belong to no other art.

[5] 'Von aller Konvention losgelöste, Reinmenschliche.' [See 'A Communication to my Friends' in *The Artwork of the Future and Other Works*, 364.]

[6] When I refer to Wagner's musical dramas, I mean always the full-grown musical dramas—*Der Ring des Nibelungen, Tristan und Isolde, Die Meistersinger*, and *Parsifal*, and not the early attempts, *Rienzi, Holländer, Tannhäuser*, and *Lohengrin*.

The words are an absolutely necessary part of Wagner's scheme, nevertheless their position in that scheme is quite subordinate. I suggested above that Wagner's plots must not be judged as if they belonged to a spoken play; much less must words, which are to be sung, be judged as if they were to be spoken. This is no new idea. In 1774, Herder, in a letter to Glück, wrote: 'A poem must be an explanation, a guide to lead the stream of the music. It must be heard, not read.'[7]

When we find much prolixity and tautology in Wagner's word books, we must remember that we are judging a small part only of a whole organism, and that a subordinate part; we must judge Wagner's words solely on the ground of how well they assist the musical expression of the dramatic idea. I do not mean that Wagner's words are always bad, and never beautiful; one of many good proofs to the contrary is Waltraute's magnificent account of Wotan awaiting his end, in the first act of Die Götterdämmerung:

So sitzt er,	He sits there,
sagt kein Wort,	speaks no word,
auf hehrem Sitze	enthroned in silence,
stumm und ernst,	stern and sad;
des Speeres Splitter	the spear in splinters
fest in der Faust;	grasped in his hand.
Holdas Äpfel	Holda's apples
rührt er nicht an.	tastes he no more.
Staunen und Bangen	Fearful and trembling,
binden starr die Götter.	The gods look on in silence.
Seine Raben beide	He has sent his ravens
sandt' er auf Reise:	forth on their journeys;
kehrten die einst	when they return
mit guter Kunde zurück,	and bring the news he awaits,
dann noch einmal,	then for the last time
zum letztenmal,	a smile of joy
lächelte ewig der Gott.[b]	will shine on the face of the god.

The duty of the words is to help the music. Where the music needs no help it would be most presumptuous of the words to offer their well-meant but clumsy assistance. There are innumerable cases where the music can explain the drama with

[7] [Henry Woodd] Nevinson, Herder and his Times [(London: Chapman and Hall, 1884)], 188.
[b] Translations from the Ring in this chapter are taken from Richard Wagner, The Ring of the Nibelung, trans. Andrew Porter (London: Faber, 1976).

no extraneous assistance. Before I give examples of these cases, I must explain the duties of that very important character in the Wagnerian drama, the orchestra. The importance of the orchestra is well typified by its physical position in the theatre between the audience and the actors. Wagner's orchestra is, indeed, half actor and half audience. In its character of actor it intensifies the action of the moment by its eloquence, and in its character of audience it comments on the action by reviving the memory of what has gone before. The first scene of *Das Rheingold* furnishes a good instance of how the music (in this case both the orchestra and the vocal melody) can intensify the action of the moment, making feasible a scene which, if it depended on words alone, would be impossible.

In writing about this scene, Mr Bernard Shaw notices that the nymphs are 'not singing ballads about the Loreley and her fated lovers, but any nonsense which comes into their heads.' A writer of spoken plays, if he had attempted this scene, would have been forced to make the Rhein-töchter say some such absurd literary ballads as Mr Shaw suggests; he could not possibly make his characters swim up and down in front of the audience and *say* nothing more interesting than 'Weia waga, woge du Welle'; indeed, if this scene depended on its words alone, there might be some justification for Sir Augustus Harris's classic solecism about a 'damned pantomime'. But when these very words are not said, but sung, they become the most natural and forcible expression of the situation (Ex. 29.2).

Ex. **29.2**. *Das Rheingold*, Scene 1.

Who shall dare to deny the beauty, the power and the 'elemental' simplicity of this scene as it stands, and how a literary flavour in the words would have spoiled it!

The orchestra as audience is even more useful to the drama than the orchestra as actor. This usefulness is due to the power of association which music possesses. All the senses can call up associations when excited, but the sense of hearing has this faculty to a greater degree than any other sense. Perhaps our fingers were freezing when we first played a certain prelude of Chopin—then that prelude will always bring the sense of chill to our fingers; or the overture to *Euryanthe* will never fail to bring vividly before us the hot stuffy atmosphere of the 'Vierter Rang' of some German opera house, where we first heard it. Very little is required to set the memory in motion; the turn of a phrase, a certain harmonic progression, the low notes of a viola—these are enough to let loose a whole train of memories, or even to bring back old and forgotten moods and frames of mind. It is this phenomenon of musical reminiscence of which Wagner makes such magnificent use. Each character and each important event in Wagner's dramas has its own music, which at first intensifies the action of the moment, and, whenever it is afterwards played, recalls that moment or that person to the hearer. I will content myself by giving two examples, out of many, of the way in which Wagner uses this system of leitmotiven to expound the drama where words would be useless for the purpose. In the first act of *Die Walküre*, Siegmund is telling the story of his life. Neither his listeners on the stage, nor his audience in the theatre know anything about him, except what he is telling them. Siegmund describes, in the well-known passage, how he returned from hunting to find that his father, 'Wolfe', has disappeared. This is all he says, and all he knows. But Wagner wants the audience to know who Siegmund's father really was. Now, obviously, no one on the stage can explain this, for the simple reason that they do not know it, so the orchestra takes the matter into its own hands. As Siegmund utters the words, 'My father I found no more', we hear in the orchestra a fragment of the 'Walhalla' theme of *Das Rheingold*, and the situation is at once clear—'Wolfe' is none other than Wotan the god (Ex. 29.3).

This example shows us the orchestra pointing to the past; but Wagner can also use his music prophetically. The leitmotif can show to the audience the way along which events are tending, the true action of the drama which underlies the apparent action. The orchestra can prophecy evil when all appears propitious, it can sound triumph in the midst of apparent defeat, it can be hopeful when everything on the stage seems most desperate; and this it does quite independently of what the characters on the stage are doing or saying. Now, in a spoken play the case is quite different; here the playwriter has to depend entirely on the apparent action of the drama to explain his purpose. By apparent action I mean all that the audience can actually see or hear on the stage. It is only through this medium that the writer of spoken plays can explain himself; he has to depend entirely on what the actors are doing or saying at any particular moment to make clear the purpose of his play. Thus, in the first act of *Die Götterdämmerung* (scene ii) the situation is this. Siegfried, wearing Alberich's ring, is greeted by Hagen, Alberich's son. Hagen, though he openly befriends Siegfried, secretly wishes his ruin. In a spoken play, what a clumsy array of asides and double meanings this tragic irony would have entailed; but, in a musical drama, Hagen need only give a plain, hearty greeting, 'Heil

Siegfried theurer Held', and it is the orchestra which reminds the audience that Alberich's ring is cursed, and that Hagen's greeting bodes not good, but evil to Siegfried (Ex. 29.4).[8]

There is another way in which the music, apart from the words, affects the drama, which must not be omitted here—that is, in its construction. It has often been said that Wagner disregarded all musical form. This is not true, even in the narrow sense in which it is intended. I shall try to show, later on, that Wagner had his recitatives and arias just as much as Bellini. But even if, from the pedantic point of view, he failed to conform to the prescribed mould in the details of his work, it was not that he disregarded musical form, but that he enlarged its scope. Wagner may almost be said to have written his dramas on a symphonic basis, with regular recurrences of the principal themes at important points in the design. This accounts for many apparent faults of construction in the plays when we read them to ourselves. For instance, one critic says: 'An audience which has already seen *Rheingold*

---

[8] The whole of this scene, apparently so quiet and uneventful, is filled with the gloomy foreboding of the orchestra.

and *Walküre*, has no need of the elaborate dialogue between Mime and the Wanderer. Siegfried's account of his boyhood, in the third act of *Götterdämmerung*, tells us nothing that we did not know before.' This redundancy is objected to because it is contrary to the canons of the spoken play. Perfectly true; but it is not Wagner who is wrong, but the canons which are inapplicable. When the whole means employed are regarded, and not a small part only, this very repetition is one of Wagner's most convincing methods of preserving dramatic unity. An opera by Mozart is a heterogeneous mass of perfectly formed units—in Wagner's drama the unit is the whole play.

All this the music can do by itself. What remains for the words to achieve? The duty of the words is to say just as much as the music has left unsaid, and no more. Now music, expressing as we have seen, emotion only, will demand least of the words at the most emotional moments, and the words will stand out most clearly in those explanatory passages where the music is all but non-existent. Therefore, the relative importance of words and music will vary exactly as the dramatic situation approximates to feeling or to mere explanation. At one end of the scale are those passages where the words are a bare statement of fact; in which cases the singer's utterances will be a near approach to speaking, and the orchestra will be almost

Ex. 29.5. *Das Rheingold*, Scene 2.

Fricka

Nur Won ne schafft dir, was mich er schreckt? Dich freut die Burg, mir bangt es um
What thee de - light-eth brings me but dread! Thou hast thy joy, my fear is for

Frei - a! Acht - lo - ser, lass' dich er - in - nern des aus-be-dun - ge-nen Lohn's! Die
Frei - a! Heed-less one dost thou re-mem-ber the tru - ly promised re-ward! The

Burg ist fer - tig, ver - fal - len das Pfand: ver -
work is fin - ished and for - feit the pledge: for -

ga - ssest du was du ver - gab'st?
get - test thou what thou must pay?

Rossini, *Guillaume Tell*, III.

silent. At the other end are those passages where the music rises to the height of lyrical intensity, and the words merely supplement the music by giving utterance to the human voice. This gamut of emotions was not invented by Wagner. It is inherent in the nature of the drama, whether musical or not. In the older opera the scale consisted of three degrees only—the bare declamation (*recitativo secco*), the scena, and the aria. This triple division finds its parallel in the spoken play. Hamlet's great soliloquy is a scena, and the passage which immediately follows it ('Soft you, now, the fair Ophelia') is *recitativo secco*, while a good instance of a regular interpolated aria is Mercutio's 'Queen Mab' speech in *Romeo and Juliet*. It is, surely, a mistake to imagine that Wagner rejected this threefold scheme. Certainly we find plenty of *recitativo secco* in Wagner, though not quite of the old-fashioned perfunctory kind. It is interesting to notice that those who stigmatize the less emotional parts of Wagner as 'dull', have not a word to say against those repulsively tedious conversations which fill up the gaps in the conventional opera. Here follow two examples of bare declamation—one from Wagner and the other from Rossini. It is not hard to say which is the most interesting (Ex. 29.5–6).

The final scene of *Götterdämmerung* and Hans Sach's monologues from *Die Meistersinger*, are instances of the scena, and no one surely will deny that Siegmund's Spring song, or Siegfried's 'Schmiedelieder' are more lyrical than 'Ah che la morte', 'Una Voce', and 'O Mio Fernando', all rolled into one.

Wagner did, indeed, break down the hard and fast lines which divided one class of dramatic utterance from another; he made it possible for a dramatic character to have more than three emotions; he also made the kind of utterance which a character shall use dependant on the dramatic needs of the moment. In the old-fashioned opera this was fixed by hidebound tradition; each actor had to have so many scenas and so many arias, with most undramatic results, as may be seen in the second act of *Don Giovanni*, where the performers crowd on to the stage, one after the other, without rhyme or reason, to work off their due quantum of singing. Wagner does not scruple to give little but declamatory music to the less emotional characters. Alberich never sings a duet with anybody, and Titurel misses a most obvious chance of a grand aria with male chorus—but then, of course, we must remember that Wagner had no deputy, as the older composers had, to write 'the arias for the minor characters'.

Having decided for the moment that we can class the different parts of the dramas under these three headings, let us see a little more in detail how Wagner treats the words in each case; first, in the case of bare declamation, and, before going any further, the question suggests itself—Why should there be any of this dry, unmusical recitative at all—why should not the essentially prosaic parts of the drama be spoken? Jacopo Peri, in his preface to *Euridice*, the first opera ever written, writes: 'I was compelled to use a tone of expression other than that of every-day speech.' This is the best answer to such a suggestion—a musical drama must never sink to the level of ordinary life. Another objection is this: speech cannot gradually merge into song; if some of a drama is to be spoken and some sung, where shall the line be drawn where one ends and the other begins?

But to return to Wagner. For the bare recitative the words are, for the moment, paramount, but they must not presume on their momentary superiority. Their duty is to state some concrete fact which is hardly amenable to musical treatment; they must never be decorative in themselves. Now, in a spoken play, even at the most prosaic moments, some attention is given to rhythm, and elegance of diction, as in this passage from *Julius Cæsar*:

> *Messala, I have here received letters,*
> *That young Octavius and Mark Antony*
> *Come down upon us with a mighty power,*
> *Bending their expedition towards Philippi.*[c]

Compare with this Isolde's command to Brangaene in the second act of *Tristan* (Ex. 29.7).

Ex. **29.7.** *Tristan und Isolde*, II. 1.

Here there is not an extraneous word. The one fact which needs expressing is expressed and no more; any decorative treatment which is necessary is supplied by the actual melody of the voice, any simultaneous embellishment of the words would be absolutely harmful. Cannot we imagine, however, how the ordinary librettist would have dragged Isolde through a dozen lines of blank verse, with metaphor and classical allusion complete; and, thereby, entirely destroyed the dramatic effect of the passage.

As we ascend the emotional ladder, the relations between words and music become more complicated; and the chief difficulty is this: sentiment and emotion can be expressed in music, but can only be indicated in words. But this verbal

[c] Shakespeare, *Julius Caesar*, IV. 3. 167–70.

indication takes a much shorter time than the corresponding musical expression; so the words must, somehow, be kept waiting while the music is catching them up. The older operatic composers adopted the simple device of repeating the words over and over again, while the music was working out its more leisurely view of the situation. Wagner rightly considered it absurd for a character in a play to have to repeat 'Ombra mai fu di vegetabile' twenty times over. But the same difficulty which had faced Handel faced Wagner also. He, too, has to keep the verbal waiting on the musical sense, not, indeed, by repeating the same words, but by repeating the same meaning in synonymous phrases, thus:

O heilige Schmach!	*Oh infinite shame!*
O schmählicher Harm!	*Oh shameful distress!*
Götternot!	*Gods' despair!*
Götternot!	*Gods' despair!*
Endloser Grimm!	*Endless remorse!*
Ewiger Gram!	*Grief evermore!*
Der Traurigste bin ich von allen![9]	*The saddest of beings is Wotan!*

The above quotation seems the merest tautology when read, but when sung it at once seems the most forcible and impressive method of reaching a dramatic climax.

This necessity of waiting on the music accounts for much of the apparent vagueness in Wagner's dramas; and as the music surges over the words, these become more vague and less satisfactory to read by themselves until a point is reached, at the most lyrical moments, where the sound of the human voice is much more important than the logical meaning of the sentences. In such cases as the great 'Song to the night', in the second act of *Tristan*, the words sink entirely into the background. When Shakspeare wishes to indicate intense emotion, he does so by tho very extravagance of his language:

> *Come, gentle night, come, loving, black-browed night,*
> *Give me my Romeo; and, when he shall die,*
> *Take him and cut him out in little stars,*
> *And he shall make the face of Heaven so fine,*
> *That all the world shall be in love with night,*
> *And pay no worship to the garish sun.*[d]

[9] *Die Walküre*, II. 2.
[d] *Romeo and Juliet*, III. 2. 20–5.

This is what Wagner has to say about the night:

Tristan, Isolde:

O sink hernieder,	*O sink down upon us,*
Nacht der Liebe,	*night of love,*
gib Vergessen,	*make me forget*
daß ich lebe;	*I live:*
nimm mich auf	*take me*
in deinen Schoß,	*into your bosom,*
löse von	*free me*
der Welt mich los!	*from the world!*

Tristan:

Verloschen nun	*Extinguished now*
Die letzte Leuchte;	*is the last glimmer . . .*

Isolde:

was wir dachten,	*of what we thought,*
was uns deuchte;	*of what we dreamed . . .*

Tristan:

all Gedenken,	*all remembrance . . .*

Isolde:

all Gemahnen,	*all recollection*

Tristan, Isolde:

heil'ger Dämmrung	*holy twilight's*
hehres Ahnen	*glorious presentiment*
löscht des Wähnens Graus	*obliterates the horror of delusion,*
welterlösend aus.[e]	*setting us free from the world.*

Here there is no attempt to depict passion by force of language. Why should Wagner use words when he had a weapon to hand ten times as sharp? Wagner was not a master of words, but a master of music; he lets music have its full sway where it so palpably dominates the situation.

To meet such varying needs as these, Wagner has devised a very elastic scheme of verse, which never hampers the music by its obtrusive rhythm, but is rhythmical enough to help on the music when necessary. It is not merely prose cut up into strips, but is really rhythmical verse, though without any mechanical regularity. In

[e] Translation by Lionel Salter in CD liner notes Wagner, *Tristan und Isolde* (Teldec 4509-94568-2, 1994), Act II, Scene 2. In the original Vaughan Williams quotes from the libretto in German as above, but omits the characters' names.

Der Ring des Nibelungen Wagner combines with this the 'Stabreim' or alliterative verse.[10]

In this kind of verse there is no rhyme at the end of the line, but an alliteration between accented syllables, all initial vowel sounds being considered alliterative. There is no regularity in the number of syllables in a line, but only in the number of accented syllables. This method of versification, borrowed from mediæval times, has obvious advantages for the purposes of the musical drama; the indefinite length of each line gives a free hand to the music; the words which are important to the sense come on the alliterated—that is, the accented—parts of the line, and, most important of all, alliteration is indigenous to the Teutonic languages. Ordinary language, even in England, abounds in pairs of words bound together by alliteration, because of their similarity or contrast of meaning, such as 'weal and woe', 'house and hearth', 'ever and aye'. The following is an example of Wagner's use of the 'Stabreim':

Immer ist Undank	*Never one word*
Loges Lohn!	*of praise or thanks!*
Um dich nur besorgt,	*For your sake alone,*
sah ich mich um,	*hoping to help,*
durchstöbert' im Sturm	*I restlessly roamed*
alle Winkel der Welt,	*to the ends of the earth,*
Ersatz für Freia zu suchen,	*to find a ransom for Freia,*
wie er den Riesen wohl recht.[11]	*one that the giants would like more.*

The one thing that is not wanted for a musical drama is 'musical verse'. A decorative scheme of artificial metres and rhymes makes the most unsuitable word-book imaginable.

That librettists of all times and all countries have hailed from Grub Street, is a truism of musical history; but, contemptible as nearly all librettos are, their real defect lies in their utter unsuitability for musical treatment, both in subject and in style. The reason of this failure is that librettists, good and bad, have always regarded the opera from the stand point of the spoken play; when they found that a good play was unsuitable, they merely substituted a bad one! The fundamental nature of the mistake has been seen more clearly in modern times, when, occasionally, an accomplished and painstaking librettist has turned out an opera book

---

[10] In *Tristan* and *Die Meistersinger*, he uses the ordinary 'end rhyme'.
[11] *Das Rheingold*, Scene 2.

in faultless Shakespearian style, consisting of a series of neat decasyllables and well-groomed lyrics, which would be ludicrous if they were not so pathetic.

Who, then, is to write the words of a musical drama? The task is not an easy one. The words of the drama, important though they be, are yet quite subordinate. They must not appear important by themselves, but only when united to the music. Who shall write poetry which shall fulfil these conditions? A poet who would undertake such work must be at a low ebb of invention. If he is to write poetry worthy of the name, he must not subordinate it to any outside conditions. He cannot entirely sink himself to save the genius of another; or, if he does so, he will be obliged to stick to such commonplaces as are sure not to be unsuitable, and from such commonplaces no good music can spring, unless, indeed, the composer, like Beethoven in *Fidelio*, practically disregards the words, and writes music to a parallel tragedy of a much deeper nature.

There is one man only who can write the words of a musical drama, and that man is the composer of the music, for the drama must generate in the music. If the music is beautiful and noble, then no more need be demanded of the words than that they should help the music, provided always that words and music spring from the same mind and the same inspiration.

The position of the words in Wagner's scheme has been much obscured by the blind fanaticism of those enthusiasts who think that, because the whole of a work of art is great, therefore each part, taken separately, must also be great. Such a congeries of perfections would only result in an enormity. Wagner himself was the last person to imagine that his art was a sum in simple addition. In one of his pamphlets he writes that such an idea only suggests to him a picture-gallery full of statues, where one man plays a sonata while another reads a poem. It is true that Wagner called himself a poet, but he uses this word in its broadest sense, to include 'Ton-Dichter', as well as 'Wort-Dichter'. It is also true that he published the text of the *Ring* separately, but in doing so he is careful to speak of his 'disinclination to have it judged as a literary production.' It is as absurd to criticise the words of one of Wagner's dramas alone as it would be to criticise the drum part alone, and the parallel may be carried further. If we were shown the drum part of the *Ring* as a complete work of art, we should not think very highly of the artist; but, considered as a part only of a large organism, we may well admire its beauty.

The Wagnerian drama is like a great building in which many parts fit into a complete whole. In this building the music corresponds to the portico, the staircases, the mouldings and traceries, while the words are the foundations and beams—all those parts of the building which are only important as supports to the whole structure. What we notice in the building are the ornamental parts; we are only occasionally conscious of the foundations and supports. So, in the Wagnerian drama the music is paramount and the words subservient; and as the subordinate parts of a building acquire a beauty of their own through their very usefulness, so do Wagner's verses become beautiful through their absolute assimilation into the whole scheme. We can no longer, as in the old-fashioned opera, ignore Wagner's words, neither must he be regarded as Shakspeare added to Beethoven. Wagner's art is a new art, and must be judged in a new way—not as a play with music, nor as a symphony with action, but as a musical drama.

CHAPTER 30

Brahms and Tchaikovsky

ST PAUL TELLS us that 'one star differeth from another in glory'; certainly no astronomer would ever think of discussing the relative merits of Sirius and the pole-star; or comparing the 'bands of Orion' with the 'sweet influences of Pleiades'. In the same way it is, in reality, ridiculous to compare those artistic luminaries which happen to appear at the same time on the horizon of the concert-room. Brahms and Tchaikovsky have nothing in common but the age in which they lived; to put them together in one article is to make a perfectly fortuitous combination of names; to compare them together to the disadvantage of either is to say that one likes a jam-puff better than a bicycle ride. Yet in England today these two names seem to have become the watchwords of the opposite camps in the party politics of music. On the one hand we hear of the 'Brahms clique' (though the 'Brahms clique' is, in reality, by no means unfriendly to Tchaikovsky); and on the other hand we hear of the 'Tchaikovsky coterie' (at whose head-quarters, by the way, one can often hear magnificent performances of Brahms). So it is hardly possible to help putting these two composers side by side and seeing what results one can obtain by comparing them; just as if one were to marry Colonel Newcome to Rosa Dartle, and see how they prospered.

Source: *The Vocalist*, 1/7 (1902), 198–200.

Before going any further I had better, to avoid misunderstanding, state my own opinion as to the relative merits of the two composers. If I had, like the 'Bezonian', to say 'under which king' or die, then I should declare in favour of Brahms. But this I should do under protest; they both have their times and seasons, we cannot afford to do without either of them; all I say is that if I *had* to do without one or the other Tchaikovsky would go by the board.

The two great points of comparison between Brahms and Tchaikovsky are depth of emotion and facility of expression. In facility of expression Tchaikovsky undoubtedly takes the lead. There was a 'musical comedy' very popular not long ago (indeed, it may still hold the boards, for all I know) in which a young lady of the name of 'Maisie' used to inform the audience that she 'gets there every time'. This is exactly the case with Tchaikovsky—he is the Maisie of music; he 'gets there every time'. Never a stroke fails; every emotion which he feels he translates into music with the readiness of a true Russian linguist. And herein lies his weakness, that the expression is often too intense for the emotion behind it; the very fact that expression comes so easily to him is apt to make him careless as to whether his idea is worth expressing. He seems unable to distinguish false sentiment from true.

How different is the case with Brahms! He has none of 'Maisie's' good qualities; over and over again he fails to get half-way in the direction that he set out to attain; so that if Tchaikovsky's fault is insincerity and glibness, Brahms' is certainly a certain long-windedness and laboriousness which often verges on the dull.

So much for expression—Tchaikovsky nearly always gets there, Brahms, as often as not, fails. Then the question arises—where do they want to get to? Is not Brahms' failure (when he does fail) owing to the immense heights which he set himself to scale? is not Tchaikovsky's success largely due to the easiness of the task which he undertakes? Brahms might well take for his motto:

What I aspired to be,
And was not, comforts me.

Even when he fails, it is interesting to see the great mind groping. And when Brahms succeeds, are not all the failures—were they a hundred times as many as they are—paid for a hundred times by such monuments of deep emotion as the Pianoforte Quintet, or the *Tragic* Overture, or such a paradise of beauty as 'Vineta', or 'Schicksalslied'? Tchaikovsky seldom really stirs the emotions—he only ruffles the surface, and, for this reason, perhaps his emotional utterances are the more quickly and evenly felt; a mere scratch pains much sooner than a deep wound. This is the case of Tchaikovsky when he succeeds. When he fails, as even he fails sometimes, the less said of the result the better. The nature of Tchaikovsky's genius leads him to the best results when he is more characteristic. Brahms is at his greatest when he is more universal. The one becomes banal directly he ceases to be characteristic; the other's individuality outlives the peculiarities of phraseology.

Among Tchaikovsky's most characteristic and, therefore, his greatest works, his Fourth Symphony seems to me to stand out supreme. It is, at all events, his greatest symphony, sharing, perhaps, the chief place among his compositions with the great pianoforte trio written in memory of Nicholas Rubinstein. The public seem to prefer the Sixth and the critics the Fifth Symphony, and have left the Fourth Symphony in the cold; but to my mind this work has a ruggedness and strength which we look for in vain in the two later symphonies. It is much more manly and much less gentlemanly than anything else Tchaikovsky has written. The tragedy of the opening trumpet call is immense, though it is quite out of proportion to the rest of the movement, with its valse rhythm and its rather trivial second subject; indeed, the whole movement is an uncomfortable mixture of comedy and tragedy; not like Schubert's great Finale in C major, which sets out as a comedy and gradually has tragedy forced upon it. This movement does not seem to know its own mind—it vacillates between the two moods, so that neither of them produce quite the effect that they might under rather different conditions. The 'pizzicato ostinato' is not only a brilliant tour de force, but is also most delightful music, while the tunes of the slow movement and the finale shine pre-eminent among all Tchaikovsky's melodies. They are redolent of Russia, the vast dreariness of the steppes, the intense isolation of the country life. We are irresistibly reminded of Turgenev's 'Sportsman's Sketches', or the farm-life in *Anna Karènina*. Would that Tchaikovsky had written more such stuff as this, and had let frock-coated sentiment alone!

The very whimsicality of this whole comparison tempts one to step further, and to pass from Tchaikovsky's Fourth Symphony to the Fourth of Brahms. This Symphony, like the other, has not found favour with the public; on the occasion of its second performance in the Gewandhaus, in Leipzig, the audience all trooped out of the hall before the last movement; perhaps it was not played quite in the way that would attract an audience. A work has very often to wait for popularity, until an interpreter comes along who will give it its true emotional significance; then, and only then, many a great work speaks to those who are ready to receive it, but whose vision has been dimmed by some bungling middleman. This Symphony has suffered as much from its friends as from its enemies; and this is especially the case in the last movement, the identical movement which proved too much for the stomachs of the Leipzigers. This movement is a kind of chaconne, or a series of variations and transformations of a short, striking, musical phrase, gradually drawing to a climax. Now, in this movement we are informed by Brahms' would-be admirers, that in the first place the theme is so difficult to follow, that the most hardened musicians are often forced to give up the chase half-way through; and that, in the second place, its great merit lies in its extreme contrapuntal skill. To this the would-be Brahms' detractors answer that a theme which cannot be made out is no theme, and that contrapuntal skill ceased to be considered music with the death of Oke-ghem in the fifteenth century. However, the truth is that this movement is perfectly simple to follow; there is no necessity to ferret out the actual notes of the original tune in each variation. Indeed, a series of short and concise epigrams, such as these, is one of the easiest musical formations to grasp at once; nor is the contrapuntal skill, as such, any greater than is displayed every day by an average conservatoire student; with this difference, that Brahms makes beautiful music out of his coun-terpoint, which the average student probably fails to do. So the critics who abuse this movement on the ground of complexity or dry learning, are proved guilty of criticising, not the work itself, but someone else's opinion on it. This, indeed, they are forced to, if, as my knowledge of critics leads me to believe, they have never heard this Finale themselves. At all events, they cannot have listened to an extra-ordinarily fine performance of this Symphony, by Mr Henry F. Wood, at the Queen's Hall, last year. The interpretation of the whole work was masterly, emo-tional, enthusiastic, and popular in the best sense of the word. And it was on this very Finale that Mr Wood concentrated all his forces. He has disproved, moreover, the old fallacy that this movement is a mere contrapuntal exercise; he showed, most clearly, that we have here a strong emotional utterance full of the most wonderful melody and the deepest feeling. For myself, I fail to understand how an audience can help recognising the grandeur of the theme at its opening, the beautiful tunes given to the flutes and cellos in the middle section, and the terrifying climax where the trombones once more return with the bare opening theme.

Of the other three movements I might say only a little. The third movement—the Scherzo of the Symphony, is decidedly the weakest movement; it is light and pleasing in itself, but it is laid out rather heavily for its subjects, giving one the impression of an elephant dancing; also it seems out of place in the whole scheme, and to be a false touch in the whole picture. The opening Allegro of the Symphony is one of those examples of intense virility and intense emotion which are so char-acteristic of Brahms at his best; and as to the slow movement, it contains a series of lovely melodies which should serve as an excellent object lesson to those extraor-dinary people who pretend to think that Brahms cannot write tunes. These two movements, at all events, require no words of explanation.

So much for the merits of this Symphony, merits which are most characteristic of their composer. This Symphony is also rife with characteristic faults, and chief among these are those of orchestration. It is quite wrong to suppose that Brahms cannot write for the orchestra; true, he does not care for luscious effects of instrumentation, but this is only that his own peculiar 'spiky' scoring suits his ideas and moods so perfectly. But sometimes, as in this symphony, he carries his dislike of instrumental butterscotch too far, and gives us instrumental vinegar instead. He seems, sometimes, almost wilful in his determination to give the wrong tune to the wrong instrument. What should be sung by the strings is squeaked by the oboe; what should stand out clear and emotional is fogged by a mass of superimposed polyphony. The intellect is of great service to the composer, but it must not be allowed to get out of hand. This is only one of the blemishes which mar the perfection of Brahms' work, but all these imperfections are the result of an almost impossible ideal. It is comparatively hard to fail when the goal is an easy one; but the greater the perfection aimed at the more glaring and obvious will be the discrepancies between the intention and the achievement. The nearer Icarus flies to the sun, the greater will be his fall when his wings fail him.

I am afraid I have digressed considerably from my original intention in this article. There is all the difference in the world between 'bread and butter' and 'bread-and-butter'; and to write an article about Brahms and about Tchaikovsky does not, perhaps, justify the title 'Brahms-and-Tchaikovsky'. So this confession of weakness brings me back to my original statement, namely, that these two composers have nothing in common, and that their association in the English mind today is purely accidental. Brahms and Tchaikovsky only met twice; all we hear of the meetings are that on one occasion Tchaikovsky did not see any merit in one of Brahms' trios, and on the other Brahms told Tchaikovsky that he could not abide his Fifth Symphony. At this second meeting, however, the two great men much enjoyed sharing a dinner. This fact we may use for our comfort; we may have found nothing in common between the two, but the very combination of names may have been food for thought.

CHAPTER 31

Ein Heldenleben

MUSICAL LONDON WILL scarcely have recovered from its state of bewilderment over Richard Strauss' *Ein Heldenleben* before the second performance, announced for today, is upon us. Perhaps prudence would have waited to correct first impressions, but I am tempted to jot down a few first thoughts about this astonishing work before it becomes ancient history.

My first impression is that Strauss' artistic position is not altered by this work. It exhibits all his strength to an intense degree, but his weaknesses also stand out as glaringly as ever. Strauss' great strength is his mastery over tones—he has chosen most happily when he calls his work a 'Tone-Poem'. Whatever we may think of *Ein Heldenleben* as music, we must admit the newness, the power, and the extreme beauty of the sounds which proceed from the Straussian orchestra. His weakness lies in the fact that he is so often content with commonplaces as the germs of his inspiration. He is like a cook who can serve up mutton with such art that he does not always take the trouble to look out for venison.

The work is divided into six sections; each, according to the Queen's Hall programme, duly labelled 'The Hero', 'His Enemies', and so on. These names do not

Source: *The Vocalist*, 1/10 (1903), 295–6.

appear in the miniature edition of the score, and I sincerely hope that they are the invention of Strauss' too eager commentators.[a] They are absolutely unnecessary to the understanding of the music: its emotional purport is quite clear throughout; indeed, these verbal explanations do actual harm, for they are apt to draw a false scent across the track—they bring a personal element into the matter. Thus in the fifth movement we are entirely absorbed with counting how many of Strauss' earlier works we can detect, and we forget all about the music. In the 'battle-scene' many people think that their minds should be entirely occupied with Strauss' victory over the Philistines; and the uglier they think the music the greater they imagine the victory, quite forgetting that, if the music were *really* ugly, and not only new, the victory would lie not with Strauss, but with the enemy.

But luckily a composer and his friends are very different people, and we can appraise and applaud his work with our minds free of all unmusical considerations. There can be no doubt, however, as to the musical splendour or the heroic nature of the opening theme. It is a curious phrase, founded on this harmony, which pervades it throughout all it extensions and modifications:

The theme, when fully harmonised, stands thus:

On this and certain secondary themes the first section is built, gradually growing to a tremendous climax and a half-close which leaves us in a state of excited anticipation. And certainly the unexpected happens.

It is as if a crowd of malignant, poisonous flies were upon us all of a sudden; the flutes, clarinets, and oboes spit and snarl, while two tubas reiterate their monotonous three notes like Pope in *Pilgrim's Progress*:

[a] The section titles in *Ein Heldenleben* are Strauss's own.

Then the snarling and groaning themes meet and fight the themes of the first movement, now become pale and careworn, till at last the heroic mood conquers and in its turn gives way to a new melody, of whose quality there can be no doubt— a song of the emotions. However, Strauss has thought fit to prelude his love-song by half-a-dozen 'false starts' interrupted by a series of remarkably dull *bravura* passages for a solo violin. I suppose that these passages are meant to prepare our minds, but why are we kept waiting so long? and why are those cadenzas so dull? However, the love-song is worth waiting for; the themes in themselves will perhaps not bear cold scrutiny, but interpreted as they are with all the warm glow of Strauss' polyphony they are magnificently emotional. At the end of this movement there happens what is, to my mind, the great moment of the work. As the love-song dies down to its final chord, we hear as if from far away the old sounds of 'envy, hatred, and malice' which before insisted so strongly. This slight touch shows Strauss to be a true poet; we are irresistibly reminded of Rossetti's sonnet:

> *And oft from mine own spirit's hurtling harms*
> *I crave the refuge of her deep embrace—*
> *Against all ills the fortified strong place,*
> *And sweet reserve of sovereign countercharms.*[b]

But peace soon gives way to war, the trumpets sound and we prepare for battle—surely the most weird and unearthly call to arms ever heard. [See p. 162.]

With this we plunge into the thick of the turmoil—sometimes one theme surges up, sometimes another; again and again the trumpets call, while throughout the heroic theme grinds along in the bass, till with a flash the victory is won, and the

[b] Dante Gabriel Rossetti, 'Heart's Haven', lines 5–8, from *The House of Life*. Vaughan Williams set this text in his song-cycle of the same title.

movement ends with a magnificent hymn of triumph. And with this we have an end of good things; the fifth movement is dull and pointless on the whole—the quotations from Strauss' own works have no emotional point—unless, indeed, the whole of his compositions (including the opera *Guntram*!) are meant to be performed in a series. As to the last movement, it seems at a first hearing comparatively weak. I cannot understand the critics when they describe this movement as 'supremely beautiful'. I can only see in it a most banal piece of sentiment which starts like bad Beethoven, and continues in the style of 'Svendserg's Romance'; of course, it is served up with all Strauss' skill, but this only emphasises the poverty of the original idea. We all know that Strauss can write noble melodies—in *Tod und Verklärung* for instance—but I should not say that this was one of them. However, on a second hearing my opinion may be quite altered.

So much for *Ein Heldenleben* itself; but how about all the extraordinary experiments in aesthetic criticism which this performance has given rise to? For instance, there is the wonderful idea that Strauss has 'three minds'—that is, that he can write down three pieces of music simultaneously, regardless of how they fit together. As a matter of fact, everything in *Ein Heldenleben* does fit, for those who have ears to hear. The notion that a composer should deliberately write down what he does not like—and this is the only valid test of 'fitness'—is, of course, sheer nonsense. Any writer who did this would not be guilty of having 'three minds', but of having none at all.

Then there is a theory that because *Ein Heldenleben* is supposed to 'mean' something, that all modern music must 'mean' something. The truth is, that this idea of a 'meaning' to music is a very old-fashioned one, and is of the same artistic value as the criticisms of the country-cousin at the Academy, who studies the titles of the pictures rather than the pictures themselves, and thinks that a picture labelled 'Love and Life' must necessarily be better than a picture which is merely called 'Nocturne', or 'Symphony'. Music is not a 'symbol' of anything else, it has no 'meaning'. True, the events of life and the facts of nature have an emotional

significance; as Carlyle says, 'If we search deep enough there is music everywhere.' When a man writes a symphonic poem, he, so to speak, distills this essence of music which is found in nature and gives us in clear language what before was only vaguely felt; but it is the external event which is the symbol of the music, not the music which is the symbol of the external event.

And, lastly, there are those absurd people who say that, because *Ein Helden-leben* is not like Mozart or Beethoven therefore it is not music. If criticisms like these had always had weight, we should still be writing music like Ockenheim! No, a man must be able to justify his point of view not by the past but by the present.

How then can we judge of a new work whether it is great or not? Will not some test like this be a good one? All great music satisfies some craving—the craving may have been felt unconsciously, but it was there; and directly the right man comes along and says the right thing, we realize at once that it is just what we have been waiting for; it seems at once to take its place in the order of things as if it had always existed; as Hans Sachs said about Walther's song:

Es klang so alt	*It sounded so old*
und war doch so neu.[c]	*and yet was so new.*

This, it seems to me, is the test of great music.

There is no doubt that *Ein Heldenleben* is new, wonderful, astonishing—but does it *satisfy* us? That is the question.

[c] *Die Meistersinger*, II. 3.

The Romantic in Music

Some Thoughts on Brahms

JOHANNES BRAHMS AND Richard Wagner divide the musical kingdom of the mid-nineteenth century between them. They each had their theories born of their weaknesses and they each of them at their greatest moments got the better of those theories.

Brahms was twenty years younger than Wagner, having been born in 1833, so that by the time he began seriously to write music Wagner's position in the world of art was decided—namely, that of the musical dramatist. How far Wagner's dramatic theories belied his practice it is not the place to discuss here; enough to say that Wagner certainly did get at his musical inspiration entirely through his dramatic instinct and at that time may well have seemed to have exhausted all the possibilities to which the Romantic movement had been pointing. It may, then, have been very natural for the younger composer to survey the field and decide that the dramatic view of music was closed and that 'a return to the classics' was the only possible step.

Whether as the result of conscious thought or not (one hopes not!) Brahms certainly did very early in his career abandon certain romantic characteristics which

Source: *The Music Student*, 2/8 (1910), 116–20.

are found in his earlier works. Of these romantic works students should study especially the beautiful Sonata in F minor (the slow movement of which has a motto), the Scherzo for pianoforte, Op. 4 (which caused Liszt to adopt Brahms as an adherent), the beautiful song 'Liebestreu' ('Faithful Love', Op. 7, No. 1) and the D minor Pianoforte Concerto.

But in 1854, Brahms retired from public life for four years (having accepted a small post in a German court) and gave himself over to study and thought, with the result that his style had very largely changed—in fact the 'return to the classics' had been accomplished. From henceforth those romantic possibilities which were so apparent in his earlier work are often sternly repressed—and though they crop up impertinently at every moment in Brahms' work—to the delight of every hearer—they often seem not to fit in with his apparently deliberately self-imposed 'classical' style.

Now what is the explanation of this often ill-assorted mixture of the classical and the romantic in Brahms' later works? The true explanation, as it appears to me, is that Brahms, who had—potentially—the noblest and greatest ideas that ever entered into a composer's mind, had not the proper technique to bring them to their full fruition.

What do we mean by this word *technique?* Technique is too often supposed to begin and end with a knowledge of 'textbook' harmony and counterpoint and 'textbook' form, founded on a very superficial study of the great masters of old. Now all this kind of technique and much more Brahms, of course, possessed in the highest degree. But such knowledge is only the beginning of real technique. To be truly a master of one's craft implies the absolute fitting of the means to the end— the knowing what you want to say and the being able to discover the best and fullest way of saying it. The composer who perhaps has found that balance between idea and expression in the highest degree is Richard Wagner. Other composers have been too facile; that is to say their power of expression goes far beyond their desire to express. To this class belong Tchaikovsky and Richard Strauss. And among the greatest composers we find that from the very height and depth of their imagination the means to carry out their huge conceptions is lacking—and in no case is this want of proportion more apparent than in that of Brahms. And nowhere is Brahms' want of technique—in the highest aspect of the word—more apparent than in the form into which he threw his inspirations.

What then are the functions of form in art? The art of composing may be said to be that of presenting those ideas which present themselves to the composer's imagination in a manner which will make their significance clear to his hearers: in fact form is one of the chief factors of intelligibility. The one and only object of form is to make the composer's dreamings intelligible. Of course when the content is

complicated the form is of necessity also complicated. But complicated form is of no value in itself; that which obscures instead of explaining the issue is no form at all.

Now this intelligibility in the classical period was arrived at by conforming to the general lines of some easily recognised pattern to which hearers were accustomed, partly through convention and partly from the innate symmetry of the pattern itself. This pattern may be roughly represented by the formula A B A. This formula seems to give a feeling of stability and unity to all forms of human activity (we find it exemplified equally in the sandwich and in the sonata); so whether it is in its origin a convention or not, it is now too deep-rooted in human nature to be ignored, and all who wish to be intelligible must more or less conform to it.

But to conform in all its details to that particular manifestation of this formula known as 'sonata form' is a very different matter. The sonata form is a pure convention. Not that this is wrong in itself; conventions are necessary at every period of art and so long as the composer himself feels that this convention does not hinder his natural flow of ideas all is for the best. But was the sonata form the best for Brahms? Was not his 'return to the classics' a piece of deliberate reasoning rather than inspired intuition? And why did Brahms apparently mistrust his intuition? Was it not because he lacked the technical power to build up the massive blocks of inspiration into an architectural scheme fitted for them and was obliged to model his works by rule and line on some ready-made plan?

It is certainly not impossible to build up great musical schemes other than that of the sonata. Probably the most perfect piece of musical form in modern times is that of the Prelude to Wagner's *Tristan*, in which, certainly, none of the special characteristics of the sonata form are present; and it is probable that if Wagner had tried to force his ideas into the sonata mould, the symmetry of his Prelude (to speak of that aspect only) would have been seriously impaired. Probably Wagner did not self-consciously think about form at all; he thought only of the content, and the best form into which to mould it grew unconsciously out of the ideas themselves. But is this so in the case of Brahms? Do we not often feel that he is self-consciously trying to stretch his ideas on to a form to which they do not properly belong? I am far from saying that Brahms did not often find the sonata form a full and satisfying mode of expression. The whole of the great Pianoforte Quintet and the last movement of the Third Symphony are wonderful examples of idea and expression going hand in hand.

But on other occasions it must be felt that Brahms' utterances demanded a different vehicle of expression than that which he was able to give them.

Brahms' ideas are essentially architectural. They require architectural treatment. He apparently had not the technique however (as much smaller composers, such as Chopin and Tchaikovsky have had), to build up a unifying scheme out of the ideas themselves; hence he was forced to fall back on the 'classical' form. Take for example the Second Symphony. The first two movements form part of one large emotional scheme—the first full of lyrical fervour and restrained emotion, and the second taking us into regions never reached by any other composer (perhaps the most romantic piece of music ever written). Obviously the Symphony could not end there; something more was required to complete the scheme. But Brahms, instead of thinking out for himself (as many inferior composers have done) the true continuation of his wonderful beginning, falls back on the conventional 'Scherzo' and 'Finale' and the last two movements have no emotional connection with the first two. The Scherzo is 'pretty' and rather insincere—bustling without being light-hearted; in the Finale he mounts his classical stilts with a vengeance, and, it must be confessed, walks rather awkwardly in them.

Perhaps the most striking instance of a want of proportion between idea and expression occurs in the Finale to his First Symphony, where the supposed necessity of a definite 'second subject' of an uninspired and rather trivial nature spoils a moving and dramatic symphonic poem dealing with tremendous issues in which the whole fate of the universe seems to be involved. This is especially the case to-wards the end of the movement, where, after a most forcible climax, built up on the famous 'Cambridge Chimes' theme, the whole emotional structure is allowed to fall to pieces so that this second subject may be re-introduced in 'orthodox' fashion.

I have purposely used the term 'symphonic poem' in this connection because I believe that it is on the lines of the symphonic poem that this Symphony and other of Brahms' great conceptions might have been carried out. On the basis of the symphonic poem, as developed by Liszt and Richard Strauss, Brahms might per-haps have achieved results more colossal than the greatest works of any composer. The symphonic poem has up to the present suffered from the fact that those com-posers who have tried their hands at it have usually lacked any distinctive musical invention. It may be said that this is a case of cause and effect. Yet it can hardly be doubted that Strauss in his 'tone poems' has laid out gigantic architectural schemes which only require to be filled out with adequate musical ideas such as Brahms alone, perhaps, could have given them.

Students are often warned against the symphonic poem as against a dangerous character. But is the symphonic poem really as black as it is painted? To try and make music a record of facts (a sort of phonogram) is of course absurd; and it must be admitted that many critics and apologists are guilty of this error. But the true symphonic poem aims at bringing the transcendental imaginings of the composer into touch with human beings by connecting them with some story, some human character or some phenomenon of nature.

As I have already pointed out, the business of the composer is to make his visions intelligible to others. His inspirations are of no use to anyone but the composer himself—and not much use to him—unless they are put before people in such a way that they will be able to correlate them with what they already know. Now this is achieved on 'classical' lines by making the music correspond in its outline with a generally recognised pattern which is accepted as giving a feeling of symmetry and unity. I am far from saying that this sense of pure pattern can ever be dispensed with in any music. But the composer has also another means of bringing himself into touch with his hearers, namely, by ranging his ideas so that they are analogous to the events of some story, some poem, some historical or ideal person or some natural phenomenon. Many people like to make up a story to any piece of music which they hear; and if it helps a student to care for Beethoven's symphonies, if he attaches a story to them, there is no reason why he should not do so. True, he may not be getting at all that Beethoven meant; but then who does? And this particularising of Beethoven's sentiment may lead him on in time to an appreciation of the universal character of his emotions. At all events it is a very poor argument against the symphonic poem to say that we could not tell, without the title, that a particular piece of music 'meant' Romeo and Juliet, or the Life of a Hero or the River Moldau. The true symphonic poem does not try to take the place of words or sights. The extraneous idea, the 'programme', is simply a common ground where the composer can meet the hearer before they start together on the voyage to unknown regions whither he is taking them.

I have in this article commented on what appear to me to be Brahms' faults rather than on his beauties. The beauties of Brahms cannot be dilated on—it would be an impertinence to do so. Brahms had perhaps the noblest and finest musical imagination that ever existed, and we who love Brahms are apt to love his faults because of the beauties which go along with them. But this is a very dangerous point of view. Just as there are violinists who think that if they scratch and play out of tune they are carrying on the 'Joachim tradition', so there are composers who imagine that if they make their orchestration muddy and ineffective, if they interlard their ideas with pedantic bits of counterpoint, if they make their form obscure and diffuse, somehow there will fall on their shoulders the mantle of nobility which Brahms wore in spite of all these things.

I should advise students not to bother about the Brahms they find obscure but to delight in the Brahms they find beautiful; there will be quite enough of that to last them a lifetime, and obscurity in itself is a fault and not a virtue. Beauties which are worth finding often shine through the setting; but that does not make the setting in itself praiseworthy. Finally, they should remember that form is a means and not an end.

I may add here a list of a few works by Brahms which will show him at his very best (as it seems to me), another in which his great invention seems partly paralysed by want of proper means of expression, and lastly a few in which Brahms appears at his worst. These classifications are founded of course purely on a personal bias and do not represent a consensus of expert opinion; nor do they pretend to be exhaustive.

1) Brahms at His Best

(a) Pianoforte music. Scherzo in E♭ minor, Op. 4; Sonata in F minor, Op. 5; 'Edward' Ballade, Op. 10; Capriccio in B minor, and Intermezzo in A♭ major, Op. 76; Rhapsodies, Op. 79; Intermezzi Nos. 2 and 3, Op. 117; Intermezzo No. 6, Op. 118.

(b) Chamber music. Pianoforte Quintet, Op. 34; Horn Trio (first movement and slow movement), Op. 40; String Quartets in C minor and A minor (opening and slow movements), Op. 51; Pianoforte Trio in C minor (opening and slow movements), Op. 109; String Quintet (slow movement), Op. 111; Clarinet Quintet (except the last movement), Op. 115.

(c) Orchestral music. Symphonies: No. 1 (slow movement); No. 2 (first two movements); No. 3 (slow movement and Finale); No. 4 (all except the Scherzo). *Tragic* Overture. Pianoforte Concerto No. 2 in B♭.

(d) Songs. 'Faithful love', Op. 10; 'Ho! Broad sword and spear', Op. 31; 'Love is for ever' and 'The May night', Op. 43; 'In summer fields' and 'The sleep walker', Op. 86; 'There among the willows', Op. 97; and many others too numerous to mention.

2) Brahms with Great Ideas Shining Through Uncongenial Surroundings

Sextet in B♭, Op. 18; Variations on a Theme of Handel, Op. 24; *German Requiem*, Nos. 1 and 6, Op. 45; *Triumph Song*, Op. 55; Symphony No. 1 (last movement); Symphony No. 3 (opening movement).

3) A Few Specimens of Brahms at His Worst, Which Should also be Studied

Most of his last movements (with some notable exceptions mentioned above), especially those of the three String Quartets and the Violin Sonata in A major. Also the Scherzos of the Third and Fourth Symphonies and the last of the *Four Serious Songs*.

CHAPTER 33

Verdi: A Symposium

VERDI WROTE OPERAS. He did not add music to plays full of superficial philosophy or bogus psychology. He carried on his drama by means of lyric song. His orchestra, it is true, has a wonderful sonority, but it is the voice on which he counts to elucidate the situation. He realised that song can carry on a plot in a way which words alone can never do.

A good example of this comes from the last Act of my favourite Verdi opera, *Rigoletto*. In case readers are not familiar with the opera I will briefly rehearse the story of the last Act (from memory, I fear, for I have lost my copy of the score).

A wicked Duke has seduced (or is about to seduce, I forget which) the daughter of his Jester, who planning revenge with several 'R's', persuades his friend, the keeper of a disreputable inn, to invite the Duke to his house, offering as a bait his, the innkeeper's, own daughter, who is quite ready to become seducee No. 2. The Duke is to be murdered and his body in a sack is to be thrown out of the window for the Jester to play with.

On the night appointed the Duke arrives and sits at a table in the inn garden, drinking wine and making love to the innkeeper's daughter, and singing to her the famous 'La Donn'é mobile', an obvious and banal tune, which it is impossible to forget. Having sung his prologue the Duke leads the girl into the house.

Source: *Opera*, 2/3 (1951), 111–12.

At this moment the Jester's daughter, Gilda, arrives and rushes into the inn after them, and it is she who gets murdered and not the Duke. Finally the Jester appears waiting outside the window. The sack is thrown down, but as he is gloating over it the Duke's voice is heard in the distance singing 'La Donn'é mobile'. He has escaped! The Jester tears open the sack and finds in it the body of his own daughter!

Here is a situation which with the aid of a striking tune can be made clear in a very short time and with very few words. Without music this would have entailed a lot of boring explanation and perhaps an extra scene. This is a real music drama.

It is curious that though Verdi's whole art derives from opera, yet his finest work, to my mind at all events, was written for the church.

Verdi's Requiem is a heap of contradictions. It gives, indeed, one of the strongest proofs that there are no canons of art. Any right-minded musician who only knew the Requiem from description would certainly condemn it. It is sentimental, as in the Recordare; theatrical as in the Dies Irae; naively melodramatic as in the Tuba mirum; absurdly onomatopæic as in the Inter Oves. Sometimes as in Domine Deus he sails perilously near to the *Café chantant*. He frankly makes frequent use of such well-worn aids to excitement as the diminished seventh and the chromatic scale. In spite, or perhaps because of all this, the Requiem is one of the stupendous monuments of art.

Verdi's art derives, as I have said, entirely from opera. We see this even in something so far removed from the stage as a church service. The Dies Irae at once suggests a stage scene. In the Mors stupebit death stalks on like a villain in an opera. In the Hostias we can see the rapt celebrant hardly daring to raise his voice in front of the Divine Mystery. The last pages of Libera Me give a vivid picture of a crowd of Italian peasants muttering their prayers.

I suppose Verdi thought it necessary to have a little counterpoint in a church work as if to challenge comparison with the academics, so he inserts two fugues, in which he manages to beat them at their own game.

Falstaff is not my favourite opera. I know it is very brilliant and skilful and that the basket scene ensemble is a miracle of stagecraft. After all, the real Verdi carried on his drama in terms of broad tune, but Boito's medicated Shakespeare hardly ever gives him a chance. Again and again the orchestra seems to be preparing us for something like the big tunes of his earlier operas, but they do not materialise.

Let us be grateful, however, for the heavenly melody with the oboe which accompanies the love-making of Ann and Fenton. Here the composer was not hampered by his librettist's sham Shakespeare, was able to rejoice in good Italian slush all about kissing!

CHAPTER 34

Arnold Schoenberg (1874–1951)

SCHOENBERG MEANT NOTHING to me—but as he apparently meant a lot to a lot of other people I daresay it is all my own fault.

Source: *Music & Letters*, 32/4 (1951), 322. This is Vaughan Williams's contribution to an obituary article containing tributes from a number of contemporary musicians.

CHAPTER 35

Sibelius at 90: Greatness and Popularity

TODAY THE WHOLE civilised world will join in celebrating the ninetieth birthday of a great composer. (I do not count as civilised those mid-Europeans who ignore Sibelius.)

Why is he great? Not because he tried to make uglier noises than anyone else, not because he invented new ways of making instruments sound other than they ought to do, not because he defied tradition; indeed his harmonic vocabulary is in the direct line from Beethoven and Schubert. Rather it is because he has never deviated from the strait path that he is truly original and will remain so when the twelve-tone apostles have become mere common-places.

As Sachs says of Walther,

Es klang so alt,	*It sounded so old*
und war doch so neu	*and yet was so new*
wie Vogelsang im süssen Mai.[a]	*like sweet birdsong in May.*

Source: *Daily Telegraph & Morning Post*, no. 31,308 (8 December 1955), 6. The original article carried this editorial introduction: 'The doyen of English composers writes this appreciation to mark the Finnish master's ninetieth birthday. In 1943, when Britain and Finland were technically at war, Dr Vaughan Williams dedicated his Fifth Symphony to Sibelius "without permission".'
[a] *Die Meistersinger*, II. 3.

It is the simple things of life which are permanent. Sibelius compared his own work to cold water, in contrast to the exotic cocktails of other contemporary composers. Sibelius remains new, just as Bach or Beethoven remain new, like the great melodies of the church and the 'immortal chants of old'.[b]

> *When old age shall this generation waste*
> *Thou shalt remain.*[c]

Nor did Sibelius ever have to starve in a garret like Schubert, or fight for recognition like Wagner. When he was only 32 his greatness was recognised by his fellow-countrymen and he was given a pension for life which enabled him to compose without the interruptions of material cares. His light has continued to shine steadily and bright; he has gone from strength to strength—from symphony to symphony—reaching his climax with the supreme number seven in 1925.

Or is number seven supreme? There is a rumour of a number eight, or even a number nine, which may, if he allows them to be heard, surpass even the glories of their predecessors.

Prigs Were Shocked

We must not forget that, in this country at all events, Sibelius first achieved fame as a 'popular' composer. *Finlandia* (1889) became a hymn tune, and *Valse Triste* (1903) was at one time played almost nightly by every restaurant band.

The Prigs' Brigade, of whom I was one, were duly shocked. How did we come to discover that we were entertaining an angel unawares? Perhaps it was Bantock, and the Birmingham Festival of 1912, when Sibelius's Fourth Symphony was first performed: or perhaps it was the persistent advocacy of Sir Henry Wood which showed us the way.

At all events, nowadays *Finlandia* and *Valse Triste* are nearly forgotten and the symphonies obtain ever more and more adherents. Nevertheless we must always remember that it was the same man, with the same outlook and the same mind who wrote both *Finlandia* and the Fourth Symphony. Sibelius has his head and his heart in heaven, but his feet firmly planted in the ground. There is a popular element in all great music, and the music of Sibelius is no exception.

[b] Matthew Arnold, 'Thyrsis', line 181.
[c] John Keats, 'Ode on a Grecian Urn', lines 46–7.

When a friend complained to Beethoven that his later quartets did not please, he did not answer that he had no wish to please, and was thinking of higher things, but that his music would please one day.

The influence of Sibelius in this country on musical thought has been most healthy, and it came just at the right moment. Our young composers seemed to be writing nothing but watered-down Wagner, or desiccated Brahms. If we go into the colleges now, and look at the work of young composers, we find that they usually start by copying out whole passages of Sibelius, which they imagine they have invented for themselves.

This is not in itself a bad thing. Every artist starts by imitating. It is very difficult to tell the early Titian from Bellini. *Love's Labours Lost* was obviously an imitation of some earlier model: we can see Haydn strongly in the early Beethoven, and Weber in the early Wagner. This absorption is a necessary part of the progress of a young musician. Great music is written, I believe, not by breaking the tradition, but by adding to it. Sibelius has shown us that the new thought which can be discovered in the old material is inexhaustible.

Sibelius is not one of the composers who sits waiting, like the scholar gipsy, for the spark from Heaven to fall.[d] For those who sit waiting for it, it never comes. The great composers have always gone in for mass production. Sometimes the result is good, sometimes bad, occasionally a masterpiece.

It has been said that he who makes no mistakes never makes anything. And this is certainly true of composition. Without the failures there would be no successes. Of all John Sebastian Bach's enormous output of music a certain amount was, of course, mere routine work, though it all showed evidence of the composer's mastery. There is a good deal of bad work in Beethoven; for example, the *Battle of Vittoria*. But he also wrote the Ninth Symphony.

Something to Say

There have, of course, been cases of enormous output without a single masterpiece; but I firmly believe it to be true that a composer who has anything to say will be able to write one piece, even a hymn tune, which Beethoven or Bach could not have bettered. There was a Welsh composer called Joseph Parry who wrote whole volumes of dreary operas and cantatas, and half a dozen magnificent hymn tunes. But,

---

[d] 'Thou waitest for the spark from heaven!...Ah! do not we, wanderer! await it too?' Matthew Arnold, 'The Scholar-Gipsy', lines 171–80.

the thing to be remembered is that unless Joseph Parry had got all the dreary cantatas out of his system, there would have been no room for the magnificent hymn tunes.

Therefore it is no lowering of our estimate of this great man to say that, as in the case of Beethoven, Bach and Schubert, a certain number of his works are just day-to-day handiwork. Meanwhile, we have the seven symphonies, *Tapiola*, *En Saga* and the string quartet *Voces Intimae*. What more can we ask for?

PART **III**

Folk Song

CHAPTER 36

Preface [to a Folk Song Collection]

THE FOLLOWING COLLECTION of folk-tunes differs from most of those hitherto printed in the *Folk-Song Journal* in that, while former collections have been gathered from one county, the present tunes represent no less than seven—namely Essex, Norfolk, Sussex, Wiltshire, Yorkshire, Kent, and even London. It is not suggested that the tunes grouped under the counties are their exclusive property— indeed the more wonderful fact elicited from the search for folk-songs is that the same tune may be heard, with hardly any variation, in Norfolk, Sussex or York- shire. This proves more than anything the fundamental character of the genuine folk-song. It will be noticed that a large proportion of the tunes in this collection are modal in character—Dorian, Aeolian or Mixolydian. I suggest that the Mix- olydian and Dorian tunes are more characteristic of agricultural districts, while Aeolian tunes belong more to towns, and trades such as fishing and cobbling—but this suggestion is merely empirical and founded on very partial evidence.

Although the field covered by the tunes in this journal is in one sense very large, in another it is very small—since it is only a small part of each county which I have searched for songs, and the time spent has been of necessity very short.

Source: *Journal of the Folk Song Society*, 2/8 (1906), 141–2.

What results might be obtained from a systematic and sympathetic search through all the villages and towns of England! And yet this precious heritage of beautiful melody is being allowed to slip through our hands through mere ignorance or apathy.

I could imagine a much less profitable way of spending a long winter evening than in the parlour of a country inn taking one's turn at the mug of 'four-ale'—(surely the most innocuous of all beverages), in the rare company of minds imbued with that fine sense which comes from advancing years and a life-long communion with nature—and with the ever-present chance of picking up some rare old ballad or an exquisitely beautiful melody, worthy, within its smaller compass, of a place beside the finest compositions of the greatest composers.

My heartiest thanks are due first to the singers of the following songs, who have always been most anxious to give me of their best and have often themselves written out the words of the ballads for me. Among these I would especially mention Mr H. Burstow, of Horsham (see Vol. i, p. 139, of the *Folk-Song Journal*), Mrs Humphreys, Mr Pottipher, shepherd, and Mr Broomfield, woodman, all three of Ingrave (Essex) and the neighbourhood; Mr and Mrs Verrall, formerly of Monksgate, Sussex, now living in Horsham. Mrs Verrall obtained the prize given in 1905 by the *West Sussex Gazette* for the best Sussex tune; the tunes being 'Covent Garden' and 'Salisbury Plain', both in this Journal. Messrs Carter and Anderson, fishermen of King's Lynn, both of them probably with Norse blood in their veins; since the fishing colony of King's Lynn are a distinct race and still talk of the rest of the town as 'foreigners'.

Secondly I must thank those who have so kindly helped me by finding out singers and helping to note both tunes and words—especially the Misses Heatley of Ingrave Rectory, Essex; the Rev A. Huddle of King's Lynn, and Mr Ansfield, gamekeeper, of Telscombe, Sussex.

And thirdly the members of the editing committee who have added valuable expert notes to this collection—namely Miss Lucy E. Broadwood (L. E. B.), Messrs F. Kidson (F. K.), J. A. Fuller-Maitland (J. A. F. M.), and C. J. Sharp (C. J. S.)

CHAPTER 37

Introduction to *Folk Songs from the Eastern Counties*

THE FIFTEEN MELODIES which are arranged in this volume are part of a much larger collection made in the Eastern Counties. It is not to be supposed that they are the exclusive property of the counties to which they are credited; all that is claimed for them is that they certainly are sung in these counties, and that most of the melodies have not as yet been discovered elsewhere. It will be noticed that, while six songs from Essex and seven from Norfolk are given, there are only two from Cambridgeshire and none from Suffolk. This means, not that these two counties are less rich in folk song than the others, but simply that time and opportunity have not yet been found to explore them. Nor do the songs collected from Essex and Norfolk represent an exhaustive search; all the Norfolk tunes come from King's Lynn and the neighbourhood, and the Essex songs from a small area near the town of Brentwood. It is to be hoped that an acquaintance with the melodies here given will incite others to explore those parts of East Anglia which are still unsearched.

I wish to take this opportunity of expressing my grateful thanks to the singers of these melodies, and to all those who helped in the work of collection.

Source: *Folk Songs from the Eastern Counties*, ed. Cecil J. Sharp, coll. and arr. Ralph Vaughan Williams (London: Novello, 1908).

CHAPTER 38

English Folk-Songs

WHEN YOUR COMMITTEE asked me to speak to you this morning they suggested the subject of British Folk-song to me. I asked them to limit the scope of this lecture to the subject of English Folk-song. I restricted myself thus for two reasons: one was that time and your patience would certainly not allow me to undertake the larger task, and besides this my own knowledge is strictly limited to the folk-songs of England, so that if I were to try to lecture on anything outside these boundaries I should simply be telling you what you could learn much better for yourselves out of books. What I am about to try to give you today is first-hand knowledge straight from the human subject, without any intervention of book knowledge at all.

For perhaps I ought to explain that I make no pretence to have any expert knowledge of archaeology or antiquarianism, or folk-lore, or any of those learned subjects which an expert should possess, but I have this excuse for standing up

Sources: *The Music Student*, 4/6–11 (1912), 247–8, 283–4, 317–18, 347, 387, 413–14; revised version in Percy M. Young, *Vaughan Williams* (London: Dennis Dobson, 1953), 200–17. The two introductory paragraphs are only found in the original version; the final four paragraphs are only found in the revised version. Otherwise there is only one discrepancy between the two versions (see note c). The first version was developed from a lecture given at the Vacation Conference on Musical Education, 10 January 1912; it was also published as a separate booklet under the same title for the English Folk Dance Society (London: Joseph Williams, 1912); and a report of a similar lecture, given to the Oxford Folk Music Society, 16 November 1910, can be found in *The Musical Times*, 52/816 (1911), 101–4.

before you today—I am like a psychical researcher who has actually seen a ghost, for I have been among the more primitive people of England and have noted down their songs and, judging from these and from songs collected by others which I have examined in the light of my own experience, I have drawn some conclusions which I will try to put before you. Moreover it is from the musical point of view entirely that I shall deal with folk-song today; I shall not try to touch the sister art of ballad poetry, though many of the conclusions which I shall attempt are equally applicable to the folk-words as to folk-tunes.

The study of English folk-song is of comparatively recent origin.[a] For years musicians and scientists, while fully recognising the existence of traditional music in every foreign country, and even in Ireland, Scotland and Wales, denied, for some inexplicable reason, there being any in England.

How it could be imagined that it was of the slightest use to practise the art of music in a country where its very foundations were absent, passes my understanding; about this I shall have more to say later on. I suppose it was considered that we were an unmusical nation, and that music was a sort of hothouse product to be imported from a foreign country and left to drag out a half-starved existence far from its home. It is difficult to see how such an art could be of any benefit to anybody. But at all events theory and practice coincided.

As late as the year 1878 Mr Carl Engel was able to write in his admirable book on national music that 'Some musical enquirers have expressed the opinion that the country people of England are not in the habit of singing—but' he adds significantly, 'this opinion would probably be found to be only partially correct if search were made in the proper places.'[b] Actually, we had sat down and said 'We are not musical—we have no folk-songs,' and nobody had taken the trouble to go three steps from home and find out for themselves!

Yes, one man at all events had taken the trouble, and had found out for himself that the country people in one small corner of Sussex were 'in the habit of singing'. This one man was John Broadwood—whose name is to be honoured in the annals of English folk-song—who went about among the people of Sussex collecting their songs, which he published under the title of *Sussex Songs*, in 1843.

Then apparently we all went to sleep again until 1889, when Baring-Gould discovered that the people of Devonshire were also 'in the habit of singing', and he made a large collection, some of which are to be found in the volume known as

[a] The 1953 version begins at this sentence.
[b] Carl Engel, *The Literature of National Music* (London: Novello, 1879), 32. This book was originally published as a series of articles in *The Musical Times* during 1878–9.

Songs of the West. About the same time Lucy Broadwood and Fuller Maitland published their well-known volume, *English County Songs*, and Frank Kidson issued his *Traditional Tunes*, obtained chiefly in Yorkshire. We had at last begun to wake up to the fact that there was melody in our midst which might any day perish with the death or the loss of memory of one man simply because no one had troubled to write it down. With the object of preventing such disaster the Folk-Song Society was founded in 1898, with the avowed object of 'collecting folk-ballads and tunes'.

Again in 1903 Cecil Sharp conceived the idea of making exhaustive investigations within a prescribed area—the County of Somerset—and found within these limits a wealth of melody which no one had heretofore dreamt of. His example has been followed by others, and such counties as Sussex, Dorset and Hampshire, as well as large tracts of Norfolk, Essex, Lincolnshire and Herefordshire have been thoroughly explored and have yielded up their treasures, while he himself continued his researches in other parts of England and among the English settlers in the Appalachian Mountains of the United States.

We have been rather late in the day in England in doing what other nations have long considered their duty. But this has not been altogether a disadvantage; most of the folk-music of foreign countries, and much of that of Scotland, Wales and Ireland, was collected and published about 120 years ago, a period when musicians had no respect for what they found, and had no scruple in altering and 'improving' their folk-songs to make them fit the supposed 'correct style' of the period: thus none of the tunes of these early collectors are above suspicion as faithful records.

But nowadays a new spirit animates the collector; he wishes to preserve and put before the public exactly what he has heard—neither more nor less—and we can be sure that whatever we find in the collections of modern investigators is an accurate transcript of the songs of traditional singers.

So now, by the efforts of a few collectors whose work is confined to almost the last twenty-five years, we have on record, roughly speaking, 3,000 tunes and versions of tunes, either printed or in easily accessible MS. collections.[c] What conclusions can we draw from this mass of material?

I said a little while back that I was trying to base my conclusions on my personal observations, so I hope you will forgive me if I start my exposition of English folk-song by giving you the account of a personal experience—namely, my

---

[c] The 1912 version gives a figure of 3,000 recorded songs; the 1953 version gives 7,000 songs.

discovery of the first (or almost the first) folk-song which I ever heard under its native conditions.

I was at that time entirely without first-hand evidence on the subject. I knew and loved the few English folk-songs which were then available in printed collections, but I only believed in them vaguely, just as the layman believes in the facts of astronomy; my faith was not yet active. I was invited to a tea-party given to the old people of a village in Essex, only twenty miles from London; after tea we asked if any of them knew any of the old songs, whereupon an old man, a shepherd, began to sing a song which set all my doubts about folk-song at rest. The song which he sang was *Bushes and Briars* (see Ex. 38.1a).

Ex. 38.1. (*a*) 'Bushes and Briars' (Essex);

(*a*)

Through bush-es and through bri - ars   I   late-ly took my— way,   All— for   to—

hear   the   small   birds   sing,   And the lambs to—   skip   and—   play.

Now it seems to me that in listening to a tune like this we are face to face with a form of music which is, first, a thing by itself, apart both in nature and origin from the written music of definite composers; and, secondly, a form of art which is not of mere antiquarian interest—not something which is merely quaint and old, but something which is beautiful and as vital now as ever it was. The best folk-tunes are dateless—they belong to every age, they exist, as Sir Charles Stanford has said 'for all time'.

Some people, of course, will have none of this. They think it impossible that among people who know no harmony or fugue or form, who often cannot even read, there should exist, self-invented, a beautiful form of art. They refuse to think this possible and refer these folk-tunes, which collectors have been lately finding, to half-remembered scraps of forgotten music by seventeenth and eighteenth century composers.

Well, to what seventeenth or eighteenth century composer can we refer such a tune as this *Bushes and Briars*? If it is merely a corruption, what must the original have been? Surely such a composer would not have died out so completely that even his *name* is not remembered?

It is, of course, true that there are a few songs which have all the outward appearance of folk-songs, and which are nevertheless traceable to printed sources. But I think I can show that their existence proves most conclusively that there is what we may call a distinctive folk-song idiom which is a thing apart.

Let me again introduce you to a concrete example. I was listening to a traditional singer in Sussex a few years ago. After he had sung me several songs he told me that he knew another, *The Miller of the Dee*. Of course what we should have expected would have been the well-known tune as it appears in a ballad opera of about 1750 (Ex. 38.1(*b*)). What he did sing to me, though evidently a version of the same tune, was very different in important particulars (Ex. 38.1(*c*)).

Ex. 38.1. (*b*) 'The Miller of the Dee', eighteenth-century version.

(*b*)

Ex. 38.1. (*c*) 'The Miller of the Dee', traditional version (Sussex).

(*c*)

Now let us examine these two versions of this tune.

The well-known version out of the ballad opera is obviously on the eighteenth-century model; and, moreover, it is built up on a purely harmonic pattern in the minor mode with the leading note well marked and a half-close at the middle cadence.

Now look at the other: here the minor mode changes to the Aeolian—the leading note is flat throughout and the middle cadence is on that very flat seventh, a purely melodic proceeding. Besides this, the whole character of the song is in keeping with other purely traditional music which we know.

How can we account for these two versions?

The most probable explanation to my mind is that this Sussex version is a true traditional form of the melody, which was bowdlerised by the ballad opera writer to fit the supposed cultivated taste of his period.

But it is, of course, just possible that some ancestor of this Sussex singer learnt this song out of a printed book and handed it down by oral tradition to his modern descendant, and that in the process the idiom has changed into one more in keeping with its singer's nature—that is to say, into the idiom we know as that of the folk-song; surely this is the most conclusive proof we can have, that the folk-song idiom, as a thing apart, does exist.

Now, some of my readers may possibly be thinking 'Why make all this fuss about the folk-song idiom? Very likely these traditional songs differ in certain respects from songs like *Heart of Oak* or *Tom Bowling* but why is it important? Why should we not lump all tunes of a simple and popular nature together and call them folk-songs?'

I believe that it is a grave mistake to ignore this difference of nature. The Germans have characteristically distinguished between the real folk-song, which they name 'Volkslied', and the song by a definite composer, but of a popular nature, such as *Rule, Britannia*, or the *Marseillaise*, which they call 'Volksthumliches Lied'. I do not want to be misunderstood; I am far from saying that folk-songs are necessarily better than the national or popular songs such as *Heart of Oak*, or that these latter are not well worth singing—it is a question not of quality but of kind. I think it is most important, not only for scientists and experts, but from a practical point of view for teachers, performers and especially for composers, that we should be quite clear in our minds whether the genus folk-song does exist as a thing apart or not, and for this reason, that, as it seems to me, the existence of folk-song (in the sense in which I am trying to explain it) is the keystone without which our whole structure of music would fall to the ground.

Let us look at the matter from another point of view. Those of us who are engaged either in teaching, performing, or writing music, find that our time is rightly largely occupied with the technical aspect of our art—with the means rather than with the end. And we are apt sometimes to forget that study, rules, practice, technique, ear-training, form, and so on, are not in themselves ends but are the means only to an end.

What, then, is that end, or perhaps I should say the beginning? Study, technique, instruction can do much, but we cannot sow seed on barren soil. There must be something to start with. What is that something? How much of our musical nature is spontaneous and unself-conscious?

Or, again. These rules and principles of form, expression and style which we learn and teach, are they merely refined systems of torture invented by cruel pedants? What is their ultimate sanction?

We can imagine the earnest student saying to himself, 'Before I take up the study of music I will satisfy myself that it is the development of something inborn in human nature, and not only a set of clever tricks; I will try and find out the absolutely unsophisticated, though naturally musical, man—one who has no learning, and no contact with learning, one who cannot read or write, and thus repeat anything stereotyped by others, one whose utterance, therefore, is purely spontaneous and unself-conscious. Will such a man be able to invent any form of music? And, if he does, will it contain the germs of those principles and rules which my professors wish to teach me? If he does, I will believe in music as an art; if not, I will devote myself with more profit to crossword puzzles.'

To such an enquirer the answer is found in the folk-song. The imaginary man becomes an actuality. We do really find in every country among those people whose utterances must of necessity be spontaneous and unsophisticated—namely, the unlettered and untravelled portion of the community—a form of musical art, unwritten, handed down by tradition, hardly self-conscious, which is their special property, and this music is not mere clownish nonsense, but has in it the germ of all those principles of beauty, of expression, of form, climax and proportion which we are accustomed to look for in the highly developed compositions of great masters.

Face to face with this fact we need no longer feel surprised that an unlettered countryman can inherit from his still more unlettered forefathers a melody like *Bushes and Briars*—adding, without doubt, to it something peculiarly his own.

I remember a distinguished musician once expressing surprise that an uneducated countryman should be able to sing 'correctly' in the Dorian mode. He might as well have expressed surprise at M. Jourdain being able to speak prose.[d]

---

[d] Jean-Baptiste Poquelin de Molière, *Le bourgeois gentilhomme*, III. iii.

Now I am far from claiming that every folk-song, or even every English folk-song, is supremely beautiful. There are dull and stupid folk-songs just as there are dull and stupid people among the community to which they belong.[1] And all folk-song is limited in its scope. We do not find, for example, folk-fugues or folk-sonatas.

Folk-music may be said to be limited in two directions—lengthways and breadthways.

Lengthways the folk-song is limited by the extent of the poetic stanza or the dance figure to which it is applied. For folk-music is always an applied art; the music is used as a vehicle for the recitation of words or for the setting of the rhythm to a dance; the traditional singer can hardly ever think of a tune without its accompanying words or dance, and he often, conversely, cannot remember words or dance without the tune.

And the folk-song is limited breadthways, in that it is purely melodic in its nature. This is certainly so as far as English folk-song is concerned, and I believe it is true of all genuine folk-song; the question of accompanying harmonies does not enter into the scheme.

Now these limitations are not without their corresponding advantages. The task of compressing one's musical imagination into sixteen bars of melody is a very different one from that of composing a symphony or a grand opera, and the result is of a very different character, and the difference becomes wider still when that sixteen bars have to be sung over and over again for perhaps ten or twenty verses of a ballad—a severe test of a tune.

So we find that a folk-tune often does not strike us particularly at first hearing; it is only when it has been repeated over and over again for a long ballad that its full beauty begins to tell.

I would, therefore, ask those who wish to study collections of folk-songs not to judge them by playing them over with one finger on the piano; first they must be heard sung to their words, and, secondly, sung several times over; one must hear the whole ballad through, for then, and then only, one will be able to judge of the quality of the tune.

And the limitation imposed on the folk-song by its melodic character carries with it freedom of a new kind, for harmonic music has its own limitations.

---

[1] It should be noted, however, that a traditional melody, if it appears dull or stupid to its singers and hearers, will *cease to exist*, while printed music remains to trouble us.

Modern music has so steeped us in harmony that we find it difficult to realise what pure melody means. It is true that the street-boy may whistle some music-hall tune at all moments of the day without any harmony; nevertheless he is unconsciously influenced by harmonic considerations: without a harmonic scheme in his mind such a tune as this would (luckily!) be quite meaningless.

Harmony has given a much wider scope to music than pure melody could make possible. But harmony at the same time confines the composer within bounds. He finds it difficult to get away from the major and minor modes, with their corresponding perfect cadences, half-closes, sharpened leading notes, and the rest.

We saw how, in the case of *The Miller of the Dee*, the presence or absence of harmonic considerations affected the whole nature of the tune. When harmony is absent the necessity for the sharp leading note disappears. The possible positions for the intermediate cadences are increased, and the whole modal system on which melodies may be built up is enlarged. It is a pity that the system of modes to which melodic music can be referred to is known as 'ecclesiastical'. This has led people to imagine that modal folk-songs are derived from the music of the church. It is only necessary to look at such melodies as *The Cobbler* or *I'm Seventeen come Sunday*[2] to be convinced that they have nothing to do with church music except in so far as they can be referred to the same modal system.

The folk-song and the plain-song are both purely melodic. That is the sum of their similarity.[3]

It is interesting to note that, with the birth of harmony, composers found the modal system unsuitable to their scheme, and the modal melodies began to be altered to fit harmonic considerations, according to the rules known as 'Cantus Fictus'. In modern times, on the other hand, musicians are beginning to find that melodies built on a purely melodic basis are nevertheless suggestive of a new kind of harmony.[4]

This, then, is the folk-song—a spontaneous, unself-conscious, unwritten musical utterance, limited in its scope, it is true, but, within its limits, often of supreme beauty, and containing in embryo all those principles which are at the basis of the fully developed art of music.

[2] See *Journal of the Folk Song Society*, 2/6 and 2/8 (1906), 10, 156.
[3] It is probable that the melodic modes conform to certain ascertainable laws of the natural rise and fall of the human voice as modified by language.
[4] That is to say, harmonisation from the melody downwards, instead of from the bass upwards, as recommended in the harmony primers.

But our imaginary objector may say here, 'Really you have not brought us much further. After all, someone must have invented the folk-song, and all the difference you can show us between this kind of music and any other is that it is partly unconscious and that it is not written down.'

But are these two differences so unimportant? And are we so certain that any one particular person must have invented a particular tune? Let us examine these two characteristics of traditional music.

The singing of folk-songs is only a half-conscious act; the tune is merely to the singer a vehicle for the words. Such a singer can hardly ever hum or whistle a tune without the words; on the other hand, if you sing words that he knows to another tune he will, as often as not, see no difference between your rendering and his.

And the folk-song obtains currency by purely oral methods. The song which you or I may have heard yesterday has been learnt by the folk-singer perhaps from his father, who learn it, perhaps, from a friend who learnt it in turn from his mother, till we finally get back to a remote period when someone invented *something*—but surely not the tune which you or I heard yesterday, but probably something very different, namely, the germ from which it sprang.

Even in the case of music which is printed, we know well that three separate players will make the same piece of music sound very different according to their different temperaments. But in the case of printed music the divergencies can never get very far, as each successive player goes back to the original printed copy. Suppose, however, that music had never been printed or written; suppose that Beethoven could only make his *Sonata Appassionata* known by playing it over to friends; suppose Liszt had heard him play it, learnt it by heart, and, years afterwards, played it to Wagner, who in his turn played what he could remember of it to Saint-Saëns, and that finally Maurice Ravel heard Saint-Saëns play his version, and went home and played his memory of it to his friends. Do you think that Ravel's version would be exactly the same as Beethoven's? Probably it would be very different. Now, who could be said to have composed that final version of what he had heard? Certainly not Ravel, for he was only playing his version of Beethoven; and I think it is unlikely that Beethoven would have acknowledged it as his. Would it not be the product of the united imagination of those five minds?[5]

[5] In this imaginary instance the united product of five very divergent minds would have a poor artistic result, but in the case of the folk-song the minds through which a tune would pass would be united by common sentiments.

We have pretty good evidence that exactly the same process has been going on on a very large scale for generations in the case of the folk-song. One man sings to several more, they sing again their versions to others; these versions, owing to the half-conscious nature of the singers, would probably vary considerably as the artistic instinct of the singer suggested, but a unity of feeling and style would be preserved (unlike the imaginary case of the Beethoven sonata), and, moreover, those variations which did not approve themselves to future generations would drop out.

And so folk-songs are handed down from generation to generation till we find, in a very short time, widely varying versions of the same tune, and, conversely, different tunes connected together by common phrases or intervals or characteristics. Thus a folk-song would appear to be a series of individual variations on a common theme. A folk-song is like a tree, whose stem dates back from immemorial times, but which continually puts out new shoots.

How far any particular folk-song is an individual creation, how far it is an exact replica of what has gone before, can never be decided. On the one hand there is evidence of the extraordinary accuracy of tradition, of which those whose lives are spent among printed books have no idea; on the other hand many folk-songs which are collected show evidence of the personal characteristics of their singer.

The folk-song collector is continually being asked two questions:

The first comes from the earnest enquirer. He always asks: 'How old do you suppose that song is?' The question I believe is unanswerable. In one aspect the folk-song is as old as time itself; in another aspect it is no older than the singer who sang it. The question of antiquity does not seem to me important; it is the question of the nature of the song which is of interest. In dealing with folk-song we are face to face with something not of mere antiquarian interest, but something which is vitally important to us today.

Then the scoffer comes along, and he says: 'I expect the old chap was having you on; I believe he made it up himself.' To which I answer that it is quite possible that to a large extent he did, and that for that reason it is all the more valuable to me.

Let us return once more to the text of my sermon—the tune *Bushes and Briars*. Here is a tune which, as far as I know, has been found nowhere else; it is, I believe, largely the personal invention of its singer—not, I think consciously invented, but out of his own unrecognised artistic instinct.

On the other hand we find individual phrases in it which belong also to other tunes. The presence of the stock phrase in folk-song has an exact parallel in the presence of the stock epithet or description in ballad-poetry. We know how in

Homer and certain parts of the Bible the same epithet or the same few lines of description are attached to certain individuals or circumstances.

Or, again, in our English ballad poetry we continually come across such phrases as

Come, saddle me my milk-white steed,
Come, bridle me my pony.

Or

Then he took hold of her lily-white hand.

Or

As I walked out one morning
So early in the spring.

So it is with folk-music. This tune, *Bushes and Briars* has, as I have said, certain phrases which it shares with other tunes—notably the opening phrase, which serves either in its simple form, or slightly varied, for the opening of many melodies. Then the opening of the third strain, again, is found in many other folk-tunes; and the final cadence with the rise of a sixth and the fall by conjunct movement on to the final of the mode may be found in other tunes also.

A most interesting parallel to this tune may be found in a carol tune, *This is the truth*, lately recovered in Herefordshire (Ex. 38.2); this is an entirely distinct tune, but of which the opening, middle and closing phrases are close variants of the corresponding phrases in *Bushes and Briars*. Here, then, we have two entirely distinct tunes but which are obviously both derived from some common source. These two tunes are good examples of the continual revivifying of the old common stem by individual flowerings.

Ex. 38.2. 'This is the Truth' (Herefordshire).

The more I see of folk-song the more important I believe the impress of the individual to be; and this fact, if it be one, may help to solve a problem which faces collectors of folk-music. Why is it that we hardly ever obtain folk-songs from any one under fifty? The practice of singing folk-songs seems to have begun to die out about the year 1860. The complaint of the old people is the same everywhere, that the younger people have not taken the trouble to learn them.

Some people may take this to be a proof that the folk-song is dead; it has done its work and is merely a relic of a past age. This I cannot believe; to my mind we have enough intrinsic evidence to show that the folk-song has plenty of vitality left. The explanation seems to me to be this: the year 1860 marks the beginning of a great increase in the means of transport and of popular education, so that, from that time onwards, the people in our remote districts became less and less dependent on themselves for their art and more and more inclined to take it ready-made from London. Thus the impulse to revivify the old stock by continual re-invention died down just as the art of playing football will die down if the modern rage for paying others to play for you continues. The folk-singer became uninventive, and the evolution of the folk-song ceased for the time. I believe, however, that this is a purely temporary check, and that the folk-song will live again in new surroundings and under new conditions.

So far I have dealt only with the nature of folk-song. May I now say a little about its value, as I believe, to twentieth-century musicians, whether performers, teachers or composers?

I have tried to put before you the theory that folk-song is an art by itself, quite different from the simplest of composer's music. I also believe that the large majority of the tunes which have been collected in England are full of character, beauty and vitality.

However, neither of these propositions is capable of absolute proof. It is quite possible for any one to deny both and to say there is no such thing as a folk-song in this sense of the word, or that, at all events, folk-songs are of no artistic value and of no scientific importance. Well it may be so; perhaps those who have actually been collectors are too near their subject to see it clearly. The outsiders can judge best. But the matter does not rest here, for surely if we have no folk-songs or none of any musical value, does it not follow that there is no music inborn in the nation? What, then, will be the use of all our institutions and associations for performing, teaching and fostering an art the very germs of which are not part of our nature? It is like trying to make an elaborate garden where no wild flowers will grow. Or perhaps I should say, to imagine it is possible to create garden flowers without the wild flowers as their prototypes. If the study of music in England is to be merely the artificial cultivation of a taste which finds no response in our own selves, far better give up this pretence of being musical and devote ourselves to anything else in which we can really achieve success.

But I do believe that the folk-song still exists as something beautiful and vital. As proof of this I may bring forward two facts: first, their extraordinary popularity with every class of hearer; and, secondly (this is a more technical proof, but none the less cogent), that folk-songs seem to take kindly to the harmony of any period at which a skilled musician may happen to treat them harmonically. Now this is not the case with 'composed music'. It would be ridiculous and out of keeping to try and harmonise a melody by Gluck in the style of Richard Strauss; the anachronism would be apparent at once. But in folk-song there is no anachronism—it seems to defy the ravages of time.

There has been, no doubt, a check. The folk-song has ceased to grow on its native soil. The art of the *folk-song* lives, but the art of the *folk-singer* is dead. That is a special art, and I would strongly advise all musicians, before it is too late, to seize some opportunity of going to hear a genuine folk-song sung by a singer who has the traditional art of singing them; it is a wonderful experience.

The folk-song in its pure state has ceased to evolve. We must take the folk-songs we have recovered as they are now; we must not venture to alter or 'improve' them; as we find them we must keep them. We may have found them at the highest point of their development, or they may have passed their climax and have begun the downward path when they were recovered. That we can never tell. It is on their face value that we must judge them. The folk-song is now on its trial under new conditions; the next few years will show the strength of its vital power.

The evolution of the English folk-song by itself has ceased, but its spirit can continue to grow and flourish at the hands of our native composers.

I do not wish to advocate a narrow parochialism in music. A composer's style must be ultimately personal, but an individual is a member of a nation, and the greatest and most widely known artists have been the most strongly national. Bach, Shakespeare, Verdi, Reynolds, Whitman—their appeal may be cosmopolitan, but the origin of their inspiration is national.

Many critics sneer at what they call 'going back to folk-song', and imagine that it is suggested that composers should devote their time to arranging traditional melodies. This is not at all what I mean.

To write rhapsodies on folk-tunes is a very good exercise for the composer, and the results may often be delightful, but to garnish our ordinary English hotchpotch of every modern composer from Brahms to Debussy with a few English folk-tunes by way of ornament will not make a national style. It is not a question (as Mrs Newmarch has wisely said) of 'playing with local colour'. The matter lies deeper than this. Let me give you an example—*Die Meistersinger*, by Richard Wagner. Here is a work using to the full all the resources of colour, of harmony, of form, of expression, which go to make up the completest art, without a touch of archaism, and alive from beginning to end with the spirit of German folk-song. In art, as I suppose in every activity, the best results are obtained by developing one's natural faculties to the highest. If an Englishman tries to pose as a Frenchman or a German, he will not only make a bad Englishman, he will also make a bad foreigner.

If the English spirit is capable of being expressed in music, let it be so expressed; if not, let us honestly give up the attempt.[e]

There are already signs that some of our younger composers are finding inspiration in their native folk-songs. If this impulse leads them to develop a school of genuinely felt and sincerely expressed music, we shall owe a great debt of gratitude to those who have pointed out the way, and especially to one man without whose work it may safely be said that the large majority of English musicians would have remained in ignorance of our own traditional art. Cecil Sharp was not the first Englishman to collect folk-songs, but it is he who first saw and proclaimed their value as a guide and stimulus to the musicians of England.

The younger composers have shown their gratitude in the most practical manner; these recently recovered traditional melodies have evidently touched many of them to the quick, and led them to look on music from a new point of view. The results are already beginning to show themselves; a concert of 'English music' need no longer mean an evening of boredom—indeed, of late, an English audience has actually been known to 'encore' an English composition. The work of this young school is still tentative and small in scope; the symphonies, oratorios, and tone-poems of a few years ago have given way to ballads, dances, 'rambles', small suites, and works on a smaller and more concise scale. This is as it should be, it is only a step back to leap further. We have made the mistake in England of trying to take over, 'ready-made', a foreign culture, a culture which is the result of generations of patient development, and of attempting to fit on to it our own incompatible conditions. This is merely to reap where we have not sown, and the end must be failure.

An art is not a matter of detached appreciation; if it is to be vital it must be a reflection of the whole life of the community. Any direct and unforced expression

[e] The 1912 version ends here.

of our common life may be the nucleus from which a great art will spring; of such expressions the folk-song is, without doubt, the most genuine and the most unadulterated, besides being in itself a complete form of art.

This growth from small beginnings will not take place all at once. We must look for signs of it, not to those musicians who are now in their maturity, but, perhaps, to students and beginners, to those whose names are still unknown. They in their turn will show the way to others, and thus there will gradually be built up a musical structure which shall have that permanence and universal recognition which is only possible to an art which has grown out of the very lives of those who make it.

CHAPTER 39

Folk-Song in Chamber Music

AS A SPECIAL subject, the influence of folk-song on chamber music is difficult to divide from that of folk-song on music in general. Chamber music is to be distinguished from other music chiefly in its scope and technique; an influence like that of the folk-song is likely to be felt by a composer equally whether he is writing symphonies, operas, or quartets.

Therefore, to trace the influence of folk-song on chamber music must, of necessity, be a rather arbitrary proceeding, consisting merely of tracing the folk influences on a composer's style generally and concentrating attention on those of his works which happen to fall under the head of chamber music.

There is, however, one class of such music which is particularly likely to be influenced by folk-song, namely, all that which is of melodic pattern and on a small and simple scale, written for a solo instrument or for two or three instruments in combination. This kind of chamber music has always been very susceptible to the influence of the folk-song.

Source: Walter Willson Cobbett (ed.), *Cobbett's Cyclopedic Survey of Chamber Music*, i (London: Oxford University Press, 1929; 2nd edn, 1963), 410–12. This is a slightly revised version of 'Influence of Folk Song on Chamber Music', in *Chamber Music*, supplement no. 8, in *The Music Student* (1914), 69–71.

There are two ways in which the music sprung from the people may be felt in a composer's work.

First: the idiom which is equally native to him and to the folk-songs of his own country may permeate his music as a whole. In this case we shall not be able necessarily to trace actual quotations from folk-song in his compositions, but we feel that his music is part of the national musical language which finds its simplest and most direct expression in his native folk-song. This is the case in all great music, which, to whatever heights it rises, always has its roots planted in its native soil.

Secondly (and this is not exclusive of the first way): composers often feel tempted to make use of actual quotations from folk music, especially that of their own country, as a basis for short pieces such as variations, fantasias, dance movements, and the like. This is partly due to the fascination which these primitive and beautiful melodies exercise over all musical minds, and partly because composers feel (unconsciously no doubt) that an occasional draught at the fountain-head will invigorate and refresh the stream of their own musical thought.

It is in this second case that folk-song has an influence over chamber music in particular; that kind of chamber music, especially, which takes the form of short piano pieces, solos for violin, and so on—pieces of a small and simple type, which are melodic in their nature or embody some striking rhythmic formula.

Among the earliest music which can properly be classified as 'chamber music' is the collection, edited by Fuller Maitland and the late W. Barclay Squire, known as the *Fitzwilliam Virginal Book*. This book consists of a number of small pieces composed for the virginals by various Elizabethan composers of note, among them being John Bull, Byrd, Dowland, Farnaby, and others. These pieces consist of fantasias and variations on tunes, most of them folk-tunes evidently popular in Elizabethan times. Such titles as *John, come kiss me now, My Robin is to the greenwood gone, Walsingham, Malt's come down, Greensleeves*, are frequent. Many of these tunes are well known to us through Chappell's great work, *Popular Music of the Olden Time*, and one of the tunes, at least, exists to this day as a Morris tune, which is even now played where Morris dancing is still a traditional art.

It is, I think, not straining a term too widely to include under the heading 'chamber music' the shorter, at all events, of J. S. Bach's choral preludes for the organ; many of these are on quite a small scale, and more suited for the chamber organ than for the great instruments of our cathedrals. In these preludes Bach has taken the hymn-tunes so beloved throughout Lutheran Germany and treated them with his own consummate art. There can be no doubt that many of these German *Choräle* are adapted from folk-tunes.

The indirect influence of the folk-song can be seen in the music of the Italian composers of the late seventeenth century—Scarlatti, Corelli, Tartini, and others—though it is the design more than the character of the folk-song whose influence is felt. The object of these early Italian composers was to produce melodic, simple and direct music, and in seeking for some easily grasped pattern on which to mould their ideas they hit (accidentally, no doubt) on the very pattern they on which so many folk-tunes are built. This pattern they enlarged and developed, and left as a heritage to the classical school of Haydn, Mozart, and Beethoven; and it was from these slender beginnings that the whole scheme of sonata form sprang, so that a direct descent from the simple folk-song to the complexity of Beethoven's Ninth Symphony is traceable—a proof, if one were needed, that great music is not something abnormal and precious, but has its roots in the common needs of human nature.

There is hardly need to speak of the folk-song influence on Haydn—he was a countryman, and the subjects of his quartets and symphonies are full of the spirit, if not of the very shape, of his own national melodies—it was the spirit of the folk-song which gave his music that vitality, coupled with simplicity, which distinguished it from the vapid commonplace of his contemporaries.

Beethoven's music, saturated though it is with the spirit of German folk-song, has, as far as the writer knows, few actual quotations from folk music. However, as regards his chamber music, the theme of the variations in his septet is said to be a Rhine *Volkslied*, and one calls to mind the *Thème Russe* in his second *Rasoumovsky* Quartet, which turns up unexpectedly, very differently treated, and under very different circumstances, in the Coronation scene of Moussorgsky's *Boris Godounov*.

Of more modern composers it is, perhaps, in certain of the works of Chopin that we find the folk-song element most strongly marked. There are two Chopins—the Parisian, the inventor of brilliant piano passages, the composer of the valses and impromptus; and the Polish, intensely national Chopin, the composer of the mazurkas and polonaises. Some of Chopin's mazurkas have a strong family likeness to actual Polish folk-songs, and his polonaises are directly founded on the national dance. In the case of Chopin there is, indeed, a special application of the folk-song influence to chamber music. The national spirit of Chopin could be expressed in no better way than in these slight forms, coupled with that intimacy of feeling which is found only in music designed for solo players.

It is hardly necessary to speak in detail of the national influences in the work of such eminently nationalist composers as Grieg, Dvořák, and Tchaikovsky. Grieg's small piano pieces are often hardly to be distinguished from Norwegian folk-songs; Dvořák's *dumky* and *furiants* are deliberately founded in form, if not in material, on the songs and dances of his native country; while Tchaikovsky has more than once used Russian folk-songs in his chamber music, notably in the theme of the Variations in his Piano Trio and in the slow movement of his Second String Quartet.

One of the most interesting developments of modern English music has been the influence of the folk-song on the style of many of our younger composers, an influence shown chiefly in their chamber music. The younger composers, however, have not been without guidance in this matter from their older colleagues. Sir Hubert Parry's delightful piano duets on British airs are too little known; and both Sir Charles Stanford and Sir Alexander Mackenzie made fine use of their own national melodies, though in the case of these two composers it is in their orchestral and vocal music that the national influence is most apparent.

Among the younger composers one of the earliest to make use of English folk-tunes was Nicholas Gatty in his early String Quartet, where the Finale takes the form of a set of variations on a Worcestershire melody. Mention must be made also of the slow movement in J. B. McEwen's splendid Second String Quartet, where the influence of Scottish idiom is very strong.

The most conspicuous use of English and Irish folk-song has been made by Percy Grainger. Grainger's work, even in his orchestral and choral music, is small in scope, and it is in his chamber music that he is most characteristic, because it is in this style of music that he can concentrate vividly all he has to say in the most concise and direct manner. His use of folk-song sometimes takes the form of varied treatment of a tune, as in his *Molly on the Shore* and *Shepherd's Hey*—sometimes, as in his *Ramble, My Robin is to the greenwood gone*, he takes a folk-song as the basis of an instrumental piece, while in the *Mock Morris* he follows the example of Chopin in his mazurkas, and has composed original music suggested in its rhythm and general scheme by our own national dance, the Morris.

It is the younger composers especially that the English folk-song has influenced. It is about twenty-five years since, through the efforts of Miss Broadwood, the late Cecil Sharp, and others, the vast wealth of beautiful melody to which English musicians are the heirs was made accessible to the world at large. Naturally, then, the older composers, to whom they were new and strange, could hardly take to them quite naturally, however much they might admire them: their style was already formed, and to them their own folk-songs inevitably remained something external. But with the younger composers it is different; they have grown up with their own national music, it has become part of their system, they have assimilated it, and with the composers of the future this may be still more so. When every child is taught his mother music with his mother tongue, the two will be equally natural means of expression, and it will be as natural for an English musician to write English music as for an English author to write the English language.

CHAPTER 40

Dance Tunes

FOLK MUSIC, LIKE all primitive art, is an applied art—a means to an end; a means of reciting a ballad or marking the rhythm of a dance. A traditional singer can seldom hum a tune of a ballad without its words; it is the words which suggest the tune to him and the tune which suggests the words; they are inextricably coupled in his mind. It is equally true that a traditional fiddler finds it difficult to remember a dance tune unless he watches the dance, and the dancer is at a loss over his steps without the tune.

THE UNSELFCONSCIOUSNESS OF ART

In this, then, traditional art is on common ground with all great art—that it is unself-conscious. Schubert was not consciously tragic in the last movement of his C major Symphony—that overwhelming cataclysm near the end of the movement would have lost half its force if it was a deliberate attempt to make our flesh creep, if we did not feel that it came nearly by accident, as the result of a purely musical development. Or to take another example: the beautiful variation of the second subject of Beethoven's D minor Sonata on its second appearance seems to be the

Source: *The Music Student*, 11/12 (1919), 453–7.

accidental result of the fact that the compass of the pianoforte did not allow of an exact repetition in the new key.

So the attitude of the traditional musician to dance or song was not that of the great artist come to show off his skill, but that of a participator in the general artistic product.

Music for a dance of some particular character was required; the musician would, apparently, call to mind any tune which was suitable, or if none were suitable he would adapt some tune, probably a song tune, to the exigencies of the dance—and it is here, in this adaptability, that the unconscious artistry of the traditional musician shows itself. Many members of the EFDS will remember with pleasure the artistic resourcefulness of Mr William Wells, the fiddler of the Bampton Morris Dancers, in adapting his music on the spur of the moment to the steps of the dancers—now going slower, now quicker, lengthening or shortening a phrase to chime in with some idiosyncracy of a dancer.

THE EVOLUTION OF TUNE

This adaptation of tunes for dancing purposes illustrates well the evolutionary nature of folk music. The process of transformation which melodies undergo in the course of their development is of course well known to students of folk song. Folk music lives by purely oral tradition. It is therefore, in its original surroundings, always in a state of flux—each new singer or player who acquires a new tune adds something individual to it; if he is dull and stupid he may spoil a good tune; if he is a fine artist and has a strong individuality he will certainly add to it something of his own—some new turn to a phrase perhaps which will glorify a tune almost out of recognition.

It must not be forgotten that the versions of folk music which collectors have stereotyped in print are always individual versions of a common theme.

There is much ignorant discussion about the 'original' or 'true' versions of traditional tunes. There is, in reality, no original of a folk tune. Traditional music is a common stem on which individual leaves and flowers are constantly blossoming. The several 'variants' of a folk song are probably at first improvisations of the moment. The collector who notes down a particularly fine variant of a folk tune may for all he knows be present at the actual birth of some artistic offspring. If these improvisations are pleasing to their inventor, or his hearers, they acquire permanency—if not, they die at the moment of birth.

A 'variant' which has all the appearance of an improvisation is to be found in the Bampton version of *Shepherd's Hey*. The second part of this version and part of the Ilmington version are given here side by side (Ex. 40.1).

Ex. 40.1. (a) 'Shepherd's Hey' (Ilmington version). Second strain; (b) 'Shepherd's Hey' (Bampton version).

(a)

(b)

'Greensleeves' as an Example

One of the most interesting examples we have of the transformation of a song tune into a dance tune is the melody *Greensleeves*. This was a well-known tune in Shakespeare's time, and he refers to it more than once[1]—and the same tune, in an altered form, was used up to modern times as a dance tune by the morris men of England.

Here (Ex. 40.2(a)) is the tune as given in Ballet's Lute Book (c. 1600). (There were apparently folk-song collectors also in those days, who noted down and arranged traditional airs, though probably in those days there was no necessity to go out collecting, one merely had to open one's window and listen).

This is obviously a singing, not a dancing, tune, and it was probably slightly sophisticated in the process of noting down. About eighty years later, the omnivorous Playford got hold of it, and introduced the following version of it into the *Dancing Master*, and, though it may be more suitable for dancing, it cannot be said that it is improved as a melody (Ex. 40.2(b)).

Then we hear no more of the tune till the twentieth century, when a rhythmical transformation of it is discovered as a traditional Morris tune. How did the Morris men get hold of this tune? They certainly had not access to the libraries

---

[1] E.g., 'They do no more adhere and keep pace than the hundredth psalm to the tune of "Greensleeves".' *Merry Wives of Windsor*, I, 2. [48–50.]

Ex. 40.2. (*a*) 'Greensleeves', as given in Ballet's Lute Book, c. 1600;

(*a*)

Ex. 40.2. (*b*) 'Greensleeves', from Playford's *Dancing Master*, 7th edn, 1686;

(*b*)

where Ballet's Lute Book and Playford's *Dancing Master* lay slumbering—it must have come down by an entirely separate tradition and be one offshoot of the same parent stem, of which the version used by Ballet so many years ago was another. The Morris version of *Greensleeves* is no longer a suave three-time melody, but a quick, exciting jig—and it is to be noticed that it is in the pure Dorian mode, which was only indicated in Ballet's version (Ex. 40.2(*c*)).

(*c*)

Those who have studied folk song will not be surprised to find yet another version, this time with the major third throughout—thus transforming a Dorian into a Mixolydian tune (Ex. 40.2(*d*)).

Ex. 40.2. (*d*) 'Greensleeves', Morris Jig–Gloucestershire.

(*d*)

FITTING NOTES TO STEPS

To the traditional dance musician the only problem to be faced was that of fitting the notes to the steps—nothing else mattered to him—and as I have already said, it is this unconscious attitude which makes for the finest art. Thus, the tune to 'Step Back' is purely choreographic in its construction, and whoever made it or adapted it to the dance had that end only in view. The climax of the dance is the 'step back' itself—and so in the tune, the key of the musical situation is found in the two repeated notes at the end of each strain (Ex. 40.3(*a*)).

Ex. 40.3. (*a*) 'Step Back', Morris Dance.

(*a*)

The problem of fitting a tune to a dance is sometimes complicated by the varying pace of the different figures of the dance. How is this difficulty got over? It is obvious that an entirely different *tempo* and often another rhythm is required for the 'Upright' and 'Capers' than that which suits the 'Side-step' and 'Jig'. To use another tune in so short a space would be to destroy all artistic unity. No, the same tune must be adapted by our resourceful Bampton fiddler and his fellow musicians to the varying needs of the dance. Sometimes it is enough to play a portion of the tune in a slower *tempo*, as in Ex. 40.3(b) and (c).

Ex. 40.3. (*b*) 'I'll go to Enlist for a Sailor', Morris Jig: side step.

(*b*)

Sometimes, however, the whole complexion of the tune is altered, nothing but the melodic curve remaining the same, as in an adaptation for dancing purposes of the well-known tune *Jockie to the Fair*, Ex. 40.3(d) and (e).

One used some years ago to hear a lot about 'transformation of themes', as if it were the invention of Liszt and Wagner—but Liszt and Wagner did not 'invent' this device, because all musical devices, if they are anything but mere tricks, are the

Ex. 40.3. (*c*) 'I'll go to Enlist for a Sailor', Morris Jig: upright.

(*c*)

Ex. 40.3. (*d*) 'Jockie to the Fair', first strain.

(*d*)

Ex. 40.3. (*e*) 'Jockie to the Fair', first strain as rhythmically altered.

(*e*)

outcome of some emotional need which can be shared alike by a world-famed composer and an unlettered countryman.

In this connection it is difficult to resist a comparison between the last-quoted example and the two versions of Siegfried's Horn Call in Wagner's *Ring* (Ex. 40.4).

The unself-consciousness of the traditional musician occasionally leads to less fortunate results—sometimes, apparently, the musical side of the folk dance fell into the hands of a poor musician, or one who was anxious to be up-to-date, and

Ex. 40.4. Siegfried's Horn Call.

who substituted the latest popular song for the tune traditionally associated with the dance. So it is not safe to assume that the music of a folk dance is always, strictly speaking, folk-music. Thus we find sword dancers at one place dancing to *So early in the morning* and country dancers in another to *I'll be a butterfly*—but these are accidental associations and not an essential part of the dance.

Playford, also in his *Dancing Master*, fished in various waters for his tunes. Most of them are undoubtedly folk-tunes; some are probably by contemporary composers; one is an adaptation of a trumpet march (*The Garter*) and a splendid dance it makes—and perhaps Playford's most wonderful feat of all is the delightful dance tune made out of Dean Aldrich's 'round': *Hark! the merry Christchurch Bells*.

It must not be imagined that all folk-dance tunes are founded on song tunes—even where we find words attached to dance tunes—these words have often been added later to fit the tune.

'Form' in Folk Dance

We can usually tell a pure dance tune by its form. In the case of a song tune the form is largely governed by the words. But in a dance tune pure and simple, there is no external consideration to influence the form, except, of course, the actual length of the dance figures; so the traditional inventors of dance tunes had to devise a form out of their own inner consciousness. It will not surprise those who realize that music is subject to the laws of evolution, to find that the form of the folk dance is in principle exactly that of a Beethoven sonata—namely (*a*) a melodic statement in which the tonal plane is constant, or, at most, changes once in the course of the section; (*b*) a period of suspense, in which the rhythmic element momentarily supersedes the melodic and in which the tonal plane is more shifting. This suspense is finally resolved by (*c*) a return, either in whole or in part, to the original melodic section.

This principle is simply (almost naively) illustrated in the following tune, Ex. 40.5(a).

Ex. 40.5. (*a*) 'Black Nag', Country Dance (Playford's *Dancing Master*, 1670).

(*a*)

The next two examples, 40.5(b) and 40.5(c), show the same plan rather more elaborated, and consist of: (*i*) a long, melodic phrase, repeated either exactly or with variation; (*ii*) a short, rhythmical, phrase, repeated on different tonal planes; (*iii*) a return either exactly or by suggestion to (*i*).

Ex. 40.5. (*b*) 'Old Mother Oxford', Morris Dance.

(*b*)

Ex. 40.5. (*c*) 'The Cuckoo's Nest', Morris Dance.

(*c*)

And finally, here is an example from Playford's *Dancing Master*, of a perfect little sonata movement in miniature—the whole principle of a Beethoven sonata compressed into eight bars, Ex. 40.5(d).

Ex. 40.5. (*d*) 'The Lady in the Dark', Country Dance (Playford's *Dancing Master*, 1665).

(*d*)

CHAPTER 41

Sailor Shanties

THE ART OF the folk-singer, like all true art, is essentially un-selfconscious—the artistic result is not openly sought, but comes, as it were, by accident. Thus Bunyan, in trying to preach a sermon, produced a masterpiece of literature; Shelley, when he thought he was reforming the world, wrote a great poem; Wagner devised inimitable counterpoint in attempting the musical portrayal of tragic passion. In the same way the sailor, with the object of improving the quality of his work, has invented the 'shanty', and it is these which Dr Terry now has collected into a volume ('Part One', I am glad to see, which means that more are to follow).[a]

Dr Terry's collection of shanties has been known to students in manuscript for many years; but now, through the enterprise of Messrs Curwen, they are given to the world, and the world will be able to see for itself the fine quality of our sea-music.

Modern developments in machinery have destroyed the original purpose of the shanty, but like the tithe-barn, the church and the castle, they remain for us as works of art, and it is as works of art, and that only, that we must now judge them. If they are merely of nautical or antiquarian interest, then their proper place is the

Source: *Musical News and Herald*, 61/1553 (1921), 683–4.
[a] R. R. Terry (ed.), *The Shanty Book* (London: J Curwen 1921).

library of the folklorist or the marine expert. In preparing a volume like this the editor, then, incurs a great responsibility, and especially if, like Dr Terry, he is an enthusiastic seaman, is subject to great temptation. On the whole Dr Terry has resisted these manfully, and he must be forgiven if, for old acquaintance' sake, he has included one or two tunes which are not up to the standard of the rest of the collection. The first duty of the editor of a book of folk-songs is that of selection. The shantyman took his material from various sources, from the folk-song, usually English, but sometimes, one would judge, South-American; from the negro melody, and occasionally from the revival hymn and the music-hall. From these the editor has to select for his purpose; in this case the purpose is to provide people with something beautiful to sing; that is the one test of the value of a book such as this. The sentimental association of the tunes, their antiquarian interest, their appropriateness as labour-songs, are not to the point. The one question is: 'Do the melodies here presented take their stand with other music as high artistic achievements?' The answer in nine cases out of ten is triumphantly 'Yes'. We have only to consider such splendid melodies as the well-known 'Rio Grande' (No. 2), and 'Shenandoah' (No. 9), and the less known, but equally fine 'Santy Anna' (No. 8), [or] the poetry of both words and music in 'Lowlands Away' (No. 6), to prove this. And these are only a few out of many. In one or two examples, perhaps, Dr Terry has not been very discriminating; we must put it down to his enthusiastic seamanship which clothes with the glamour of association tunes which the cold hard world will judge as not being worthy of the rest of the collection.

A task of almost equal difficulty to the one of selection is that of a suitable setting. Dr Terry has decided, in common with other folk-song editors, to add a simple accompaniment for the pianoforte. In this, I think, he is right; the folk-song in its original surroundings is, of course, purely melodic, but a volume like this is a deliberate attempt to take the folk-song out of its own surroundings and let it take its chance as music, pure and simple. The folk-song implies more than it says, and the editor has to embody these implications in his pianoforte accompaniment. This is a task which requires the highest qualities, both of the heart and the head; of the heart, because absolute sympathy with the subject is necessary; of the head, because consummate musicianship is necessary. Of Dr Terry's musicianship there can be no doubt. For proof we have only to turn to his work at Westminster Cathedral, where in the face of unparalleled difficulties he has maintained the great traditions of true choral style, and has obtained for the cathedral music an European reputation. Dr Terry's musicianship is, then, above suspicion, and so there seems to be no need for him to mark the 'consecutive fifths' in No. 21. A musical progression either sounds well or it does not. If it sounds well, there is no more to be said; if it does not, it will not sound any better for having attention drawn to it. Luckily we are able to judge of Dr Terry's musicianship in other ways than by his ability to recognise 'consecutives' when he sees them. The settings of 'Billy Boy' (No. 1), 'Johnny come down' (No. 4), 'We're all bound to go' (No. 13), 'Hanging Johnny' (No. 19), 'Hilo Somebody' (No. 20), 'Tom's gone to Hilo' (No. 24)—all splendid tunes finely arranged, are sufficient proof of the editor's taste and culture. But sometimes Dr Terry seems afraid of his own musicianship—perhaps he is over-anxious to show that a Doctor of Music is also a human being, or, paradoxically, his sympathy obscures his musicianship. Let us take one or two examples: the pianoforte prelude to that splendid tune, 'What shall we do' (No. 14), or the setting of 'Reuben Ranzo' (No. 22), and 'Clear the Track' (No. 5). What has happened in these cases? I think it is that Dr Terry has here mistaken the nature of his task. He seems to say: 'I will add to these songs the unsophisticated kind of setting which the original singer would appreciate.' But surely this is a piece of false reasoning? The shantyman, like all true artists, was building better than he knew, and it is the business of the arranger to find the true harmonic equivalent which is implied in the tunes, and which the singer unconsciously suggests, and not that sort of setting of which the sailor would self-consciously approve.

A good wine needs no bush, and when there is such good wine it seems ungracious to quarrel with the label; but there are one or two points in Dr Terry's preface which cannot pass unnoticed. A good deal of space has been devoted to the awful fate which will apparently pursue those who say 'Hog-eye'd' instead of 'Hog-eye'—this seems to me over-elaborated; again, was it necessary to write nearly a page on the spelling of the word 'shanty'? Shakspeare still lives, though his name is spelled in six different ways, and the splendid tunes in his book will survive being described as 'chantys', or even—*horribile dictu*—'chanteys'. On one rather technical point I find myself in disagreement with Dr Terry. He writes as if there were such a thing as the 'origin', or authentic version of a folk-song. But where is this original? The folk-song is continually in a state of flux, each singer makes his own version, and the one which is most worth preserving is not the oldest but the best. The shanty, doubtless, had a version which was best suited to its immediate purpose, but that purpose, as Dr Terry admits, is now gone by; and if it so happens that the 'twirls and twiddles' on which Dr Terry pours his scorn, actually improve the tune, as such, why not preserve them? I can imagine the 'amusement and contempt' of the medieval chansonnier when he found his gay little spring song converted into the 'Tonus Peregrinus'; but does Dr Terry therefore consider that this magnificent melody is unworthy of a place in the music of his Church?

Dr Terry is unhappy because folk-song collecting has, in his opinion, ceased to be 'artistic', and become 'commercial'. I hope that readers of the *Musical News and Herald* will buy copies of his delightful book by the thousand—it will repay them over and over again, and will prove to Dr Terry that the 'commercial' result is not incompatible with the 'artistic' aim. But from what I know of folk-song collecting, of the immense labour and time which such a book as this involves, not to mention the actual cash expenditure which the work of collecting and arranging entails, I think Dr Terry may rest assured that his work will remain a labour of love.

CHAPTER 42

How to Sing a Folk-Song

MUSIC CAN BE applied to poetry in two ways; either the music can illustrate in detail each passing mood or idea of the poem—or it can merely supply a melodic equivalent to the metre and rhythm of the words. The former is the 'dramatic' method much in favour with the romantic composers of the nineteenth century. The latter is the 'strophical' method and views music as a means of declaiming poetry beautifully. Both methods have produced the greatest art. Schubert's 'Prometheus' is an example of the dramatic method, his 'Sylvia' of the strophical.

Now the traditional ballad or folk song—in England at all events—is always strophical. Not only is ballad music looked upon by traditional singers merely as a convenient and beautiful way of reciting a ballad, but the ballad poetry itself is looked on as nothing else than a convenient and beautiful way of telling a story. The art of the traditional folk-song is (like all great art) unconscious. The beauty of our folk-music, like that of our castles, our barns, our churches, grew out of its utility. Now there can be no doubt as to the traditional method of singing a ballad. Clearness of diction, perfection of melodic outline and beauty of phrasing, these are the prominent characteristics of the best traditional singers' art. The art of the ballad singer is a lost art—we cannot recapture it—at the best we can parody it,

Source: *The Midland Musician*, 1/4 (1926), 127.

imitate the externals, the dialect, the closed eyes, the curious prolongation of certain syllables—but heaven forbid that we should do so.

But we can, if we wish to, apply the fundamental principles of the ballad singer's art to our own interpretation of folk-songs; and the essential characteristics of the ballad singer's style is summed up in the word 'impersonal', the singer must be absorbed in the song. This is certainly true of what is now called 'community' singing. To deviate one moment from our subject, we know the terrible results of the 'personal' element applied to congregational singing—such vandalisms as the following rendering of a well-known hymn as recommended, I believe, in a popular hymnal;

(ff) In life, (pp) in death, (p) O Lord (cresc) abide with me.

This 'impersonal' principle is largely applicable to solo singing as well—we all know the drawing-room singer who in the *Bailiff's Daughter of Islington* will make a 'dramatic' pause or a whining rallentando on the words 'She is dead, sir, long ago'—to the utter ruination of the outline of the melody and the whole spirit of the ballad. (I have actually heard a singer who transposed the well-known tune to the minor mode at this point!)

After all, the whole essence of a ballad is that it is sung to the same tune throughout—and the essence of a good ballad tune is that it can bear numerous repetitions; indeed, a fine ballad tune only begins to show its quality when it has been repeated several times—its effect is cumulative. This cumulative effect must obviously be lost if the tune be cut up by continual pauses, rallentandos and 'dramatic' ejaculations.

The tune's the thing, and each time we 'dramatise' a folk-song we must necessarily do violence to the tune.

I am far from denying that there are some great artists who can ignore these principles with success—but they do so not because they ignore them but in spite of their ignoring them. A great artist like Jean Stirling Mackinlay often delights us with her dramatic renderings of folk-songs—but she shows her art at its highest (and its most difficult) achievement, when she sings the *Cherry Tree Carol* in a simple white dress without gesture, without nuance—when she lets the beautiful words and tune speak for themselves.

CHAPTER 43

The Late Mr Frank Kidson

KIDSON WAS A lineal descendant—musically speaking—of Chappell, but he had probably more knowledge and certainly more accurate knowledge than his ancestor. But their point of view was the same; the supreme authority was always the printed source: they both distrusted tradition. In this Kidson differed from many other writers on folk-song including Cecil Sharp himself, who considered that folk-song is kept pure and vital by oral tradition.

It follows, from Kidson's point of view, that all traditional deviations from a printed copy are 'corruptions'. Other thinkers consider it doubtful whether one can always refer to a printed copy as an 'original' version; they think rather that a printed version of a ballad or tune is often itself a distorted version and that folk-songs can be more readily found in their pure and idiomatic form in the minds of traditional singers.

An interesting example of these different points of view may be seen in the notes on the 'Sheepshearing Song' in Sharp's *Folk-Songs from Somerset*.

Kidson's attitude to this question may be seen in his introduction to his *Traditional Tunes* (p. xiv), where, however, he pays a tribute to the wonderful accuracy of tradition.

Source: *Journal of the English Folk Dance Society*, 2nd ser., 1 (1927), 51.

Kidson's great knowledge of printed sources enabled him to dispose of such spurious 'folk-songs' as 'Caller Herrin', and to restore to their true traditional origins tunes like 'The Arethusa' long supposed to be the compositions of eighteenth-century musicians (see his articles on these tunes in *Grove's Dictionary of Music*).

It must be remembered that Kidson's collection of eighty-four traditional tunes was published in 1891 when folk-song was an unknown quantity except to a few experts and enthusiasts and when 'educated' musicians, at all events in England, despised everything which could not show its trademark.

In his introduction to his collection Kidson thinks it necessary to apologize to the profession for his 'homely ditties'. Nevertheless, we realize all through his preface that he was one of the first to recognize the beauty inherent in our traditional song.

CHAPTER 44

Lucy Broadwood: An Appreciation

IN 1843 IT occurred to the Rev. John Broadwood to pay attention to the songs which were sung at Harvest Homes and other festivities in his little Sussex village. When the local organist saw the tunes he was much shocked, said they were all wrong, and insisted on altering some of the cadences to fit in with the current harmony primers. How could the reverend gentleman think there was anything worth recording in the songs of these rough and uncultivated boors? Besides, it was well known that we had no music in England, except of course the dutiful copies of Mendelssohn and Spohr which were to be heard at Exeter Hall. Mr Broadwood meekly acquiesced, but in his heart of hearts he knew that he was right, and that in the words of Hubert Parry: 'True style comes not from the individual but from the products of crowds of fellow-workers, who sift, try, and try again, till they have found the thing that suits their native taste; and the purest product of such efforts is folk-song, which, when it is found outlasts the greatest works of art and becomes a heritage to generations.'[a]

This love of folk song and the belief in its importance Mr Broadwood passed on to his niece Lucy Broadwood, who added this to her brilliant talents as pianist,

Source: *Journal of the Folk Song Society*, 8/31 (1927), 44–5.
[a] See Parry's address to the inaugural general meeting of the Folk Song Society in 'A Folk-Song Function', *The Musical Times*, no. 673 (1899), 168–9.

singer, composer and essayist. Among a stiff-necked generation of unbelievers she believed in the beauty and vitality of our own national melody.

The first fruits of her love of English folk song appeared in 1893—the well-known *English County Songs* edited by herself and Fuller Maitland. The graceful musicianship of her pianoforte accompaniments to these songs showed, as do also her few published original compositions, a strongly marked inventive gift.

In the great flood of wonderful melody which has been undammed in England during the last twenty-five years we are apt to forget that there were strong men before Agamemnon; but *English County Songs* (together with *Songs of the West* and Kidson's *Traditional Tunes* which all appeared within four years of each other) deserve pride of place as pioneers. If it had not been for these early collections who knows but that the necessary impetus to further research would have been lacking and that our great wealth of national melody would have been lost to us for ever?

When the Folk-Song Society was founded in 1899 Lucy Broadwood threw herself whole-heartedly into its work, and in 1904 became *de jure* what she had been for some years *de facto*—both honorary secretary of the Society and editor-in-chief of the *Journal*. From that time to now every *Journal* has had the advantage of her editorial care and supervision. It is only those who have worked with her who know the amount of energy and hard labour that this double task has involved. It is not generally recognized how much the well-ordered correctness of our *Journals* owes to her untiring editorial care. Besides this she was always ready to place her great knowledge (ranging from eighteenth-century song-books to Apocryphal gospels) at the disposal of the Society, and the *Journals* are full of her learned and illuminating comments. She has also generously contributed material for two *Journals* (No. 5, Songs from Sussex and Surrey; No. 10, Songs from Ireland) as well as numerous variants of tunes contributed by other collectors. The present number of the *Journal* is the last which will contain the name of Lucy Broadwood as one of its editors and we say goodbye gratefully and regretfully. We shall sadly miss the familiar initials 'L. E. B.' inevitably following some illuminating note or the correction of some well-worn fallacy.

Lucy Broadwood's 'output' (if one may use the word) as a collector is not large but it is choice. She loves the songs with an almost personal affection, and she has naturally shrunk from bringing into the glaring light of publicity these songs which grew up in the stillness of the countryside and which it has been her delight to ponder over in the quiet of her study. But she realized, as all earnest folk-songists do, that we hold these treasures as trustees only, and that we are bound to offer them back to those to whom they belong in the hope that they will be worthy of them. So in 1908 she determined to publish a large portion of her collection fitted with her own felicitous pianoforte accompaniments, under the title of *Traditional Songs and Carols*. Rumour has it that there is also a collection of beautiful Gaelic airs known at present only to a privileged few. Is it too much to hope that in the comparative leisure which will now be hers that she will find time to issue these also to the world?[b]

[b] Although Broadwood remained an active participant in the folksong movement until her death in 1929, she published no new collections after this 1908 volume.

CHAPTER 45

Ella Mary Leather

BORN MARCH 26TH, 1874. DIED JUNE 7TH, 1928

A good folklorist requires to be scientifically accurate, artistically imaginative and humanly sympathetic. It is the combination of these qualities that makes the success of Mrs Leather's *Folklore of Herefordshire*.

This book is now a recognised authority on folklore and archaeology, while a complete number of the *Journal of the Folk Song Society* (No. 14) testifies to her power of discovering lovely melody in the usual unpromising circumstances.

As to her human sympathy, one only had to accompany her, as was more than once my privilege, on a folk-song collecting expedition among the gypsies of Herefordshire, to be astonished at her friendly reception by these proud and suspicious people. She understood them and they understood her; they knew that both she and Colonel Leather were willing and anxious to help and advise them in all their difficulties, and in return they gave her of their best.

One of these expeditions remains clearly in my memory. It was a cold, clear September night and we stood by the light of a blazing fire in the open ground of the gypsy encampment; the fire had been specially lighted to enable us to note down tunes and words in the growing darkness. Then out of the half light there

Source: *Journal of the Folk Song Society*, 8 part 2/32 (1928), 102.

came the sound of a beautiful tenor voice singing 'The unquiet grave'. It was a
memorable experience.

As far as I know the tune has not yet been printed, so I give it as we heard it
then, though when the same singer sang it again some years later he had considerably altered the rhythm (Ex. 45.1).

Ex. 45.1. 'The unquiet grave'.

CHAPTER 46

Folk-Song

ANY ART IF it is to have life must be able to trace its origin to a fundamental human need. Such needs must prompt expression among people even in their most primitive and uncultivated state. To this rule the art of music is no exception; Parry has pointed out that the universal law of evolution demands that we should be able to trace even the most elaborate compositions of Beethoven or Wagner back to some primitive germ. This primitive, spontaneous music has been called 'folk-song', a rather awkward translation of the German word 'Volkslied', but nevertheless a word which stands for a very definite fact in the realm of music. It has been said that if we did not know by experience of the existence of folk-song we should have to presuppose it theoretically to account for the art of music.

Fortunately theory is borne out by practice. We find that unlettered and untravelled people have both the desire and the power to express themselves musically and these attempts at musical expression are not mere clownish nonsense, nor are they, as we are sometimes told, degraded reminiscences of 'cultured' music, but are something *sui generis*; moreover, among these spontaneous expressions are to be found melodies which are the most treasured possessions of our art—such melodies as 'Searching for Lambs' (England), 'Ca' the Yowes' (Scotland), 'The

Source: *Encyclopaedia Britannica*, ix (14th edn, London: Encyclopaedia Britannica, 1929), 447–8.

Londonderry Air' (Ireland), 'Innsbrück Ich musz dich lassen' (Germany), 'Magali' (Provence), are ample proof of this, and these are only a few examples out of hundreds.

Moreover, as we have already seen, the folk-song must of necessity bear within it the seed of all the future developments of the art. Such a tune as 'The Lady in the Dark', from Playford's *Dancing Master*, exhibits in miniature the same ground plan as many a movement from a Beethoven symphony: indeed this tune has been described as a 'Symphony eight bars long'.[a]

Folk-music has, of course, its limitations. To start with, folk-music like all primitive art is an applied art, the vehicle for the declamation of a ballad or the stepping of a dance, and it is, therefore, bounded by the structure of the stanza or the dance-figure. Secondly, folk-music (at all events that of the Teutonic and Latin races) is non-harmonic; there is nothing but the melodic line.

But these limitations have their compensating advantages. A tune which is only eight bars long, and which has to be repeated as often as twenty times to accompany a ballad or a dance, must have certain peculiar qualities if it is not to become wearisome; and we find that the best folk tunes only show their true quality after several repetitions.

Again, the purely melodic character of traditional song gives it a wide range of outline, impossible to melodies which are bound by the progressions of underlying harmonies. Melodies of an harmonic nature are almost always in the major or minor modes, but in folk-song other modes, chiefly the Dorian or Mixolydian, are frequent.

The fact that these modes are also to be found in another great body of purely melodic music, namely the plain-song of the Roman church, has led to the assumption that 'modal' folk-songs must be 'ancient', or even derived from mediaeval church music. On the propriety of dubbing a folk-song 'ancient' or 'modern' more will be said later; as to the supposed derivation from plain-song, surely the simple explanation is that folk-song and plain-song, being purely melodic, are based on the same principles; surely no similarity except that of mode can be traced between such tunes as 'Seventeen come Sunday' and 'Jesu dulcis memoria'.

A further and very important limitation of folk-song must be mentioned, namely that it survives by purely oral tradition. By our hypothesis the inventors and disseminators of folk-music are unlettered, and are therefore unable to stereotype their inventions by means of reading and writing. It is on this that the whole nature of folk-song and all questions of its origin and development depend.

[a] See Vaughan Williams's own article, 'Dance Tunes' (Chapter 40).

It is sometimes held that the word 'folk-song' should be used in what is called a 'broad' sense so as to include not only genuinely traditional music, but all those songs of a popular character which are habitually sung by the people of a country. But, in fact, the difference between these two classes of music is a real and scientific one, which is properly recognized by the Germans in their distinction between a 'Volkslied' and a 'Volksthümlicheslied'. What common denominator can be found which will cover, on the one hand, such a song as 'Tom Bowling' and, on the other, the 'Lazarus' tune in *English County Songs*? In the one case we can judge the date and even guess at the composer; but who can date a folk-song? Indeed, a folk-song is neither new nor old; it is like a forest tree with its roots deeply buried in the past but which continually puts forth new branches, new leaves, new fruit.

Collectors are often asked by would-be intelligent enquirers as to the age of some folk-song, as if the question of age were either important or relevant. Others (sceptics) suggest that the traditional singer 'made it up himself'. The answer to this, of course, is that quite possibly he did to some extent 'make it up himself', although this in no way adds to, or takes away from, its scientific or artistic value. It is not the question of age or authorship that is important in a folk-song but that of spontaneity and beauty. When a collector nowadays hears a song sung by a traditional singer he may be pretty sure that, if the singer is a true artist, he will have unconsciously added something of his own to what he sings. A folk-song then is always grafting the new on to the old. This is the answer to the question: 'How old is that folk-song?' A folk-song is neither new nor old because it is continually taking on new life; it is an individual flowering on a common stem.

This brings us to the vexed question of the 'communal growth' of folk-song; and here it may be pointed out that much useless derision has been wasted over a supposed theory of 'communal origin'. No one has ever laid it down as an indisputable proposition that folk-song has a communal origin, though even this is not so impossible an idea as some people suppose. No one insists that some individual must have invented every word of our language. Who invented 'father' or 'plough' or 'sun' or any other of the words that belong to primitive life? If we admit communal authorship in our language, is it not even more probable in such an intangible matter as music?

However, it is not necessary to prove the communal origin of folk-song in order to argue in favour of its communal growth. It is well known that when a rumoured fact or story becomes spread about it soon is circulated in various altered forms and this in spite of the fact that everyone who repeats the story is anxious to repeat it correctly. How much more then will a song become altered by oral repetition when each new singer is bound only by his artistic predilections? If he thinks he can improve the song, why should he not do so? If he finds it too difficult why should he not simplify it? Thus a folk-song evolves gradually as it passes through the minds of different men and different generations.

Nor will this gradual change ever be a process of deterioration, because those versions of the tune which are distasteful to others will die a natural death. Here then is a clear case of the survival of the fittest. A tune which has been handed down from father to son through many generations will represent the united imaginations of thousands of men and women through hundreds of years of evolution.

This then is the much discussed 'communal growth' theory, and it is borne out by the facts. Collectors know well that numerous variants of the same tune have been found in different parts of the country and, conversely, that tunes have been found which are quite distinct from each other, but at the same time have features that point to a common stock. Thus Grimm's famous apophthegm 'a folk-song composes itself'[b] is not, after all, a piece of misty emotionalism but represents the hard commonsense facts of the case.

---

[b] 'Ein Volksleid dichtet sich selbst'. W. Grimm, *Altdänische Heldenleider* (Heidelberg, 1811), 541, quoted in Carl Engel, *An Introduction to the Study of National Music* (London: Longmans, Green, 1866), 13.

CHAPTER 47

Cecil Sharp's Accompaniments

IT HAS SOMETIMES been questioned whether Sharp had the creative impulse in music, but his accompaniments to my mind clearly show that he had. His creative impulse came from the tune he was setting. That is why his settings are often better than those of more technically gifted arrangers, because they come to the task as composers and let the suggestions started by the tune run away with them, and so forget the tune itself. This is especially bad when the arranger deliberately sets out 'to make something of' the tune. In all the best of Sharp's accompaniments it is the tune that counts and the arrangement falls into its proper background. In some cases his accompaniments look wrong, and sometimes even when played by themselves seem awkward, but they stand the important test, that they make the tune sound right. It is true that Sharp had little of the conventional technique of pianoforte accompaniment, as taught by professors of composition, but he developed a technique of his own whose complete success was only hindered, I think, by his fear of the harmony professor. He was so anxious for the songs to get known that he sometimes did not venture to produce an accompaniment which would be considered 'not correct'. And as he was not able entirely to assimilate this 'correct' style

Source: A. H. Fox Strangways and Maud Karpeles, *Cecil Sharp* (London: Oxford University Press, 1933), 217.

his accompaniments sometimes seem to halt between two opinions. If he had let himself go regardless of this more of his work might have been up to his best standard, but it might not have been so acceptable to the education authorities.

Occasionally, and only occasionally, his accompaniments seem to be bad. When this is so I put it down to the fact that he was so anxious for people to sing the songs, that he feared to provide an accompaniment which was beyond their mental, emotional, and technical equipment. As examples of first-rate accompaniments I suggest 'The Cuckoo', 'The Drowned Lover', 'The Water is Wide', the morris tune, 'Leap Frog' (Field Town), and 'Jenny Pluck Pears'. Of the second class, not entirely satisfactory for reasons I have given, 'Searching for Lambs' and 'A Rosebud in June'. Among those I presume to condemn are 'The Trees they do grow high' and 'Sellenger's Round'. But in nine cases out of ten the total result is satisfying and beautiful, and this after all is the only valid test.

CHAPTER 48

Arthur Somervell

JUNE 5TH, 1866–MAY 2ND, 1937

Arthur Somervell was a pupil of Parry and Stanford and was one of the first products of their contention that the musician's art should be the consummation of a liberal education. This liberal education Somervell obtained at Uppingham School and King's College, Cambridge.

It was from Parry, Stanford and Hadow that he learnt to look on folk-song as the foundation of musical culture and when he became a power in the educational councils of the nation he lost no time in putting that theory into practice.

Unfortunately in those days opinion on the true nature of folk-song was very inchoate and in a Blue Book published in 1906, while on the one hand the use of folk-songs in schools was strongly advocated, at the same time the list of songs printed to support this view contained many tunes which had no connection with true folk-song, thus vitiating the whole argument.[a]

This caused a strong controversy between Somervell and Cecil Sharp whose views which are, or should be, those held by the EFDSS, were clear and

---

Source: *Journal of the Folk Dance and Song Society*, 3/2 (1937), 152.

[a] The Blue Book in question, *Suggestions for the Consideration of Teachers* (London: HMSO, 1905), was presented to Parliament by the Board of Education. The songs listed in that report were published in Charles Villiers Stanford (ed.), *The National Song Book* (London: Boosey, 1906).

uncompromising. Folk-songs are those made by the people and grow to maturity by oral tradition; they must not be confused either theoretically or practically with songs written *for* the people by popular composers.

This difference of opinion led to a personal estrangement between the two men which lasted a few years, but to the infinite credit of both they came together again and at the famous symposium held at Stratford in 1912 Somervell and Sharp stood shoulder to shoulder in their fight for the recognition of the folk-dance as a true art to be taken seriously and Somervell later became a warm and active supporter of our Society.

Somervell was a skilled composer with a poetic mind. It is early days yet to prophesy as to the fate of his larger works, but there can to my mind be no doubt that such things as 'The Shepherd's Cradle Song', 'The Grasmere Carol', and the 'Air' for Violin will be loved wherever beautiful melody is appreciated.

CHAPTER 49

Cecil James Sharp (1859–1924)

SHARP, CECIL JAMES (1859–1924), musician, author, and collector and arranger of English folk-songs and dances, was born in London 22 November 1859, the eldest son of John James Sharp, slate-merchant, by his wife, Jane Bloyd. He was educated at Uppingham School and at Clare College, Cambridge. He had inherited a love of music from his father, and in his early days had studied music, practically and theoretically. While at Cambridge he entered fully into the musical activities of the university. After taking his degree (a third class in the mathematical tripos), Sharp went in 1882 to Adelaide, where he held the legal post of associate to the chief justice of South Australia. He was also during this period assistant organist of the cathedral and conductor of the Philharmonic Society. From 1889 to 1891 he was co-director of the Adelaide College of Music. While in Australia he composed two light operas and some smaller pieces. Early in 1892 he returned to England. In 1893 he married Constance Dorothea (died 1928), daughter of Priestley Birch, of Woolston, near Kingsbridge, Devon, and had one son and three daughters. He became conductor of the Finsbury Choral Association (1893–1897), music master at Ludgrove School (1893–1910), and principal of the Hampstead Conservatoire of Music (1896–1905). From 1910 to 1912 he held no official position. From 1912 to

Source: *Dictionary of National Biography, 1922–30* (London: Oxford University Press, 1937), 761–3.

1924 he was director of the English Folk-Dance Society. From 1919 to 1923 he held the post of occasional inspector to the Board of Education with special reference to the teaching of folk-dance. In 1923 he received the honorary degree of Mus.M. of Cambridge University. He died at Hampstead 23 June 1924, after a short illness.

Such are the external facts of Sharp's career, but interest centres in the last twenty-five years of his life and in the gradual growth under his influence of the knowledge of the English traditional arts of music and dancing. In 1902 his experience as singing-teacher at Ludgrove School led him to prepare and publish *A Book of British Song*. This contains both traditional melodies (gleaned from William Chappell's *Popular Music of the Olden Time*, 1838, and other printed sources) and 'composed' music of a simple kind. It was probably his work on this book which led Sharp to realize the essential importance of traditional art, and in 1903 he decided to find out for himself how far traditional music survived in England and what was its quality. His first experiment was made in September 1903 at Hambridge, in Somerset, where, with the help of the vicar, the Rev. C. L. Marson, he made an exhaustive search of the neighbourhood with surprising results. A selection from the songs which he discovered, called *Folk-Songs from Somerset*, was published in 1904 and aroused great interest. That such beautiful and vital melodies should have been sung for generations in 'unmusical' England was indeed a remarkable discovery.

Opinion had, however, been ripening. (Sir) Hubert Parry [q.v.] had in 1893 published his *Art of Music*, in which he applied the theory of evolution to music and showed the line of succession from the simplest of folk-tunes to the most elaborate symphony. Already, also, a certain number of traditional melodies had been collected. In 1898 the Folk-Song Society had been founded, and in 1904 Sharp was elected on to its committee. Nevertheless, his ideas were not cordially welcomed by the leading members of the society, whose ideal was that of quiet research, while Sharp was above all a teacher and a propagandist. He used scholarship and research as a means to an end; for he believed in folk-song, not as a relic of the past, but as a thing of living beauty. These simple and lovely melodies have awakened in thousands of people a musical consciousness hitherto dormant. In 1906, after the Board of Education had published a list of recommended songs for children in which no distinction was made between songs which were traditional and those which were merely popular, Sharp vainly urged the Folk-Song Society to make a protest.

Meanwhile Sharp persistently pressed the claims of folk-song by lectures, articles, and letters to the newspapers, thereby arousing some bitter opposition. In 1907 he tabulated his experiences in his book *English Folk-Song: Some Conclusions*. The theories set out therein are not new, nor do they pretend to be so. They are the logical conclusions of the evolutionary theory of music and that of the communal authorship of folk-song already vaguely formulated by others. It should be noted that Sharp claimed communal authorship, but not communal origin, for the folk-song. He held, together with Jacob Grimm and others, that folk-music, developing as it does by purely oral tradition without being stereotyped by print or writing, tends to evolve as it passes through the minds of generations of singers; that therefore no individual singer can at any given moment be said to be the author of the song, but that it truly represents the communal mind of those to whom it belongs. Moreover, he held that the law of the survival of the fittest applies here, and that the process is one not of disintegration but of evolution.

All this time Sharp was collecting more songs and publishing the cream of them in further volumes of *Folk-Songs from Somerset* (five series, 1904, 1905, 1906, 1908, and 1909). His example fired others, and it soon appeared that there was hardly a village in England where this native art did not survive.

Sharp's final adventure in search of songs was his visits to the Southern Appalachian Mountains in North Carolina, Tennessee, Kentucky, and Virginia in 1916 to 1918. In these remote parts of the United States there lives a people descended from early English colonists segregated by natural surroundings from the rest of the world. They have preserved the customs, speech, and above all the songs, which they brought with them from England in the early eighteenth century. When Sharp heard of this community he characteristically determined to get at the facts of the alleged survivals, and he paid several visits (lasting forty-six weeks in all) to the Appalachian Mountains, although he was in indifferent health and had to make his investigations in circumstances of the most primitive discomfort.

Sharp noted down altogether nearly five thousand tunes and variants, about one-third being collected in the Appalachian Mountains. Of these he published some five hundred for use with pianoforte accompaniment, and a further thousand are printed in the *Journal of the Folk-Song Society* and other scientific publications. The rest remain in his manuscript books which he left to Clare College, Cambridge. These figures conclusively dispel the idea that Sharp imagined that all folk-songs were of equal value.

The other main subject of Sharp's activities was the folk-dance, in which he was practically first in the field. This was a much more difficult problem than the folk-song, for it takes only one man to sing a song while it takes six to dance a morris, and by the time Sharp began to collect there were few complete morris 'sides' left. Most of the dances had, therefore, to be reconstructed from the explanations and partial demonstrations of old and infirm men. Further, there is no recognized notation of the dance as there is of the song; so the only thing to do was to invent a notation for the purpose. Sharp's first dance researches, dating from 1905 (he had previously, in 1899, noted the tunes of several morris-dances from Headington, Oxfordshire), were in the Midlands, the home of the morris-dance. In 1910 he turned his attention to the corresponding ceremonial dance of northern England, the sword-dance. Less artistically important, but, as it proved, socially more far-reaching, was the country dance. This is not a ceremonial dance for experts, but a form of social enjoyment; moreover it is danced by both sexes, whereas the morris and sword dances are traditionally danced by men only. Sharp collected some examples of the country dance from living tradition, but most of those which he published were transcribed by him from the seventeen editions of John Playford's *Dancing Master* (1650–1728). Here his unfailing instinct enabled him to select those dances which reflect the spirit of tradition, even though some of them have no doubt been consciously worked on by individuals.

Sharp was, of course, not content merely to collect; he also wanted to teach, and between 1907 and 1914 he published over three hundred dances with their tunes. He recognized, however, that these things cannot be learned from books only. In 1905 he had come into contact with Mary Neal and her Espérance club for working-girls in Cumberland Market, London; and it was here that practical folk-dance teaching was first undertaken. For a time Sharp and Miss Neal worked together; but the object of the Espérance club was social regeneration rather than artistic excellence. Miss Neal held that Sharp's interpretation of the dances was formal and pedantic and robbed them of the joyousness which it was the object of her club to encourage: Sharp considered that the joy of doing a good thing well was the ultimate object to be secured. So the two parted company, and Sharp found new allies in the Chelsea College of Physical Training, where he established a school of folk-dance in 1909.

In 1911 Sharp founded the English Folk-Dance Society, the object of which was to 'preserve and promote the practice of English folk-dances in their true traditional forms'. From this time forward his life became that of an inspiring teacher and an efficient and autocratic organizer, and with the exception of a few flying visits to discover new folk-songs and dances and the expeditions to America already recorded, the rest of his life was devoted to the society which he founded. The English Folk-Dance Society prospered far beyond his expectations, and since his death it has gone on growing. In 1931 the membership was 1,689, besides fifty-two local branches (including two in the United States) with a membership of over 20,000, and early in 1932 an amalgamation with the Folk-Song Society was effected.

On Sharp's death a fund was opened to build a house where his memory could be kept alive by preserving, practising, and teaching folk-songs and dances. In June 1930 Cecil Sharp House in Regent's Park Road, London, was opened, and on its foundation-stone are inscribed the words: 'This building is erected in memory of Cecil Sharp who restored to the English people the songs and dances of their country.'

Sharp won the admiration of all who came into contact with him, even those whom his uncompromising methods of controversy had antagonized before they got to know him. His absorption in his mission did not prevent him from taking an intelligent interest in all that was going on in the world, about which he always had something pregnant to say. In politics he inclined to the Fabian socialist view. His favourite composers were Beethoven, Wagner, and Handel. He suffered all his life from ill-health, but this only added to the energy with which he worked for the causes that he loved.

A portrait by Sir William Rothenstein hangs in the library at Cecil Sharp House.

CHAPTER 50

Traditional Arts in the Twentieth Century

WE ARE CONTINUALLY being told in the press and elsewhere that the EFDS is concerned with the 'revival' of something old and past, either, as our dangerous friends put it an attempt to recapture the quaint old manners and customs of our forefathers so as to teach a lesson to our modern wicked youth, or as our rather less dangerous detractors say an attempt by a few long-haired men and short-haired women to galvanize into a sham life a dead and happily dead past.

Is there any truth in these accusations? If there is, then it is time we shut up shop and left the business to a few librarians and curators.

But we all believe that this is not so; we believe that folk song and dance are living forces which have something to say to the youth of this generation. However, we cannot just accept this opinion, we must prove it both by word and deed.

The revival of folk song and dance has been active for nearly forty years, therefore few of us can remember the early excitement when this mine of melody and movement was first explored and its treasures revealed.

Here at last was song which fulfilled the highest canons of art and yet could be understood by all; melody moreover which fitted the peculiar shy undemonstrative Anglo-Saxon nature. Here were dances in which the cricketer or the sportsman

Source: *English Dance and Song*, 2/6 (1938), 98–9.

could take part without feeling he was 'making a fool of himself', moreover they were dances which required the athletic skill of which he was proud, and that type of well co-ordinated body which is so different from the specialised muscles and distorted limbs of the ballet dancer. The young man, nauseated by the drawing-room ballad, found here songs he could sing to his friends in the evening and these songs were fitted with accompaniments by Cecil Sharp and others which his sister or his girl friend could easily manage on the parlour pianoforte. Here was no conscious return to 'Olde England', no theorizing about 'national' art or about religious origins, but simply something which filled a crying need in the artistic consciousness of the ordinary man and woman.

The folk dance and song stand or fall for us of the twentieth century entirely on their intrinsic merits. When placed against the songs of Brahms and Strauss, the pianoforte music of Debussy, the ballet, the drawing-room dance, do they hold their own by their vitality and beauty? This is the important question and indeed to my mind the only one. We must not make a parade of worthless music or clumsy, dull dancing merely because it belongs to the 'folk': we must not lower our standard in deference to the supposed needs of 'common' people. In artistic matters the supply creates the demand; if we continually give people something a little better than what they would without prompting ask for, then we shall gradually raise the standard of artistic excellence throughout the country, and for this standard there can be no better guide than the best of our traditional art. This is one of the ways in which our folk song has evolved in our time, more perhaps in the spirit than in the letter, by setting a standard—to our singers, our dancers, to our composers and even our audiences—the standard of the three great 'S's' Simplicity, Serenity and Sincerity.

Nobody wants an obscurantist policy; it should not be the object of our Society to recreate outward accidents of folk song and dance. The folk song as a concert singer sings it, the folk dance as a member of the EFDS dances it, is necessarily something different from the same tune or dance when collected from a traditional singer or dancer. The one question to be asked is—is it (in the words of a famous classic) a 'good thing'? I notice in the May number of this journal a suggestion by a distinguished member of our Society that we consider evolution outside our scope; but surely the dance has evolved whether we wish it or no from the first moment that Cecil Sharp taught, to a girl from a factory, steps which he had learnt from a country labourer. I am certain that Sharp realized that what he taught these early pupils would in the end become something very different from what he saw danced at Headington or Bampton and that he did not wish it otherwise. The university man, the city clerk, the school girl, the society beauty all react differently to the stimulus of the song and dance: the result will be superficially different from what the countryman danced for Sharp and his successors, but if we are true to our tradition they will be essentially the same. The countryman, so far as he still dances at all, will probably evolve his own variants on tradition, but it by no means follows that evolution on his lines is to be a model for us all. Each flower on a rose tree differs from the other, but they obtain their life and their beauty because they are attached to the same stem; if they are entirely broken off they will wither and die.

There is a tendency at present in our Society to be frightened at the word 'folk', largely owing to the silly misunderstanding of our objects by cheap and brainless journalists. We must not be ashamed of our birthright: if we do not believe in what our Society stands for we had better give up altogether. I admit that the word 'folk' in this sense is a hybrid word borrowed from the German, though by itself it is good English ('we are his folk he doth us feed')[1] but it stands for something very definite in our national life. If we are ashamed of the word we may soon become ashamed of what the word stands for. We must not court popularity by denying our faith.

---

[1] A modern editor of this hymn has altered 'folck' into 'flock'. He must have been a member of the EFDS.

CHAPTER 51

The Justification of Folk Song

CECIL SHARP COLLECTED over 5,000 tunes. Of these he published about 500 as being of genuine artistic value: a certain amount more he printed in scientific volumes for their archaeological or anthropological interest; the rest—that is the large majority—remain to this day in manuscript books.

Why did he do this? Because he saw that a tradition is not worth preserving unless it has certain permanent qualities which make it alive for the next generation.

The English Folk Dance and Song Society has two sides to its activities: the study of traditional art and its practice. For the student a folk tune may be worth preserving for its historical or archaeological interest—for the singer and dancer there is only one test—is it beautiful? If I did not believe that in preserving our songs and dances we were perpetuating beauty I should have welcomed the bomb which did its best to destroy Cecil Sharp House.

This beauty is not to be perpetuated by mere slavish imitation of the traditional singer or dancer—a tradition may be half-forgotten or may be corrupted or be obscured by inefficient performance. The true artist—and that is what we must all learn to be—must learn to pick out the beauty which lies behind—to adapt the tradition to his own needs and develop, if possible, something even more beautiful and vital out of the tradition which has been handed down to us.

Source: *English Dance and Song*, 5/6 (1941), 66–7.

I have no hesitation in saying that a fine performance by the Headquarters Morris Team of the EFDS is something more beautiful, more monumental and alive than what now remains to us of the 'genuine' folk dancers' performances. It may be conscious art—but I fear that such an accusation leaves me cold. We are no longer unsophisticated in the twentieth century and some of the finest art is the most conscious. A sort of sham naturalism would be the lowest depth of self-consciousness.

I admit that there is a sort of impersonal detachment about the true traditional dancer or singer which we cannot achieve. But we certainly must not try to achieve it by an imitation of the external accidents which that detachment involves—the fixed far-away look of the dancer or the tightly shut eyes of the singer—which are probably not, as some people imagine, a sign of mystical exaltation but simply come from the effort of memory which the singer or dancer must evoke.

Also we must be careful not to preserve the weaknesses in the letter of the traditional artist in our desire to capture the strength of his spirit. Van Gogh was a very great artist—but he had an unfortunate habit of drawing everything crooked: later artists, failing entirely to understand his inner power, imagined that if they also drew everything crooked they would be as great artists as Van Gogh.

People who have been brought up in the EFDS tradition, when confronted with (say) the Bampton Dancers, profess to find in them something which we lack—of course they do! EFDS members are not agricultural labourers but university students, businessmen, clerks or school-teachers and they naturally react differently to the stimulus of traditional song and dance. The countryman moves his legs and arms in the dance in obedience to his artistic intuition—we, with our different minds must also obey our artistic intuitions. On the basis of the beauty which we see behind these movements we must evolve something which appeals to us and so by an individual flowering on a common stem evolve something even more beautiful.

It may, however, be argued that the very existence of the EFDS rests on the belief that man is capable of creating beauty and that in primitive art we have beauty in its truest form made by people who, in the words of Hubert Parry: 'made what they liked and liked what they made.'[a] Here I think we have struck

---

[a] See Parry's address to the inaugural general meeting of the Folk Song Society: 'The old folk-music is among the purest product of the human mind...In the old days they produced music because it pleased them to make it, and because what they made pleased them mightily, and that is the only way in which good music is ever made.' From 'A Folk-Song Function', *The Musical Times*, no. 673 (1899), 168–9 at 168.

a dangerous half-truth. It is indeed paradoxically true that traditional art has a peculiar quality of its own which more sophisticated art cannot aspire to and at the same time is the foundation on which all developed art must build if it is to be a firm and lasting structure.

Therefore it is our duty though we may not be able to drink at the spring head to make sure that our stream of art flows clear and undefiled from its source. But we must be sure that we have found the spring head and not a muddy trickle.

May not some particular movement of a dance or form of a melody which we have discovered to our joy in a hitherto undiscovered country be a debased version of a pure original? I believe in the communal evolution of the folk song—but that belief involves the possibility of individual disintegration. Folk singers and dancers are, after all, human beings and if there are great artists among them there are also dull practitioners. We must make sure when we sit at the feet of a folk dancer that he is a great artist and not a dull practitioner. A tune or dance once beautiful may well have been disfigured into dullness by passing through the mind of a dull-witted individual who has robbed it of its character and vitality. If we are wise and experienced we may be able to see the light shining through the dimmed glass—but we must be careful not to mistake the pale reflection for the true light.

The task of the EFDS is twofold: scientific discovery and artistic presentation. In the first we may be omnivorous; in the second we must be selective. Every tune and every dance which is genuinely traditional must be carefully preserved—but only that which has beauty and vitality, or at all events makes for these things must be practised by us. There is a dangerous tendency rife among members of the EFDS to take to its bosom everything which is supposed to be 'folk' regardless of its artistic value. But surely our only justification for existence lies in the proof that tradition can make for beauty. Not all traditions are good: will anyone uphold the killing of harmless squirrels on Good Friday because it is traditional? Surely such a custom is more honoured in the breach than in the observance.

It is not as if we had only poor material to choose from. When we have more beautiful tunes and dances than we can possibly cope with, why neglect these for a dreadful tune like the 'Oyster Girl' merely because it is played by a 'folk' musician. As a matter of fact the 'Oyster Girl' is not even a traditional tune but is a popular song which was at some period tacked on to a traditional dance by a mean-minded fiddler. I can only imagine that we suffer from depraved musical taste when we find this tune apparently preferred to hundreds of beautiful tunes and accepted as part of the canon because it is erroneously supposed to be 'folk'.

Those of us who are now 'digging for Victory' know that when the seedlings begin to appear above the ground it becomes necessary to 'thin them out' so that only those which have strength and health and are likely to bear fruit shall be left growing—the others will not only be useless themselves but will impair the vitality of the strong ones. We must apply this 'thinning out' process to our traditional art. To do so requires the imagination of the artist, the experience of the scientist and the skill of the expert. Their judgment should be supreme in our counsels. Their task is to wash away the dross and discover the pure gold underneath. I suggest that we accept their ruling which is guided by artistic insight and ripe experience which few of us possess.

When I was at school, the rules of Latin Grammar were set out in a series of rhymes which we had to learn. At the end of the rhymes there came the following four lines:

> *N.B. The rules grammarians make*
> *Poets and fools alone will break;*
> *So, if you break the rules and know it;*
> *The question is—are you a poet?*

CHAPTER **52**

Let Us Remember . . . Early Days

I HAVE BEEN invited to describe my early reactions to folk song. This article will have to be largely all about myself. I wish it could be otherwise, but such are the commands of the Editor whose willing slaves we all are.

I think I must have first come across our English folk songs through Stainer and Bramley's *Christmas Carols New and Old*. Stainer and Bramley's contained some pretty poor stuff; nevertheless, it was the means of introducing to the public for the first time some of our most beautiful traditional melodies.

That must have been in the early eighties when I was about 10. I used to go with my family every Christmas to stop with an Aunt. My Aunt had been much bitten by the William Morris movement. She frescoed sunflowers on her walls and put bottled glass in her windows. One of the by-products of this movement was the cult of the Christmas carol. My Aunt was a first-rate musician and her children were also musical and we used to gather round the pianoforte in the evening and sing 'Stainer and Bramley'. I especially remember the 'Cherry Tree' carol tune which has remained a fragrant possession all my life and is, to my mind, much more beautiful than later discoveries to the same words.

My next contact with folk song must have been about 1888 when I was at school and was ordered by the master in charge of entertainments to organise a

Source: *English Dance and Song*, 6/3 (1942), 27–8.

'Welsh Concert'. I bought Boosey's *Songs of Wales* and thus got to know such lovely tunes as 'David of the White Rock' and the 'Marsh of Rhuddlan'. I believe that I even concocted a march out of some of the tunes which was played at the concert. This must have been my first essay in 'folk-song' composition. But my real awakening to folk song did not come till 1898 when *English County Songs* came into my hands and I lighted on the 'Lazarus' tune as it is given there.[a] When one comes across something great and new, if it is great enough, one's attitude is not of surprise but of recognition, 'but I have known this all my life'. I felt like this when I heard later Wagner, when I first saw Michael Angelo's *Night and Day*, [and] when I first visited Stonehenge. I immediately recognised these things which had always been in my unconscious self. The tinder was there, it only wanted the spark to set it ablaze. I believe this is true of all great art, however new and strange; it does not cause amazement but one greets it as an old friend.

So when I first played through 'Lazarus' I realised that this was what we had all been waiting for—something which we knew already—something which had always been with us if we had only known it; something entirely new yet absolutely familiar.

Es klang so alt	*It sounded so old*
Und war doch so neu.[b]	*And yet was so new.*

This is how our folk song can stimulate the composer. We have been laughed at for trying to form a national style by tacking on that bit of English folk song to a hotch potch of Wagner, Tchaikovsky, and Debussy. For those who use the folk songs purely mechanically this criticism may be just, but to those who find in our tunes that which no other music can give them, the love of these tunes is a freeing and not a restraining influence, setting free new ideas, new vistas and new possibilities.

By this time I was thoroughly obsessed by the folk song. I went berserk on the flat seventh and the sharp sixth and the Mixolydian cadence. My revered master, Stanford, one of the greatest teachers, was much worried by my flattened leading notes. He declared, if I remember right, that the flat seventh was purely theoretical and was in practice always corrected by 'musica ficta'. Later on, when I went to Max

[a] Vaughan Williams states elsewhere that he first encountered 'Dives and Lazarus', as printed in *English County Songs*, in 1893, the year that volume was first published. See 'A Musical Autobiography' in *National Music and Other Essays* (2nd edn, Oxford: Oxford University Press, 1987), 177–94 at 189.
[b] Hans Sachs, *Die Meistersinger*, II. 3.

Bruch, he was equally worried and said 'Sie haben eine Leidenschaft für die Kleine Septime' [He has a passion for the flat seventh].

All the same, I felt that I was right, but I had no proof. How was I to get it? Then, one day about 1900, Miss Lucy Broadwood asked me to see the songs she had collected in Sussex. Then indeed I saw the flattened cadence in all its glory but still I was a doubting Thomas and I wanted first-hand evidence. In 1903 the chance came. I was at that time, greatly daring, giving a course of lectures on folk song in a town in Essex. I knew precious little about it and the little knowledge I had was entirely out of books. I was like a psychic researcher who has never seen a ghost. But soon the ghost walked. At the end of the lectures a lady from a neighbouring village asked me to a tea-party to which some of the older people were to be invited. At that party I heard 'Bushes and Briars' sung by a shepherd and my education was complete.

It must be difficult for the younger generation who now take these things in their stride, to realise the excitement with which we collectors heard these beautiful tunes sung in their true conditions. Is it surprising that we went all 'folky'; that we longed to do for our English tunes what Liszt had done for Hungary, Brahms for Germany and Grieg for Norway? There is an objectionably smug type of musician who thinks he has condemned a piece of music when he has called it 'folky', but after all, why shouldn't we be folky? It only means that we are letting a breath of fresh air into these smuggeries which is naturally dreaded by those who inhabit them.

It can be well imagined that I was not slow to bore all my friends with my discoveries, but one man I decided not to bore because I did not believe he would be interested and that man was Cecil Sharp. I believe that just then he would not have been interested. He had not yet made personal contact, which was essential to him before he could catch fire, but very soon the ghost was to walk for him too. Hardly had I decided that Sharp would 'not be interested' when I received an invitation from him to hear the folk songs he had collected in Somerset, sung by Miss Mattie Kay at a lecture in Hampstead. That lecture set the world ablaze. Before that we had not theorised much about folk song. We just enjoyed them and did not care much where they came from or where they were going to, but now the welkin rang with 'communal origins' and the nature of the folk and their place in the scheme of world reconstruction. From henceforth one had to be definitely pro or anti folk song. It was a case of 'Under which King, Bezonian? Speak or die.'

I have now traced my story from the dim mists of legend to the clear light of recorded history and will leave it to my successor to carry on the tale.

CHAPTER **53**

Preface [Celebrating the Foundation of the Folk Song Society]

FIFTY YEARS! AND it seems but yesterday that those pioneers founded the Folk Song Society; and yet, in those fifty years a silent revolution has transformed our musical life. Silent, because though our sound may have gone out into all lands it has not yet penetrated the thick hide of the cheap journalist who still adds 'folky' to 'Wigan' and 'mother-in-law' in his stock of stale witticisms, and even a University professor quite lately, in a scientific article referred to folk song as 'the mumblings of toothless rustics'.

Nevertheless, we of the EFDSS realise the change of heart which has taken place in the plain man of music, and it is the plain man whom we wish to capture; the experts are already converted. Let us then hold in pious memory the names of Baring-Gould, Broadwood, Kidson and others, the strong men before Agamemnon without whose spade-work it is doubtful if Cecil Sharp would have had the incentive to initiate his great campaign. It is these pioneers who brought the grist to the mill. Today our mills turn merrily, but without that substratum of knowledge,

Source: *Journal of the English Folk Dance and Song Society*, 5/3 (1948), p. v.

research and artistic imagination our summer schools, our morris rings, our Albert Hall festivals, would be as sounding brass and tinkling cymbals.

Let us then praise these famous men, the fathers who begat our Society, who found out the musical tunes of our country and preserved them for us as an imperishable heritage.

CHAPTER 54

Lucy Broadwood, 1858–1929

THE FOLK SONG has so many facets that it is not surprising few people can see all sides of the subject at once. Some are interested in the tune, some in the words, some in the anthropological and historical implications of the song. It is not given to many to have the literary culture, the scholarly accuracy and the artistic imagination to see the folk song as a whole.

Lucy Etheldred Broadwood, a direct descendant of 'Tschudi and Broadwood' was born in 1858 and spent much of her early life in country surroundings at Lyne in Sussex, but the Broadwoods had also a town house which was visited from time to time by many musical celebrities from Europe including Liszt, whose playing of double thirds filled her with admiration. This combination of rural background and urban culture was the basis of her character. In addition to her wide knowledge of literature and painting she showed a great talent for music. She was an excellent pianist and a most artistic singer, her inventive mind was shown in her accompaniments to her collection of folk songs and a few original compositions which though slight in texture show considerable musical imagination. Moreover her friends have always treasured in their memories her singing, especially of folk song and Purcell, to her own accompaniment. Circumstances made it unnecessary for

Source: *Journal of the English Folk Dance and Song Society,* 5/3 (1948), 136–8.

her to adopt the professional career for which she certainly had the aptitude, but in 1893 her name suddenly sprang into public recognition as the collaborator with J. A. Fuller Maitland in the now famous *English County Songs*. This may be said to be the starting point of the modern folk song movement. For the first time people who had accepted without question the aphorism that 'All folk tunes are either bad or Irish' had their eyes opened to the beauty of our English national music. Perhaps in view of later discoveries *English County Songs* does not contain a large proportion of first-class melodies, but we must remember that what astonished people at that period was, in the words of Dr Johnson, 'that it was done at all'. Surely a volume that contains such gems as 'Lazarus' and 'My Bonny Boy' deserves a high place in our national treasury.

Lucy Broadwood's interest in folk song was inherited from her uncle, The Reverend John Broadwood who in 1843 had published a small volume of Sussex songs collected by himself. This book, if we except the earlier carol collection of Sandys and Davies Gilbert marks the beginning of folk song collection in this country, though it must be admitted that for nearly forty years this little book bloomed in the desert.[a] The time was really not quite ripe and it is interesting to note that Mr Broadwood—much as he loved the tunes himself thought it necessary to apologise for this 'Silly Sooth sung by Spinners and Knitters in the Sun'. It is on record that the organist who was entrusted with the pianoforte accompaniments to the songs complained that the modal intervals in some of them were 'incorrect' and should be altered. Luckily Mr Broadwood was insistent and the tunes were printed faithfully as he heard them.

In 1898, largely as a result of *English County Songs*, Baring-Gould's *Songs of the West* and Kidson's *Traditional Tunes*, all of which appeared within a few years of each other, it was decided to inaugurate The Folk Song Society. At first the proceedings were rather of a dilettante and 'tea-party' order. The members were largely professional singers, musical journalists and the official heads of the profession, most of them not distinguished for their knowledge of folk song, however eminent they might be as performers and composers.

For a time the Society languished, but in 1904 Lucy Broadwood became its Secretary and the editor of its *Journal*. Both thereupon took on a very different

---

[a] These two collectors published separately: Davies Gilbert, *Some Ancient Christmas Carols* (London: J. Nichols, 1822); William Sandys, *Christmas Carols, Ancient and Modern* (London: Beckley, 1833). However, their names often appear together, especially in R. R. Terry (ed.), *Gilbert and Sandys Christmas Carols with Six Collateral Tunes* (London: Burns, Oates & Washbourne, 1932).

aspect, the Editor herself contributed a whole number of the *Journal* from her own collection of songs from Sussex and Surrey (No. 4, 1902); later there came a collection of Irish songs (No. 10, 1907) and Songs from Ireland and Scotland (No. 19, 1915). She also edited for the *Journal* Miss Tolmie's monumental collection of Gaelic songs (No. 16, 1911). Besides this the volumes were full of her learned and stimulating comments. Her knowledge ranged from eighteenth-century song-books to the Apocryphal Gospels. The initials L.E.B. inevitably followed some illuminating note or the correction of some well-worn fallacy. Particularly notice-able are her masterly comments on 'The Bitter Withy' (No. 9, p. 302), 'Christ made a trance' (No. 14, p. 13) and 'The Carnal and the Crane' (No. 14, p. 24).

Lucy Broadwood loved the songs she had herself collected with an almost personal affection and she shrank from bringing into the bright light of publicity songs which had grown up in the stillness of the countryside and which it was her delight to ponder over in the quiet of her study. Her own quiet Sussex country, its ways and its people were dear to her, and her love of them, rather than any theories about the 'folk', led her to love our country tunes. She never, if she could help it, used the word 'folk song'. It is indeed a terrible hybrid. We find we cannot get on without it, but we do not love it any more for that. At all events Lucy Broadwood never generalised about the 'folk'. It was not an *a priori* theory which led her to study the folk-song, and she was quite out of sympathy with Cecil Sharp's gen-eralisations about 'the peasant'. She misunderstood what she thought to be his patronising attitude of the townsman towards the countryman, an attitude incom-patible with the intimate affection of those, who, like herself have lived all their early life among country things and country people.

We must not, however suppose that Lucy Broadwood had a merely dilettante and sentimental affection for country songs. She combined the accuracy of the scholar with the imagination of the artist. Her great knowledge and wide reading enabled her to trace both words and tunes to their obscure origins, and she oc-casionally took a malicious delight in pinning down some supposed folk tune to its source in a Vauxhall composition by Hook or Arne. Once indeed, she made up a pseudo folk song, words and tune, and completely took in Fuller Maitland (per-haps not a very hard task) who told her that it was a fine song and that he was making a pianoforte accompaniment for it for inclusion in *English County Songs*. Needless to say, he was undeceived before it was too late.

To her, folk songs were largely a matter for the study[;] treasures to be pondered over in solitude and only occasionally to be displayed to the chosen few. This was probably nearer to the countryman's view of his own songs than the wholesale pop-ularity which we advocate nowadays. He treasures them as precious possessions, and Lucy Broadwood felt it almost a betrayal of trust to bring them into the glaring light of the concert room and theatre, or to make them a cog in the educational wheel. It may therefore be readily understood that Cecil Sharp's great campaign for disseminating the folk song broadcast wherever English people sang found little sympathy with her. For one thing she thought he was in too much of a hurry, which perhaps was true. His early volumes of folk song arrangements certainly show signs of haste. As she wittily said, her family motto had always been *Chi va piano va sano*. She also saw the danger of premature popularity which she thought might lead to vulgarisation; in fact that quantity might tend to spoil quality. But she realised, as all who care for folk song do, that we hold these treasures as trustees only, and that we are bound to offer them back to those to whom they belong in the hope that they will be worthy of their inheritance. So in 1908 she determined to publish a large portion of her collection fitted with her own felicitous pianoforte accompaniments under the title of *Traditional Songs and Carols*.

It was inevitable then that two minds such as Lucy Broadwood's and Cecil Sharp's, having so much power but so different ideals could never coalesce, and it is not surprising that when Cecil Sharp founded the English Folk Dance Society in 1911 Lucy Broadwood did not give it her support. For one thing the folk dance had little attraction for her and she once described the Morris as 'grotesque'. Further, the Society was concerned with action rather than with theory and therefore was not in keeping with her attitude of mind. But such activities are of no worth unless they are based on scientific knowledge and accurate observation, and it is always to be regretted that the EFDS could not command her wide knowledge and musical understanding.

For the Folk Song Society, which she helped to found, Lucy Broadwood was a devoted and tireless worker in all she undertook to do, whether as adviser, Secretary, Editor or President: many singers can testify to the unstinting manner in which she imparted to them the art of singing and to all those who were fortunate enough to gain her sympathy she was a firm and generous friend.

CHAPTER 55

Appeal on Behalf of the English Folk Dance and Song Society

'THE LAND WITHOUT music'—thus our friends on the continent used to describe us.

Are we really the land without music? Well—we have done our best to deserve the title. Incredible as it may seem we have taken it for granted that, while every other nation had its own songs and dances, born of the hearts and minds of its own people, yet England had none, and was obliged to obtain its music from abroad.

However it gradually began to dawn upon us that our own people also were making their own songs and dances.

This music which lived in the hearts of our people was gradually discovered by musicians who were able to write it down and thus preserve it, for before that the songs had only existed in the minds of their singers.

The chance came in 1904 when Cecil Sharp went down to Somerset and found that there, as indeed all over England, almost every village had its songs and dances—songs of classical beauty and dances that only an Englishman could dance.

Now these songs and dances were in danger of being forgotten by the younger generation and Cecil Sharp saw at once that this precious age-old heritage must be

Source: BBC Home Service, 24 September 1950. From script held in BBC archives.

preserved in permanent form before it was too late and not only preserved but given back to the people, not as a mere relic of the past, but as a living art, and he spent the rest of his life collecting and giving back to his fellow countrymen the music which they, in their ignorance and carelessness, had so nearly lost.

When, worn out by his labours, Cecil Sharp died in 1924, we built in his memory a house where anyone who wished could come and sing the songs and dance the dances. There was a large hall for singing and dancing—class rooms for teachers and a library for study—here young men and women were trained to go all over the country and offer back to the people these English treasures. The supposed moribund art of our people was returning to triumphant life.

Cecil Sharp House was ready in 1930 and for ten years it [grew] and prospered, then the enemy, hoping to make us once again a land without music dropped a bomb on our beautiful house; but our music and our dances he could not destroy and sheltered by the ruins of Cecil Sharp House we have managed to limp along.

Now the time has come to rebuild our home. This will cost £34,000 and all but £5,000 has already been subscribed—not a large sum by modern standards—I believe that if everyone who has ever felt the exaltation of a folk song or a fiddle tune or a morris dance would forego one visit to the cinema for the sake of Cecil Sharp House the result would be more like £50,000 than £5,000.

We hear a lot nowadays about 'filling the gap'. Will you help to fill this gap—you will then be enabling our country to realize to the full the potentialities of great and lasting art.

Please send your donations to me:

Ralph Vaughan Williams, at Cecil Sharp House, 2 Regent's Park Road, London, NW1. Good night and thank you.

CHAPTER 56

Preface to *Index of English Songs*

A DISTINGUISHED SCIENTIST once told me that in his opinion a book without an index was a bad book, whatever its contents.

On that showing *The Folk Song Journal* has been a bad book for over fifty years. Now through the skilful and devoted labours of Mr White it has become a good book.

No longer will researchers have to perform that maddening task of hunting through the contents tables of each volume only to find that the enquirer on whose behalf they were searching had said *volume* three when they *meant* part three.

We must not, however, forget the excellent subject indexes made by Miss Cra'ster which appeared sporadically in the early days of the *Journal*, but these, useful as they are, cover only a few volumes. Is it too much to hope that we may one day have a complete subject index either from the present compiler, or from someone equally devoted and skilful, if indeed there be such a person!

Source: E. A. White (compiler), *An Index of English Songs Contributed to the Journal of the Folk Song Society 1899–1931 and its Continuation the Journal of the English Folk Dance and Song Society to 1950*, ed. Margaret Dean-Smith (London: English Folk Dance and Song Society, 1951), p. vii.

CHAPTER 57

Address to the Fifth Conference
of the International Folk Music Council

I AM HERE today in a dual capacity. First, as President of the English Folk Dance and Song Society, I have the pleasure and honour to greet here the members of the International Folk Music Council, both from foreign parts as well as from this country, and to offer them a welcome to Cecil Sharp House. I have also the honour to be the President of the International Folk Music Council, and to thank the Director and members of the EFDSS for their hospitality; so I appear indeed to be welcoming myself.

The EFDSS, as I daresay you know, exists for the purpose of preserving and disseminating the folk songs and dances of England in their traditional forms. This, our Society, under the able guidance of its director, Mr Kennedy, has striven to do. As I imagine is the case in all similar societies, the disseminators and the preservers do not always see eye to eye. The disseminators are so anxious that the whole country should take a practical part in our discoveries that they are sorely tempted to put quantity in the place of quality. The preservers, on the other hand, are too apt to allow folk song and dance to become a dead art, an affair of libraries and dry discussion.

Source: *Journal of the International Folk Music Council,* 5 (1953), 7–8.

I venture to think that in our Society we have managed to keep the balance. We do not bother those people, especially the young, who come to enjoy themselves singing and dancing, with boring discussions on origins and modes and comparative folklore. On the other hand, we try to keep the scientific side strong so as to make sure that what these young people practise is genuine and not bogus. That is our ideal.

On reading through our latest report I have come to the conclusion that all our societies, including our English Society, are suffering from a bad attack of broadmindedness. This so-called 'broadmindedness' is really a form of snobbery. We English are first-rate artistic snobs—we cannot believe that any artistic effort is good unless it comes from another country. This is called being 'broadminded', with the result that we get all our painting from France, all our music from Germany and all our dancing from America; and moreover it gets diluted in the process so that the result is neither good English nor good foreign. This shows itself particularly in the tendency to call everything, whether song or dance, which is popular, 'folk song or dance'.

I have no quarrel with popular music, but I do feel that our International Council should confine itself to what is truly traditional. Of course there must be border-line cases—traditional dances which have acquired non-traditional tunes, and traditional tunes which have become allied to non-traditional words. But this does not affect the main question as to the distinct cleavage between the true folk song composed *by* the people and the popular song composed *for* the people. It is the former with which this Council has to deal.

It was, I think, Lord Haldane who said that he could not define an elephant but that he knew one when he saw it. I feel the same with folk song, and for the moment we will leave it at that.

In the course of the many formidable essays to which we are to have the pleasure of listening during this conference there will probably be acrimonious discussion on this point and may I not be there to hear. I want to enjoy folk songs and not to quarrel about them.

And this brings me to another point which I gather from our report. As I have already said, the duty of a Folk Song Society is not only to preserve but to disseminate. As preservers it is our duty to place on record, whether by print, manuscript or the gramophone, everything which we can pass as genuinely traditional; but when it comes to the question of dissemination we must discriminate. The people whom it is our mission to make acquainted with our folk music are not experts. They have, and quite rightly, no interest in variants and parallels and folklore. What they want to do is, like your President, to enjoy the songs and dances.

Now what are they to enjoy? I believe and I think we all believe, that we wish folk song and dance to be better known because it makes people acquainted with beauty—or at all events, to find out by practical experience what is beautiful in their own lives. I believe that folk music has in it the possibilities of the greatest and purest beauty. But of course there are dull songs and dances, just as there are dull people who have passed them on in former generations. Indeed, when we get to the borderline cases we find material which is actually cheap and vulgar.

Now there is a tendency at present to think that everything that is danced in the village hall or sung in a public house is FOLK, and therefore to be encouraged. This is another fatal example of dangerous broadmindedness. Even if we went back 200 years, when folk song existed in all its purity, we should be much disappointed if we imagined that every festive labourer would roll home singing 'John Barleycorn' or that every heartbroken swain would console himself with 'The Green Willow', or that every seduced young woman would nurse her baby to the tune of 'A Bold Young Farmer'. If we should have had to discriminate then, much more must we discriminate now.

Our duty then is twofold. Only that which is genuinely traditional must be preserved, and all that must be recorded in our libraries and museums; but only that which has the germs of great art must be let loose on the simple-minded public whom we invite to sample our wares.

CHAPTER 58

Cecil Sharp: An Appreciation

IT IS NOW nearly fifty years since Cecil Sharp startled England with *Folk Songs from Somerset*. We knew vaguely, already, that we had some traditional tunes in this country and that some of them, such as 'Dives and Lazarus' and 'My Bonnie Boy', were very beautiful. But such a wealth of beauty as this volume, containing, to mention only a few, 'High Germany', 'The False Bride', 'Searching for Lambs' and 'The Crystal Spring', was something we had never dreamed of. And where did it all come from? It was not a bit like Purcell or Arne or Bishop or Sterndale Bennett. Nor apparently could we trace it to watered-down reminiscences of Schubert or Mendelssohn. It must therefore be indigenous. But that was absurd. We knew, on the best authority, that folk music was 'all either bad or Irish'. But Sharp believed, and we believe, that there, in the fastnesses of rural England, was the well-spring of English music; tunes of classical beauty which vied with all the most beautiful melody in the world, and traceable to no source other than the minds of unlettered country men, who unknown to the squire and the parson were singing their own songs, and as Hubert Parry says, 'liked what they made and made what they liked'.[a]

Source: Cecil Sharp, *English Folk Song: Some Conclusions*, rev. Maud Karpeles (3rd edn, London: Methuen, 1954), pp. v–vi.

[a] See Parry's address to the inaugural general meeting of the Folk Song Society: 'A Folk-Song Function', *The Musical Times*, no. 673 (1899), 168–9 at 168.

Of course there were strong men before Agamemnon, and there were collectors of folk song, in a small way, before Cecil Sharp. Indeed, if it had not been for these fore-runners, Sharp could not even have started his great work. In the domain of theory, Parry had applied the Darwinian theory of evolution to music, and had proved the necessity of folk song. It remained for the big man to come along and combine theory and practice in one.

There was already a Folk Song Society in existence which discussed our traditional melodies over a cup of tea in a dilettante spirit, and had to admit, rather shamefacedly, that some of these tunes sung by simple-minded rustics were 'sweetly pretty'. And in the domain of the ballad Allingham had suggested, tentatively, the idea of communal growth. Parry had theoretically traced the evolution of music from the primitive tune to the elaborate symphony. It was left to Sharp to declare, in no half-hearted manner, that here was something of supreme beauty which had grown up, as part of our life, with our language and our customs. And he set to work both by precept and practice to enable, at all events, the younger generation to recapture their great heritage of song which their fathers had nearly let slip through their fingers. The result was astonishing. Here were tunes obviously of the highest beauty which were nevertheless easy to understand and easy to sing. Sharp, who had no idea of hiding his light under a bushel, published several volumes of these wonderful tunes which the average amateur could easily sing, and fitted them with accompaniments which their sisters or girl friends could easily play. But Sharp's mind was set on the younger generation, and he insisted, after some trouble with the authorities, that folk song should be taught in school. So the battle was won and a folk song is now a house-hold word.

And how about the creative musician? Sharp in this book, *English Folk Song: Some Conclusions*, writes:

> Now...we have the musical ability, and we have the folk song: our first obvious duty is to see that the latter is restored to the nation as soon as may be...When every English child is, as a matter of course, made acquainted with the folk songs of his own country then, from whatever class the musician of the future may spring he will speak in the national musical idiom.

This prophecy has come true. It is not mere accident that the sudden emergence of vital invention among our English composers corresponds in time with this resuscitation of our own national melody. Of course there has been a reaction. The younger generation declare that folk songs had no influence on them. But much as they may dislike it, they can no more help being influenced by these melodies which have permeated the concert room, the school room, the stage and even the church, than they can help speaking their own language. It is not something antique and quaint which Sharp has galvanized into a semblance of life. It is something which has persisted through the centuries, something which still appeals to us here and now and, if we allow it, will continue to develop through all the changes and chances of history.

CHAPTER 59

Preface to *International Catalogue of Recorded Folk Music*

FOLK MUSIC IS one of the good things of this world which, like freedom, health and prosperity, we value most when we are in danger of losing it. And the present interest in folk music occurs at a time when in almost every country of the world it is being influenced and often submerged by the flood of mechanized music which increases daily. There is, however, no need for despondency, for the very agencies that have been the enemies of folk music are being pressed into its service, as is shown by this catalogue. Through the processes of mechanical recording, folk music is not only being preserved but it is being made available for study and enjoyment by a wider circle than has ever before been possible. Through its medium the art of the 'mute inglorious Miltons' can now be conveyed not only to their fellow-countrymen but to lovers of music throughout the whole world.

Folk music lends itself to many different kinds of treatment. It can be 'arranged' for concert performance, its themes can be developed and employed in original composition, or it can be performed without embellishment merely for the enjoyment of the singer or instrumentalist. These are all legitimate ways of treating

Source: Norman Fraser (ed.), *International Catalogue of Recorded Folk Music* (London: Oxford University Press, 1954), p. iv.

folk music, but if we are to maintain its true spirit, we must have the opportunity of studying from those musicians who are in the direct line of tradition. The printed or written notation on which we have hitherto had to rely gives us the form and substance of folk music, but, however accurate it may be, it cannot portray all the subtle nuances of intonation, rhythm and ornamentation which give the style and character of the folk musician's art.

No one can tell what the folk music of the future will be, or whether indeed folk music as the product of oral transmission will continue to exist. That is a question for posterity. All we can do is to hand to posterity the fruits of our own generation. This catalogue shows that we still have a big task before us and it is one that will brook no delay.

CHAPTER **60**

Martin Shaw

TONIGHT WE CELEBRATE the eightieth year of Martin Shaw, and it is my privilege to speak to you about him. Perhaps we are not sufficiently aware that when Martin Shaw visits us and gives us of his wisdom and insight we are entertaining an angel. He is not, to outward appearance, at all like a professional musician; he seems, superficially, to be much more like a cultivated dilletante: he is a fine organist, pianist and composer. He comes of professional stock, to whom art is something serious and means thoroughness and hard work. He inherits from his father the devotion of his talent to the service of the church, believing, as we all ought to believe, that the very best in painting, literature, architecture and music is alone worthy of the cause he serves. How often can we say this of our church services? In our music at all events, are we not often content with something that both in conception and execution, would not be tolerated by secular standards? Incidentally,

Source: *The Diocesan Magazine* [St Edmundsbury and Ipswich], 42/6 (1955), 85–7. The source describes this article as an address given by Vaughan Williams in St Mary-le-Tower Church, Ipswich, 22 October 1955. The extent to which this published text represents what Vaughan Williams said is unclear. Ursula Vaughan Williams writes that Ralph prepared a script, as the talk was to be printed in the Diocesan magazine, but, 'when it came to the point he delivered a much more fiery oration, practically a commination service on the basis of "cursed be the congregations, choirmasters, and organists who do not listen to Martin".' See *R. V. W.: A Biography of Ralph Vaughan Williams* (Oxford: Oxford University Press, 1984), 367.

I believe that the same might be said about our church literature, and that there is even a movement on foot to dethrone the superb language of our English Bible and to substitute for it something more in the style of the popular press.

Martin Shaw has devoted himself to the cause of church music from the time he met Percy Dearmer, and they worked together to rescue our church music from the slough of despond into which the Victorian fondness for sacharine insincerity had led it. Are we doing our part to welcome our angelic stranger as we should? I think that his quality is being slowly recognised. Even Whitehall has at last stirred in its slumber and has given Doctor Shaw tardy and grudging recognition. I think we can do better than that.

Shaw shows us the way, not only by precept but by practice. His anthems and services are models of what such things should be; particularly I should like to give my tribute of praise to his beautiful Passion Cantata, *The Redeemer*, which ought to be sung every year in every church by a competent choir, and thus replace the sentimentalities by composers with ridiculous names which at present mar our Lenten services. You will know him best by his hymn tunes, such tunes as Riley ('Songs of praise the angels sang') and Marching ('Through the night of doubt and sorrow'). which are deservedly popular. He had the courage to depose 'John's Brown's Body' in favour of his fine Battle Song for the words 'Mine eyes have seen the glory...' At the bidding of Percy Dearmer he even made a tune for Whitman's 'Pioneers', with complete success.

I feel that I cannot speak to you about Martin Shaw without paying a tribute to Joan Shaw, who has stood by him for better for worse through a long and arduous life, always there to help him in those periods of despondency which come to every artist, and always ready to smooth away the difficulties which a man of his temperament must necessarily encounter. I cannot praise her better than by quoting what Martin once said to me in conversation—'What should I do without Joan?'

Here then is one who for a time was your Musical Adviser, but without your aid he could do nothing. Artistic appreciation must be creative. Are you putting something of yourself into the music you hear and sing? Are you going half way to meet your leader? Or is your attitude one of hostility, indifference, or, at most passive acceptance? Everyone taking part in a church service has his share. The priest must read his part beautifully, simply and intelligently, and as director of the whole service he must make sure that nothing creeps in that is unworthy. He must remember that in church music an expert is available to advise and guide him, and he must not let presumptuous ignorance over-ride knowledge and experience. Then there are the principal singers, the choir, and their instructor. These may not always have supreme skill, but they can work hard to make all as perfect as possible.

Choirs are apt to spend their energies on a showy anthem and neglect a beautiful and thoughtful rendering of the psalms and responses.

Finally we come to the people. They also have their share. Sometimes they only have to listen. Let them listen with intelligence, and as I have already suggested, go half way to meet the reader or singer to whom they are listening. It is in the congregational hymn that they have their opportunity. The organist and choir are too apt to treat the congregation as their hereditary enemies; but these trained musicians have their chance in the anthems and voluntaries; in the hymn it is their duty to lead and accompany the people sympathetically. I admit that this is difficult unless you, who are of the congregation, co-operate intelligently. Do you do so? Or do you prefer to remain wallowing in the mire and making no effort to arrive at something nobler and cleaner? Do you study your part at home? Do you attend congregational practices at which you can learn new tunes which may at first appear difficult or distasteful, but will, if well chosen, come to exercise their power over you?

This is not only a musical issue but a moral one. A bad tune, no less than unworthy words, connotes a low moral atmosphere. No doubt it requires an effort to rise to the level of a fine but austere melody. It is easier to languish sentimentally in some of our worse popular tunes. It is up to you, guided by your priest and choirmaster, to establish a good tradition. Here is Martin Shaw ready to advise and help you—but without your co-operation he can do nothing.

CHAPTER **61**

Preface to *Folksong—Plainsong*

FATHER GEORGE CHAMBERS' masterly treatise ought really to be unnecessary. Hubert Parry in his *Evolution of the Art of Music* has proved conclusively that music obeys the laws of heredity, and that a Beethoven symphony is in the direct line of descent from a primitive folk song.[a] Surely, what is true in general must be equally true in particular, and the plain song of the church derive from the song of the people.

It is perhaps lucky that our bat-eyed musicologists have not recognised this, and that it has been necessary for Father George Chambers to write this delightful, learned, and, to my mind, entirely persuasive essay. Of course the musicologists cannot altogether ignore the connection between plain song and folk song, but they have put the cart before the horse and imagine that the music of the people is the debased descendant of that of the church. In their opinion the written word was impeccable and oral tradition fallible. But in truth the clerk may make errors in his copying while the memory of the unlettered countryman is sure.

Source: G. B. Chambers, *Folksong—Plainsong: A Study in Origins and Musical Relationships* (London: The Merlin Press, 1956), p. v.
[a] (London: Kegan Paul, 1896; first published as *The Art of Music*, 1893).

279

One of the most interesting chapters of this book contains convincing proof that the 'Jubilus' is not an ecclesiastical parallel to the coloratura of the prima donna, but has developed out of the wordless melismata of primitive people when their mystical emotions got beyond words. This is only one instance of the deep research and thorough scholarship which pervades the book.

CHAPTER 62

The Diamond Jubilee
of the Folk Song Society

THIS YEAR WE celebrate the sixtieth anniversary of the foundation of the Folk Song Society. To some of you this may seem a long time; to me, it seems criminally short. To think that up to sixty years ago we were allowing a great tradition to disappear before our eyes, or rather, before our ears! Every nation, except our own, recognized that in their national music they had a treasure, which, owing to changing conditions, must vanish unless it was rescued at once. And this was done, and usually with public help. But in England we had no national music, no folk songs—at least, so the squire's daughter and the vicar's wife declared. They were of the opinion that their tenants and parishioners were 'quite unmusical'. It is true that at the beginning of the nineteenth century a few people saw through the surface, and were beginning tentatively and apologetically to preserve what remained of their local song. Among the collectors was one whose name is famous in the annals of folk song—John Broadwood, who made a small collection of Sussex songs, published privately in 1843. These early collectors had little notion of the *artistic* value of what they were preserving. Then, about 1890 appeared two epoch-making books, *Songs of the West* and *English County Songs*. Baring-Gould, Fuller Maitland and Lucy Broadwood recognized the beauty of their collections, and fortified by the theories of Parry and Hadow, declared them to be the foundation of

Source: *Journal of the English Folk Dance and Song Society*, 8/3 (1958), 123–4.

national art. This led on by natural sequence to the foundation of the Folk Song Society in 1898, with the avowed object of preserving our national heritage of song from extinction.

The Folk Song Society was at first a small body of enthusiasts who issued every year a slim, privately printed Journal. This was a beginning but it did not go far enough. It was left to Cecil Sharp to discover that what belonged to the people—and what they were very nearly cheated out of by so-called education—must be restored to them. This led to Sharp's famous folk-song campaign in which he won the battle of folk song against the violent opposition of most educationists.

To this discovery Sharp added another, namely that the classical beauty of our Morris, Sword and Country dances was worth preserving, side by side with our songs. So, in 1911, Sharp founded an English Folk Dance Society to preserve and popularize our beautiful dances. Twenty-one years later the two Societies amalgamated and under the title of the English Folk Dance and Song Society, they have gone from strength to strength under our energetic and imaginative Director, Douglas Kennedy. So that in this year of Diamond Jubilee we are able to take the Albert Hall three times over for an enthusiastic audience, while all over the country similar folk song and dance festivals are testifying to our national recognition of our rediscovered art. Nor has collecting come to an end; many younger members of our Society are hard at work making new discoveries. There may be still much to do. And the Society has not neglected the scientific side of its work; we are gradually, as funds allow, completing a library and museum which are already known to experts all over the world.

One last word—do not think that we are exploiting our traditional art merely because it is old, or quaint, or of scientific interest. All these things are true, but they would be as nothing if our songs and dances were not beautiful, and not only beautiful in themselves but a sure foundation on which a more developed art can be built. Our own folk song and dance has proved, beyond doubt, that we are not 'the land without music'; this assurance has given us all a feeling of self-confidence which has already borne fruit, and will continue to grow if we only give it a chance. I should like to quote a passage from a well-known writer who knew nothing about folk song and may not have even heard the word:

In *A Room of One's Own* Virginia Woolf writes: 'Masterpieces are not single and solitary births, they are the outcome of many years of thinking in common, of thinking by the body of the people, so that the experience of the mass is behind the single voice'.[a]

[a] (London: Hogarth Press, 1929), 98.

CHAPTER 63

The English Folk Dance and Song Society

IN 1958 THE English Folk Dance and Song Society is celebrating the Diamond Jubilee of its older half—the Folk Song Society, which was founded in June 1898. Of those who brought the movement to birth no one now remains in the Society, and few names on the first list of members are those of people whom today we would associate with folk music—their distinction lies in other fields, Elgar, Grieg, Parry, Stanford, the great violinist Joachim, Mrs Lawrence (later Lady) Gomme— these are some of the names we find on the first committee. Two great figures in folk music were, however, there from the beginning. Mr Frank Kidson, a shy Yorkshire bachelor with a unique knowledge of seventeenth and eighteenth-century song and dance collections, had already compiled over fifty-four volumes of a manuscript *Index of Airs* (now in the Mitchell Library, Glasgow). He is probably best known as joint editor with Alfred Moffat of a large number of *Minstrelsies* of different parts of the British Isles, but his great service to the Folk Song Society lay in his vast knowledge of sources which was readily at the disposal of the editors of the Journal. Miss Lucy Broadwood, whose uncle, the Rev. John E. Broadwood had been the first to publish in 1843, a book of songs collected 'from the mouths of the peasantry', had, by 1898, already collaborated with J.A. Fuller-Maitland (also a

Source: *Ethnomusicology*, 2/3 (1958), 108–12.

founder member of the Folk Song Society) in producing *English County Songs*, still one of the most useful collections of folk songs. For the rest of her life, Miss Broadwood was one of the pillars of the Society, as its tireless Secretary, frequently as Editor of its Journal and, for the last few months of her life, as its President.

The Journal was the pivot of the Folk Song Society's work. At first it was merely a record of the proceedings at the Annual General Meetings of 1899 and 1900, at which papers were read, illustrated by songs, but with the publication in 1901 (*Folk Song Journal* No. 3) of fifty-two songs collected in Sussex by Mr W.P. Merrick and annotated by Miss Broadwood and Mr Kidson, the character of the Journal changed and the pattern was established that is still basically followed today in the *Journal of the English Folk Dance and Song Society*. From the beginning the Folk Song Society set itself the task of 'the collection and preservation of songs, ballads, and tunes, and the publication of such of these as may be advisable,' and soon after adopted the rule that the Society should 'publish only such traditional songs as have not hitherto appeared in print, but have been handed down orally.'

My own connection with the Society dates from 1904, the same year that Cecil Sharp (a member since 1901) was invited to join the committee. Among other distinguished collectors to join the Society in the first decade of the century were Percy Grainger, H. E. D. Hammond, Dr George B. Gardiner, and George Butterworth, one of the most promising young men to be cut down by the First World War. Grainger's fame as the writer of popular piano pieces based on some of our best English folk tunes has obscured the fact that he was one of the pioneers of folk music recording. In 1906 he took an Edison Bell phonograph to Lincolnshire and on the basis of this work wrote an article on 'Collecting with the Phonograph' and contributed to *Folk Song Journal* No. 11 (1908) with elaborate transcriptions of his recordings which indicated all the singers' variations from verse to verse. Miss Anne G. Gilchrist, whose knowledge of tunes has been unsurpassed and whose contributions to the Journal from 1906 onwards make it one of the great repositories of English musical scholarship, and Miss Frances Tolmie, who joined in 1908 and whose collection of Hebridean folk music was published as *Folk Song Journal* No. 16 (1911) just after her death, should finally be mentioned.

Enough has been said about the Folk Song Society for it to be clear that it was not concerned only with *English* folk music. From the first the outlook of the Society was firmly non-geographical, and although a large part of the material contributed to its Journal was collected in England it was not exclusively so and there are, besides the Tolmie Collection, two sets of three Journals devoted to songs collected by A. Martin Freeman in Ireland (Nos. 23–25) and to the Clague Collection of Manx Folk Music (Nos. 28–30).

The English Folk Dance Society reached its majority in the year of the amalgamation. Founded at the close of 1911 by Cecil Sharp, its activities were practical rather than academic, and, whereas the Folk Song Society existed to preserve English folk music through the publication of material exactly as it had been collected, the English Folk Dance Society set out by instruction and demonstration to give back to the people of England their heritage of folk dances that were all but forgotten. Within six months branches of the Society had been formed in Oxford, Liverpool and Manchester, in Gloucestershire and Suffolk.

The Society's methods of work were explained by Cecil Sharp in the first Annual Report: 'if the Society is to fulfill the object with which it was founded its executive must be prepared to provide demonstrations whenever and wherever they are wanted; to supply lecturers; to recommend adjudicators for Folk-Song and Dance Competitions; to meet the growing demand for competent instructors by the systematic training of teachers ... in fine to lose no opportunity of popularizing our native songs and dances, while maintaining the standard of execution.' Classes were organized regularly in London and elsewhere. Vacation Schools were arranged at Stratford-upon-Avon, examinations were held and certificates given; lectures and special demonstrations brought the work of the Society into the public eye. Within a few years branches were formed in most counties of England, and specially qualified teachers went to the United States to help the New York branch, founded in 1915 (and still flourishing as The Country Dance Society of America under the direction of Miss May Gadd).

Apart from two years in the United States, when he discovered a whole body of English songs and dances preserved among the Appalachian mountain communities, Sharp remained at the helm of the English Folk Dance Society until his death in 1924. So closely had he been identified with the Society that it seemed in danger of foundering without him; but he had chosen for his successor Douglas Kennedy, a vigorous young Scot, who with his wife Helen and her sister Maud Karpeles, had been in the Society from the beginning.

Reorganization of the Society brought new strength. A further stimulus was added by the decision to build a memorial to the founder—a headquarters which would accommodate the offices, provide suitable halls for dancing and a library for the books bequeathed to the Society for the use of its members. Cecil Sharp House in north-west London was opened on June 24th, 1930 and two years later opened its doors to the Folk Society.

The coming together of the two societies, both concerned with the preservation, study and furtherance of English traditions of folk music but using different methods, has proved a happy union and one that it was possible to forge without a break in continuity on either side. The *Folk Song Journal* acquired a new title but continued publication under the same editor, Mr Frank Howes, who had succeeded Miss Lucy Broadwood shortly before her death in 1929, assisted by an editorial board consisting largely of members of the Folk Song Society. Its policy and high standard of scholarship remained the same, while the contents were broadened to include articles on dance traditions and allied customs. The English Folk Dance Society's teaching activities continued. Perhaps only the joint society could have brought about such a successful blending of study, organisation and exciting entertainment as the International Folk Dance Festival and Conference held in London in July, 1935, an event that had far-reaching effects, not the least being the founding of the International Folk Music Council in 1948. Although it would be invidious to seek a hard and fast distinction between the popular and scientific elements in the Society's work, it may be said that the majority of its members come to its dances, classes and festivals for recreation and enjoyment, and that a small and serious body of people look to it as a focus for research. The library, which is based on Cecil Sharp's own unique collection of rare books on dance and song, is a specialist archive of books, manuscripts, photographs, prints, disc and tape recordings and films available to the public for consultation. It operates as a reading room, as a general information service on folk music and allied subjects and as a repository for the field work of collectors. The most recent and most important collection to be bequeathed to the Society consists of the manuscripts of Miss Anne Gilchrist who died in 1954 at the age of 91.

The great period of folk-song collecting in England came to an end during the First World War; collectors continued to go out into the field, but it was felt by the middle of the twenties that there was little left to collect except variants of songs already well known. The search for surviving folk dances continued after Cecil Sharp's death in 1924 and to it was added the collecting of texts of Mumming plays. Important discoveries and texts, and re-assessments of earlier material were published in the Journal, and many texts, tunes and descriptions were deposited in the Library. Then with new developments in electronics during the war, came the recording machine which placed a new tool in the hands of the experienced collector and also brought the possibility of collecting folk music within the grasp of those who had not received the formal training of a musician. In 1952, with the collaboration of the Society, the BBC embarked on a five-year scheme of collecting as much as possible of the surviving folk traditions of the British Isles. Probably no-one at the beginning of the scheme, foresaw the vast amount of material that was brought to light. Hundreds of field recordings of British folk music were added to the Library at Cecil Sharp House by courtesy of the BBC. Amateurs all over the country were stimulated, for good or ill, to do their own 'collecting' and a new pride and interest in their own songs and tunes was aroused among the country folk and townspeople, who, not so long ago thought them of little account compared with the latest popular 'hit' heard on the radio or gramophone.

On the dance side the recording machine is supplemented by the cine-camera and in recent years the Society has experimented with this medium, not only for archival purposes but also as a means of transmitting by visual impact the essential character of folk dance technique.

War, peace, economic pressure and fashion have all affected the Society's fluctuating fortunes. But there is no doubt of the influences, both hidden and apparent that it has exerted on our national life. For years English folk dances and songs have been taught in schools as a matter of course; young men and women turn to English dances for their recreation; local traditions of Morris and Sword dancing, and other seasonal rites have received fresh impetus, or have been brought to life again by the interest aroused by the Society's activities; fertilized by native folk airs English music has thrown up vigorous new growth. And this is more than ample fulfillment of Sir Hubert Parry's modest hope, expressed in his Vice-Presidential address at the inaugural meeting of the Folk Song Society in June 1898 that 'we shall preserve much precious folk music from being lost and . . . that before long we shall find England more satisfactorily represented in folk-song collections than has hitherto been the case.'[a]

[a] This message was repeated by Parry at the first general meeting of the Folk Song Society. See 'A Folk-Song Function', *The Musical Times*, no. 673 (1899), 168–9 at 168.

CHAPTER **64**

Introduction to *Classic English Folk Songs*

AN OLD SUFFOLK labourer with a fine folk song repertory and a delicate, rather gnat-like voice, once remarked: 'I used to be reckoned a good singer before these here *tunes* came in.' The *tunes* he spoke of with such scorn had come in with a vengeance, and it seemed that his kind of songs, once so admired, would be lost under the flood of commercial popular music. However, folk songs are tough, and show an obstinate will to survive. Of recent years, they have begun to reassert themselves in places where formerly only *tunes* were heard, and now it seems that many young people, whose musical nourishment had been limited to whatever came to them in canned form from the Charing Cross Road, are looking to folk music for something that they can take and re-make as their own. The ceilidh, the folksinging party, is becoming a part of urban social life, and the voice of the revival folk-singer makes itself heard in youth hostels, city pubs, skiffle cellars, even in jazz clubs. It is a curious but welcome phenomenon, this revival of folk music as a city music. It seems that many taking part in that revival have come to appreciate British balladry through their interest in jazz. A search for the roots of jazz leads to American folk song, and a search for the origins of American folk song leads the

Source: R. Vaughan Williams and A. L. Lloyd (eds.), *Classic English Folk Songs* (London: English Folk Dance and Song Society, 2003; first published as *The Penguin Book of English Folk Songs*, Harmondsworth: Penguin Books, 1959), pp. ix–xii.

astonished enthusiast back home to his own traditional music. It is to the partisans of the new folk song revival that this book is first addressed, but we hope, too, that our selection will contain some delightful surprises for those who have been singing folk songs for years.

The songs we have chosen are all taken from the *Journal of the Folk Song Society* and its continuation, the *Journal of the English Folk Dance and Song Society*. The Folk Song Society was founded in 1898, as the culmination of the work of Baring-Gould, Lucy Broadwood, Fuller Maitland, Frank Kidson, and others in rescuing the beautiful traditional music of England from oblivion. The Folk Song Society and its successor, the English Folk Dance and Song Society, have published annually, as their *Journal*, a small volume of the songs discovered by their members. Many of the songs have found their way to a wide public, being printed in settings for voice and piano, for choir, or in other forms. We have included none of these in the present volume, but have confined ourselves to songs and variants unpublished outside the pages of the *Journals*. Thus, this book consists of versions of songs that have hitherto remained in what is practically a private collection. We have found our choice hard to make, for in this book we have room for only a small portion of the 2,000 or so British traditional melodies contained in the *Journals*. Reluctantly, we decided to leave out all occupational and seasonal songs, such as Christmas carols, harvest songs, and sailors' shanties. These may be included in a future volume.

This is a book to sing from. To make the songs singable, the editorial hand has been used where necessary. We assure our readers that the melodies have not been doctored, but are as the collector took them from the traditional singer. With the words, the case is rather different. Music is a matter of emotion, words of logic. If a bad singer mars a tune, we either keep it as it is, or leave it out; in no case do we alter it. However, if a forgetful singer omits verses or lines, or knows the song only in imperfect form, we do not hesitate, in compiling a book for popular use, to complete the song from other traditional sources. Phillips Barry, a responsible American folk song scholar, speaks for us: 'Different obligations bind the maker of a scientific work to be thrown to the lions of scholarship and the maker of a practical work for people who like singing. . . . The editor of a practical work has the right and is under the duty to make both singable and understandable the song he edits. . . . Both singer and scholar, nevertheless, into whose hands the book may fall, have today a right . . . to know both the extent and the sources of editorial changes and restorations.'

Accordingly, in several instances we have collated various versions of song-texts, whether recorded from oral sources or printed on broadsides. Where we have done this, we say so in our notes, and we give the source of our borrowing. In very rare cases, and only where it seemed otherwise very hard to make the text fit the tune, we have ventured to cancel a few words, or to add interjections such as 'oh' or 'and', in order to complete the scansion of a line. In most cases, irregular lines have been left irregular, for therein lies some of the beauty of folk song; any folk singer worth his salt delights in variation, and some of the happiest rhythmical effects may come from making the tune fit the words instead of adapting the text to the tune.

In a few cases, we have shortened songs that seemed overlong for what they had to say. On the other hand, we have not hesitated to include words, verses, or whole texts which earlier collectors prudishly modified or omitted as being objectionable. The old habit of cleaning-up or even entirely rewriting the texts led to the false supposition that folk songs are always 'quite nice'. The folk singer has no objection to plain speech. He is likely to be forthright in his treatment of the pleasures and pains of love, though he may class some songs as 'outway rude' which we think quite harmless. In restoring song-texts that had hitherto been published only in bowdlerized form, we have referred to the collectors' original manuscripts.

We have said that the melodies represent the songs as the collectors reported them. The remark needs some qualification. In a few cases the *Journal* versions showed errors of musical grammar, and these have been corrected. One or two tunes needed re-barring. Several of the melodies have been transposed, in the interests of orderliness and singability. Otherwise, we have been at pains to preserve the collectors' impression of what their informants were actually singing. It must be confessed that when, perhaps under the influence of modern convention, a singer has weakened certain phrases of a fine modal tune, the temptation to 'correct' his singing is great. We have resisted that temptation. In one instance, however, it may be considered that we have cheated slightly. The singer of No. 29, *The Grey Cock*, constantly sang a final F on the recording. Her son remembers that she used to sing a final D. The D preserves the modal character of this beautiful tune, whereas the F comes as a disappointment. In our transcription we have retained the D, but have indicated the F as a variant.

We would like to give a few suggestions for singing the songs in this book. The ideal way to sing an English folk song, of course, is unaccompanied. Our melodies were made to be sung that way, and much of their tonal beauty and delightful suppleness comes from the fact that they have been traditionally free from harmonic or rhythmic accompaniment. They are best suited to stand on their own, and we rather agree with the Dorset countryman who commented on a professional singer of folk songs: 'Of course, it's nice for him to have the piano when he's singing, but it does make it very awkward for the listener.'

However, for those to whom the unaccompanied voice seems naked, there is no harm in adding a few supporting chords on the pianoforte, guitar, or other instrument, provided the chords are in keeping with the style of the tune. Special care needs to be taken when accompanying modal tunes, where the chords should be strictly in the mode. As to which instruments should or should not be used for folk song accompaniment, this is entirely a matter of choice. The fashionable guitar has no more traditional sanction than the less fashionable pianoforte. The concertina, mouth-organ, fiddle, banjo, zither, spoons, bones, even the harmonium have all been used as accompaniment to country singers without necessarily resulting in a performance that sounds more 'right' than that given by the voice unadorned. On pages xxi and xxii we print a few examples of the way in which, in our opinion, the songs might be harmonized. But we hope that our readers will sing the songs unaccompanied as much as possible.

It should not be necessary to impress on our readers that this volume does not offer them what is mere clownish nonsense or only of antiquarian interest. Béla Bartók, who knew more about folk music than any other musician of our time, once said: 'Folk melodies are a real model of the highest artistic perfection. To my mind, on a small scale, they are masterpieces just as much as, in the world of larger forms, a fugue by Bach or a Mozart sonata.'[a] We believe that the songs in this book are not only full of classical beauty, but are the foundations on which all more matured musical art must be built. This has been recognized in every country except England; and even here we are beginning to realize that, in the words of Virginia Woolf (a writer who knew nothing about folk music, but whose words are extraordinarily applicable to our case): 'Masterpieces are not single and solitary births, they are the outcome of many years of thinking in common, of thinking by the body of the people, so that the experience of the mass is behind the single voice.'[b]

So, in singing these songs, you may not only have great enjoyment, but you may be showing to some mute inglorious Milton the way which will lead him to musical self-expression. Sincerely, we wish you joy.

---

[a] 'The Folk Songs of Hungary' (1928) in Benjamin Suchoff (ed.), *Béla Bartók Essays* (Lincoln: University of Nebraska Press, 1992), 331–9 at 333. 'According to the way I feel, a genuine peasant melody of our land is a musical example of a perfected art. I consider it quite as much a masterpiece, for instance, in miniature, as a Bach fugue or a Mozart sonata movement is a masterpiece in larger form.'
[b] *A Room of One's Own* (London: Hogarth Press, 1929), 98.

PART **IV**

BRITISH COMPOSERS

CHAPTER 65

Sir Hubert Parry

IT IS A great privilege to have the opportunity of paying my tribute in these pages to the memory of Sir Hubert Parry.

It was because he was a great man that Parry was a great teacher and a great composer. Many years ago it was my good fortune to be for a short time his pupil. I still often go out of my way to pass his house in Kensington Square in order to experience again the thrill with which I used to approach his door on my lesson day.

Walt Whitman says: 'Why are there men and women that while they are nigh me sunlight expands my blood'.[a] Parry was one of these. You could not hear the sound of his voice or feel the touch of his hand without knowing that 'virtue had gone out of him'. It would not have mattered what we went to learn from him—it might have been mathematics or chemistry—his magic touch would have made it glow with life. Half-a-dozen of his enthusiastic, eloquent words were worth a hundred learned expositions.

Parry taught music as a part of life. Was it necessary for life that every part should form an organic whole? so it must be in music: there must be no mere filling up, every part must have its relation to the whole, so that the whole may live. Can

Source: *The Music Student*, 11/3 (1918), 79.
[a] 'Song of the Open Road', line 97, from *Leaves of Grass*.

we trace in life a process of evolution from the germ to the complete organism? So must we read the story of music. Is a nation given over to frivolity and insincere vulgarity? We shall surely see it reflected in the music of that nation. There was no distinction for him between a moral and an artistic problem. To him it was morally wrong to use musical colour for its own sake, or to cover up weak material with harmonic device. This is what Parry taught, and this is what he practised; later composers have followed after strange gods: they have gathered new sounds from Germany, bizarre rhythms from Russia, and subtle harmonies from France. Into these paths Parry has not followed, not because he could not, but because he would not; he remained staunchly himself, and amidst all the outpouring of modern English music the work of Parry remains supreme.

The secret of Parry's greatness as a teacher was his broad-minded sympathy; his was not that so called broadmindedness which comes of want of conviction; his musical antipathies were very strong, and sometimes, in the opinion of those who disagreed with them, unreasonable; but in appraising a composer's work he was able to set these on one side and see beyond them. And it was in this spirit that he examined the work of his pupils. A student's compositions are seldom of any intrinsic merit, and a teacher is apt to judge them on their face-value. But Parry looked further than this; he saw what lay behind the faulty utterance and made it his object to clear the obstacles that prevented fullness of musical speech. His watchword was 'characteristic'—that was the thing which mattered.

When other duties forced Parry to give up his pupils the younger generations of English musicians suffered an irreparable loss. True, his influence is more widely felt now than it was then; hundreds of students have passed through the College of Music, hundreds have read his books, have heard his lectures, have sung his music—none of these but must to some extent have realised what Parry was and what he stood for; but they are the most fortunate who knew Parry in the earlier days, when *The Glories of our blood and State* and *Blest Pair of Sirens* were new, the years which saw *De Profundis* and *Job*: those who came under his influence in those times it is who can realise most fully all that Parry did for English music.

CHAPTER 66

Charles Villiers Stanford, by Some of His Pupils

IN STANFORD'S MUSIC the sense of style, the sense of beauty, the feeling of a great tradition is never absent. His music is in the best sense of the word Victorian, that is to say it is the musical counterpart of the art of Tennyson, Watts and Matthew Arnold.

A composer cannot always be master of his inspiration, but he can see to it that his tools are always of tempered steel. This was preeminently the case with Stanford, so that whenever a true inspiration came to him he was ready for it and it was doubtless this perfection of workmanship which helped to give such compositions as the *Stabat Mater*, the Prelude to *The Travelling Companion* and the *Songs of the Fleet*, a beauty which is, I believe, imperishable.

Source: *Music & Letters*, 5/3 (1924), 195.

CHAPTER 67

Introductory Talk to Holst
Memorial Concert

I WANT TO speak to you for a few minutes about the great composer, Gustav Holst, whose music you are to hear tonight.

Holst was a visionary but, at the same time, in all essentials a very practical man. He himself used to say that only second-rate artists were unbusinesslike. It is the blend of the visionary with the realist that gives Holst's music its distinctive character.

Besides being a composer he was a great teacher, a wonderful friend, a helper and counsellor to all who needed it. His teaching and his friendship we can no longer experience directly, but the works of art which are the connotations of a fine character are with us for ever and will, I firmly believe, be loved more and more as time goes on.

Holst's life gave the lie to the notion that a composer must shut himself away from his fellows and live in a world of dreams. Holst was, it is true, a dreamer—his whole nature, and the music which exemplifies his nature, seem to be hovering on the verge of an unseen world. But he never allowed his dreams to become

Source: Bernard Shore, *The Orchestra Speaks* (London: Longmans, Green, 1938), 139–41. Broadcast in BBC national and regional programmes, 22 June 1934.

incoherent or meandering. He loved life—in the best sense of the word—too much and he loved his fellow creatures too much to allow his message to them to appear in vague or incomprehensible terms.

Partly of necessity and partly from choice he lived in the common world of men. While he was still young, he was strongly attracted by the ideals of William Morris and, though in later years he discarded the medievalism of that teacher, the ideal of comradeship remained with him throughout his life. He wanted to work with and teach and to have the companionship of his fellow-beings.

His music is sometimes described as mystical, and rightly so, but we must not imagine from this something precious or vague. His texture, his form, his melody is always clear-cut and definite. Whenever he puts pen to paper, the signature Gustav Holst is clear to read in every bar of the music.

It is sometimes true of English composers that though they may have fine and poetical ideas, yet they lack that final power of realization which is a necessary part of a complete work of art. But it is emphatically not true of two English composers that we have lately lost, and I think for the same reason in both cases: namely, that Elgar and Holst learnt their craft not so much from books and in the study as from practical experience and from the nature of their material.

Already in his student days Holst had to eke out his meagre scholarship money by remunerative work, and he deliberately chose not to shut himself up in the organ loft or to give half-hearted pianoforte lessons to unwilling pupils, but to go out into the world armed with his trombone, earning his living where he could, playing now in a symphony orchestra, now in a dance-band, now in a Christmas pantomime at a suburban theatre. In later years came other activities, teaching and conducting. It was these experiences which gave him that grip of the facts of music which helped to build up his wonderful technique.

To many men this constant occupation with the practical side of music would have been a hindrance to inspiration, but to Holst it seemed to be an incentive. The fact that his creative work had often to be crowded into the short two months of a summer holiday gave him his great power of concentration and the intense will to evoke at all costs those thoughts that lay in the depths of his being.

Holst had no use for half-measures, whether in life or art. What he wanted to say he said forcibly and directly. He, like every other great composer, was not afraid of being obvious when the occasion demanded it—nor did he hesitate to be remote when remoteness expressed his purpose. But whether he gives us the familiar chords and straightforward tunes of 'Jupiter' or leads us to the farthest limits of harmony as in 'Neptune', his meaning is never in doubt—he has something to tell us that only he can say and he has found the only way of saying it.

CHAPTER 68

A Note on Gustav Holst

GUSTAV HOLST WAS a great composer, a great teacher, and a great friend. These are really only different aspects of the same thing—his pupils were his friends, his friends were always learning from him, his music made friends for him all over the world even among those who had never seen him, and will continue to make more friends for him in the years to come.

A naval officer was once visiting a lonely station on the Yorkshire coast inhabited only by a storekeeper and his wife. 'You must be very lonely here,' he said. 'Yes, we depend a lot on our wireless.' 'What do you enjoy most on the wireless?' 'Beethoven and Holst.'

Beethoven and Holst have this in common, that they are both uncompromisingly direct in their utterance. Holst never fumbles; he says what he means without circumlocution; he is not afraid of a downright tune like both the tunes in 'Jupiter'. On the other hand, where the depth of the thought requires recondite harmony he does not flinch. The strange chords in 'Neptune' make our 'moderns' sound like milk and water. Yet these chords never seem 'wrong', nor are they incongruous; the same mind is evident in the remote aloofness of *Egdon Heath* and the homely tunes of the *St Paul's Suite*.

Source: Imogen Holst, *Gustav Holst* (London: Oxford University Press, 1938), pp. vii–ix.

This downrightness produces a certain pungency of effect which is I believe an offence to some pusillanimous aesthetes. His music probably does not appeal to the aesthete nor would he wish it so, but it does appeal to the storekeeper on the lonely Yorkshire coast.

Holst's art has been called cold and inhuman: the truth is that it is supra-human, it glows with that white radiancy in which burning heat and freezing cold become the same thing. But though his music lives in mystical regions yet it is never indefinite or shadowy; indeed, it may be a fault that it is occasionally too clear cut—a sharp outline where perhaps a vague impression would have sufficed. Those who knew him see him in his music. He was a visionary but never an idle dreamer. He seemed sometimes to be living away from the world of the senses, but as he himself said, 'Only second-rate artists are unbusinesslike.' He would lose himself hopelessly on a holiday, but he never missed an appointment. Though he seemed sometimes to be living in a world of his own, yet if a friend or even a stranger wanted help, advice, or even a rebuke, he was there to give it. His music reaches into the unknown, but it never loses touch with humanity.

In artistic matters clarity was his watchword. He simply could not understand slovenly workmanship, half-hearted endeavour, or artistic dishonesty.

Holst was a leader in the revolt against the riot of luxurious sentiment which marked the decadence of the Romantic period, but his early love of the true Romanticists Bach and Wagner prevented his ever succumbing to the poverty-stricken aridity of modern pseudo-classicism.

Much, however, as he loved Wagner, he is never 'Wagnerian'. Much as he loved Bach, he was never tempted to write those dreadful exercises in 'Bach up to date' which have lately become the fashion.

Holst inherited the English tradition of adventurous comradeship in the arts; that spirit which made Weelkes and Byrd and Wilbye throw off the shackles of Italian academicism and experiment in strange rhythms and harmonies. Nevertheless he did not succumb to that taint of amateurishness which is the fault which these good qualities breed.

Whatever his hand found to do he did it with his might.

CHAPTER 69

Gustav Theodore Holst (1874–1934)

HOLST, GUSTAV THEODORE (1874–1934), composer, whose original name was Gustavus Theodore von Holst, was born at Cheltenham 21 September 1874, the elder son of Adolph von Holst, a music teacher in Cheltenham, by his first wife, Clara, daughter of Samuel Lediard, solicitor, of Cirencester. The von Holsts were of Swedish origin though long settled in England. The painter Theodor von Holst [q.v.] was Gustav's great-uncle.

At an early age Holst began to learn the violin and the pianoforte. His favourite composer in these days was Grieg. Soon after entering Cheltenham Grammar School he read Berlioz's *Orchestration* and with no further instruction started to set Macaulay's *Horatius* to music for chorus and orchestra. However, his father discouraged composition and wished him to be a virtuoso pianist, but neuritis prevented this and at the age of 17 he was allowed to study counterpoint with G. F. Sims of Oxford.

In 1892 Holst obtained his first professional engagement as organist of Wyck Rissington, Gloucestershire. At the same time he conducted a choral society at the neighbouring Bourton-on-the-Water. Next year saw the first public performance of

Source: *Dictionary of National Biography 1931–1940* (London: Oxford University Press, 1949), 441–3.

his work in Cheltenham, the music for an operetta, *Lansdowne Castle*. As a result of this success his father sent him to the Royal College of Music where he studied composition with (Sir) C. V. Stanford [q.v.]. At this time he got to know the later works of Wagner and heard Bach's B minor Mass; thenceforth Bach and Wagner became his passion until in later years the influence of English folk-song and of the Tudor composers tended to weaken the Wagnerian supremacy although Bach was never dethroned.

Meanwhile Holst had made himself proficient on the trombone and was able to eke out his modest allowance by playing on seaside piers and in a 'Viennese' dance band. The trombone took him right into the heart of the orchestra, an experience which was the foundation of his great command of instrumentation.

In 1895 the Royal College awarded Holst a scholarship. This meant free tuition but only £30 a year for 'maintenance' and his life at this time, partly on principle, but chiefly from necessity, was almost unbelievably frugal. Owing to this his neuritis became so bad that he could not hold an ordinary pen and his eyesight suffered severely. These two weaknesses persisted throughout his life. Out of his poverty, however, there grew indirectly his love of the English country. He could not afford train journeys and used to walk to his various destinations. His habit of long walks never left him. They were his relaxation after a spell of hard work and a prelude to new periods of inspiration.

In 1898 Holst became first trombone and répétiteur to the Carl Rosa Opera Company and shortly after joined the Scottish Orchestra as second trombone. Thus ended his *status pupillaris*. His student compositions had grown in competence but, although his intimate friends saw something beneath the surface, his work did not, in itself, show great originality or force. Strangely enough the germ of the future Holst seems to be found in his early children's operettas; otherwise he was content, unconsciously perhaps, to lay the foundations of that incomparable sureness of touch and clarity of texture which mark his mature writing.

It was now that Holst discovered the feeling of unity with his fellow men which made him afterwards a great teacher. A sense of comradeship rather than political conviction led him, while still a student, to join the Kelmscott House Socialist Club in Hammersmith. Here he met Isobel, daughter of an artist Augustus Ralph Harrison, and he married her in 1901. They had one daughter, Imogen, who followed her father's footsteps as composer and teacher.

Mysticism had always attracted Holst, and he had read Walt Whitman and Ibsen. In 1899 with no other training than a little 'grammar school' Latin he learnt enough Sanskrit to make translations of the Vedic hymns for musical setting. On these followed the *opera di camera,* 'Savitri' (1908), also on a Sanskrit subject: this was first performed at the London School of Opera under Mr Hermann Grunebaum in 1916. These works, although mature, were but a foreshadowing of something greater—*The Hymn of Jesus*—written in 1917 and first performed at the Queen's Hall in 1920.

In 1903, although still comparatively unknown, Holst decided to give up the trombone and devote himself to writing music. He soon found that man cannot live by composition alone and he became music teacher at the James Allen Girls' School, Dulwich, and at the Passmore Edwards (later the Mary Ward) Settlement, where he gave the first English performances of several Bach cantatas. In 1905 he was appointed director of music at St. Paul's Girls' School, Hammersmith. Here he did away with the childish sentimentality which schoolgirls were supposed to appreciate and substituted Bach and Vittoria; a splendid background for immature minds. In 1913 a sound-proof music room was built at the school where he could work undisturbed. The first work written in these rooms was the *St. Paul's Suite* for strings (1913) dedicated to the school orchestra.

St. Paul's was a clean slate, but at Morley College for Working Men and Women in South London, where Holst became musical director in 1907, a bad tradition had to be broken down. The results were at first discouraging, but soon a new spirit appeared and the music of Morley College, together with its off-shoot the 'Whitsuntide festival' held at Thaxted, Essex, and elsewhere, became a force to be reckoned with. The 'Holst' room stands as a memorial to his work there which was carried on in the same spirit by his successors.

The year 1914 marked the inception of Holst's most famous work, *The Planets*, a suite for orchestra, each movement being suggested by the astrological attribute of a planet. This was completed in 1917. A private performance was given in 1918 under (Sir) Adrian Boult as a parting present to the composer on his departure to the Near East. The war had brought Holst great misery; he tried in vain to enlist and he began to think that he was useless; then the Young Men's Christian Association invited him to organise music for the troops in Salonika. In view of this official appointment he decided to discard the prefix 'von' from his name. He returned after a successful year abroad to find, rather to his dismay, that he was becoming a popular composer. The American orchestras were fighting for the first public performance of *The Planets* which was produced at the Queen's Hall in 1919 and followed there by *The Hymn of Jesus* in 1920.

Holst went back to his sound-proof room and in 1919 composed the *Ode to Death* (a setting of a poem by Whitman), considered by many to be his most beautiful choral work. He also finished in 1922 his opera *The Perfect Fool*. This was played to a crowded house at Covent Garden in 1923. The audience was puzzled and did not understand his peculiar sense of humour, so well appreciated by his friends. However, the splendid ballet music has remained in the repertoire.

From 1919 to 1924 Holst was professor of composition at the Royal College of Music and he held a similar post at University College, Reading, from 1919 to 1923. An accident while conducting at Reading caused concussion. Disregarding this he went to America in 1923 in order to conduct at the musical festival at the University of Michigan at Ann Arbor, but on his return his old enemy, insomnia, became alarming and he was ordered complete rest. This enabled him soon to restart composing, first an opera, *At the Boar's Head*, founded on the Falstaff scenes of *Henry the Fourth*, and set almost entirely to English dance tunes (produced by the British National Opera Company at Manchester in 1925), and second and more important, the 'Keats' Choral Symphony, written for the Leeds Festival of 1925. Its strength and power were obvious but it had no popular success and an entirely inadequate performance in London did not help it. Holst's dread of popularity seemed to drive him back upon himself. A certain aloofness appeared in his music; for instance, in *Egdon Heath* (1927, first performed in 1928), written as a homage to Thomas Hardy. Even those who understood him best found it difficult to assimilate at first, although they are gradually coming round to the composer's own opinion, that this was his best work. However, some gracious smaller compositions belong to this period, notably the Seven Part-Songs for women's voices (1925–1926), settings of poems by his friend Robert Bridges.

Holst's position as a composer is testified to by the Holst festival held in his native town of Cheltenham in 1927 and by the award of the gold medal of the Royal Philharmonic Society in 1930. He was also invited to lecture at Harvard University and to conduct his own compositions in Boston. This (his third) visit to the United States of America (1932) was interrupted by illness, but he recovered quickly and he returned to England apparently well though without some of his old energy. At this time he wrote the Six Choral Canons which are a puzzle to many although some have succeeded in plucking out the heart of their mystery.

In these later years Holst's constant companion was his daughter, and whenever they could meet, he and his lifelong friend, Dr Ralph Vaughan Williams, would spend whole days discussing their compositions. Holst declared that his music was influenced by that of his friend: the converse is certainly true.

Holst again fell ill in 1932, although he was able in 1933 to write the 'Lyric Movement' for Mr Lionel Tertis, the violist. He died in London of heart failure following an operation 25 May 1934. His ashes were buried in Chichester Cathedral, close to the memorial to Thomas Weelkes [q.v.] whose music he greatly loved.

Holst's music has been called cold and inhuman: it is only cold from its burning intensity. It is true that he sometimes seemed to be living in a world removed from human beings, but he never lost touch with his fellow men.

A portrait of Holst, by Bernard Munns, is in Cheltenham Public Library, and a drawing, by Sir William Rothenstein (1920), is at Morley College.

CHAPTER 70

Foreword to *Eight Concerts of Henry Purcell's Music*

WE ALL PAY lip service to Henry Purcell, but what do we really know of him?
One or two anthems and services are perfunctorily done occasionally in our
churches just to make the service list look respectable. About half-a-dozen of the
songs appear in vocal recitals, the Covent Garden Opera Company, more one
suspects out of piety than affection, produced *The Fairy Queen* amidst complete
public apathy, and occasionally, for much the same reasons, we revive *King Arthur*,
and this is all, apparently, that we can do for the great genius who enriched our
lives with such lovely tunes as 'Fairest Isle' and 'How blest are shepherds', with
such moving tragedy as *Dido and Aeneas*, such astonishing virtuosity of expression
as 'The Blessed Virgin's Expostulation' and such ecstatic fervour as the 'Evening
Hymn'.

I mention only the better known music, but there are equal treasures which till
quite lately have lain hidden in manuscripts.

The Purcell Society has, I believe, at last almost completed its labours, carried
on by the devotion of a few experts who gave their scanty leisure to the work and

Source: Harold Watkins Shaw (ed.), *Arts Council of Great Britain Commemorative Book of Eight
Concerts of Henry Purcell's Music* (London: Arts Council of Great Britain, 1951), 7.

were entirely neglected by the State or the public. Meantime, Austria, Germany, Italy and France have all produced at the public expense complete and critical editions, not only of their great masters, but also of their lesser lights. In this country we have too long allowed one of the greatest geniuses of music to languish unwept, unhonoured and almost unsung.

Therefore, these programmes, to which this collection of essays refers, are to be welcomed and commended as offering, during the Festival of Britain, a wide range of music rarely heard which will demonstrate the power, vitality and originality of one of Britain's greatest composers.

CHAPTER 71

Gustav Holst: A Great Composer

GUSTAV HOLST WAS a great composer, a great teacher, and a great friend. These are really different aspects of the same fact. It was his intense human sympathy that fostered his musical invention. It was the same spur of sympathy which made him at once the teacher and the friend. He could not but be friends with those whom he taught; similarly, he could not help, by his very presence, teaching those who were his friends. In one of his lectures he speaks of the almost mystical unity which must necessarily exist between master and pupil, between friend and friend.

Art and craft are travellers alongside of each other. It is obvious that craft is of no use except as a handmaiden of art. But it is equally true that an art cannot reach its full fruition unless the craft develops along with it. In England we do not always realise this. Our musicians are often too much the gifted amateur; and when they really get down to business they fumble and lose their way. In this country our young composers have not those practical opportunities of learning their job as répétiteurs, stage conductors, and general assistants in the opera houses and concert rooms. Holst realised this, and—partly from necessity, but largely from choice—he refused to view the world from the dignified eminence of the organ loft, but rushed into the mêlée of life armed with his trombone and picking up a living where

Source: *The Listener*, 51/1318 (1954), 965–6.

he could: sometimes in a travelling opera company, sometimes playing in a pantomime or in the pier band. At one time, indeed, he spent his summer dressed up as a Blue Hungarian, where he was admonished with a rude word by the manager to speak broken English. Another part of his practical education was an engagement as accompanist and répétiteur to the Carl Rosa Opera Company. And he finally found his true vocation, other than that of composer, as a teacher at Morley College and St. Paul's Girls School. The result of this unconventional but practical training was that theory and practice always met in him. Indeed, he never forgot the theory that he had imbibed from Stanford and Rockstro, but he implemented it by the live experience of the band room and the rehearsal pianoforte. The result is that sure touch of his texture which is so lamentably absent in many contemporary composers.

It is this very sureness of purpose which makes his music distasteful to some of the less bold hearted of his critics, who seem to think that the tunes from 'Jupiter' and *St. Paul's Suite* are little less than an insult to the intelligence of the intelligentsia. But Holst gets his own back in 'Neptune' and *Egdon Heath*, with harmonies compared with which the wildest efforts of our young 'moderns' are so much milk and water.

Holst's watchwords were economy and clarity. One really grows out of the other. He always used to declare, with characteristic humour, that these qualities grew out of the neuritis in his arm which forced him to write no more notes than were absolutely necessary. His superb technique enabled him to achieve both these qualities. Many of us have to hide our want of skill under a mass of musical verbiage. But not so Holst. As in his life, so in his art. He knew what he wanted and he understood the means to achieve it. It was only when the end was not important that he relaxed. He would lose himself hopelessly on a holiday walk, but he never missed an appointment. He used to say that only a second-rate artist is unbusinesslike. Did this artistic clarity occasionally lead to starkness and coldness? Some people seem to think so. Yes, Holst is cold occasionally, but it is the cold which approximates to intense heat. He is accused of being inhuman. Rather, he was supra-human. His real life seemed to be set in the world of vision. But though a visionary he was never a mere dreamer. The very clarity of his purpose and the means of his art saved him from this. *Egdon Heath* is a case in point. I confess that at first I found it a hard nut to crack. But I hope that I have now cracked it, and it is certainly well worth cracking. I remember, when he first showed it me, I felt that the very definiteness of his melodies were out of keeping with such an impressionistic conception. But I was wrong. It is only those who have no melodic invention who have to resort to vague twilight.

If we look at Holst's work as a whole we find that those delightful tunes which he wrote for children's operas when he was little more than a boy, tinged as they were perhaps with Sullivan and Grieg, are yet the true ancestors of those strong melodies of *The Planets* and *The Perfect Fool* ballet. And in those same early works we find a hint of what was to develop later into the mysticism of 'Neptune', and the choral song *To the Unknown God*, and *The Hymn of Jesus*. In later years the mystical element was prone to oust the simply melodic. But those later years also produced *Hammersmith* and the *Brook Green Suite*.

To my mind *The Planets* marks the perfect equilibrium of these two sides of his nature. From the straightforward tunes of 'Jupiter', which even those awful people who sing in their baths would, I believe, manage, down to the strange colours—we can hardly call them harmonies—of 'Neptune': passing through the schoolboy rampage of 'Uranus' with its organ glissando, and the ineffable peace of 'Venus', it is all pure Holst. And we may note in passing that 'Venus' is a good example of the continuity of Holst's musical idiom, because here we find, though not an actual quotation, yet a distinct development from a theme in his early work, *The Mystic Trumpeter*, where that poem also deals with peace. Some timid souls are frightened at the frank melodiousness of 'Jupiter', and are almost afraid that it is rather vulgar. I wonder what these same people make of the Finale of Beethoven's C minor Symphony? But apparently Beethoven, being a classical German, is allowed to do what he likes, while Holst, being a modern Englishman, has to do what he is told.

Needless to say, the orchestration is masterly; so masterly, indeed, that it is not noticeable. It is only second-rate orchestration which causes the hearer to sit up and say—what wonderful orchestral colour. The choral composition of Holst which I like best, even better than *The Hymn of Jesus*, is his setting of Whitman's 'Ode to Death', from *The Memories of President Lincoln*. Here we find extreme mysticism combined with beautiful and simple melody in an ideal marriage. It is not easy to perform. The orchestration is pared down almost to leanness; in fact, it is orchestral chamber music, though a large orchestra is used. And each member of the chorus ought to be a fine musician. The truth is that Holst had built up his choral technique on his experience of the teachers and pupils at St. Paul's Girls School, whom he apparently taught to be able to sing anything in tune; therefore the voices in this Ode are often left entirely unsupported, without those comfortable doublings by clarinets, bassoons, and horns which Parry, for example, almost invariably added to his unaccompanied passages, after a first, disastrous rehearsal. And I have to confess that I often had to ask the composer's leave to add a few notes to the orchestra to help out my chorus, some of whom were not archangels.

It is a great privilege to me to be allowed to speak about my old friend. I first met him about 1895, when we were both at the Royal College of Music, and he started the ball by quoting Sheridan's *Critic*. This, for some reason, broke the ice and seemed to seal our friendship, and almost from that time onwards we used to meet at frequent intervals and give each other composition lessons. He was an unsparing critic; further, he had absolutely no use for half measures. Any makeshift or make-believe left him just dumb and puzzled, and I often regret that I had not the courage to show him some of my work because I thought it would seem to him insincere. But what he would have said would have helped me greatly though it might at the time have hurt me.

Thus my argument comes round full circle. When Holst became my friend he also, inevitably, became my teacher. And anyone who troubles to look carefully into my work will realise how much I learned from him as a composer. I learned from him chiefly by the simple process of cribbing. Holst used to say that he cribbed from me: I could never perceive this myself. But I could give you chapter and verse of the places where I have borrowed from him. Personally, I can see no harm in cribbing. Composers whose thoughts run on parallel lines, especially if they are master and pupil, or even great friends, will often find that the lines converge and become identical. This, I hope, will explain my borrowing from Holst, and I am indeed, not ashamed, but proud, of it.

CHAPTER 72

The Teaching of Parry and Stanford

WITH THE PERMISSION of the organizers of this Concourse and by your leave, Mr Chairman, I propose to enlarge the scope of this talk so as to include Hubert Parry as well as Charles Villiers Stanford. In my early days these two stood together as the two forward-looking English musicians. Nowadays the bright young things of music seem to have forgotten them,—they do not even know how to spell Stanford's name! But in my belief these two will come back to us when many of our latest blunderbusses have proved mere flashes in the pan.

I had the honour to be a pupil of both these great men. I went to Parry as a lad of 17, and naturally absorbed him wholesale. Then came three years at Cambridge and technical instruction from Charles Wood and others, so that by the time I became a pupil of Stanford's I was musically more mature and did not fall under his spell as completely as I did under that of Parry.

Source: Ralph Vaughan Williams and Gustav Holst, *Heirs and Rebels: Letters Written to Each Other and Occasional Writings on Music*, ed. Ursula Vaughan Williams and Imogen Holst (London: Oxford Unversity Press, 1959), 94–102, ascribed the erroneous date of 1957. The talk was broadcast as 'The Teaching of Parry and Standford', on BBC Third Programme, 1 January 1956. The broadcast is a shortened version of a lecture given at the Composers' Concourse in 1955 (see Peter Starbuck in KC, 292).

Let us take Parry first. Many more recent writers, for instance Arnold Bax and Philip Heseltine, entirely misunderstood Parry; they were deceived by his rubicund bonhomie and imagined that he had the mind, as he had the appearance, of a country squire. The fact is that Parry had a highly nervous temperament. He was in early days a thinker with very advanced views. I remember, for example, how in the early nineties he accepted Ibsen with delight. He was one of the early champions of Wagner when other thinkers in this country were still calling him impious. His life of Wagner, published in the early eighties in his *Studies of Great Composers*,[a] is masterly, putting him in his high place, long before the time when Bernard Shaw and his satellites imagined that they had discovered him. His early radicalism subsided in later years to a broad-minded conservatism. He would take the trouble to listen to Schoenberg, even in his old age. Naturally he did not like him, but he was willing to test him; though, after hearing the *Five Orchestral Pieces* he is reported to have said 'I can stand this fellow when he is loud, it is when he is soft he is so obscene.'

In 1891 when I first went to Parry he was indeed an out-and-out radical both in art and life. He introduced me to Wagner and Brahms—which was quite contrary to curricula then obtaining in academies. He showed me the greatness of Bach and Beethoven as compared with Handel and Mendelssohn. He once discovered with horror that I did not know the Finale of Beethoven's 'Appassionata' Sonata, so he sat down and played it to me, pointing out as he went on, how the development grew to a great climax. It was a wonderful performance and I shall never forget it.

In the year 1891 there were early performances of *Siegfried*, under Mahler, and Parry generously lent me a copy of the pianoforte score, [which was] hard to obtain in those days. I remember how amused, but pleased, he was when I showed him a song which I thought I had composed, but was really a passage out of the third act of *Siegfried*. It was a setting of Browning's *Summum bonum*. He praised its insight, but said it was too much like *Siegfried* to be allowed to pass!

Parry was always on the look-out for what was 'characteristic'—even if he disliked the music he would praise it if he saw that it had character. I remember once I showed him a piece in which, by pure carelessness, I had repeated a note in a scale passage; Parry, as his custom was, had kept the piece back to look at it in the week, and he said to me 'I have been looking at that passage for a long time to see if it was just accident, or something characteristic.' I nearly died of shame.

Parry never tried to divorce art from life: he once said to me 'Write choral music as befits an Englishman and a democrat.' This attitude towards art led to an

---

[a] (London: G. Routledge, 1886).

almost moral hatred of mere luscious sound. It has been said that Parry's orchestration was bad; there may have been occasional carelessness and hurry, but I think the truth was that he occasionally went too far in mere eschewal of orchestral effects. Some years ago I was sitting next to Elgar at a rehearsal of Parry's *Symphonic Variations*, I said 'I suppose many people would call this bad orchestration.' Elgar replied angrily 'Of course it's not bad orchestration; the music could have been scored in no other way.'

Parry's generosity is well known: I have already told you how he used to lend valuable music to his pupils, which was not always returned. The story of Parry and the Elgar *Variations* is well known, though it was persistently ignored by Bernard Shaw in his attempts to draw a picture of Elgar persecuted by mysterious people whom he invented and called 'The Academic Clique'. But perhaps the following story is not so well known; Parry had for a pupil Richard Walthew, who one day showed him a setting of Browning's *Pied Piper*. Parry thought so well of it that he determined to try to get it a public performance. But Parry had already nearly finished a setting of his own of the same words. What did Parry do? He just put his own setting away in a drawer and said nothing about it to Walthew for whom he obtained his public performance. I think it was twenty years before Parry allowed his own setting to be performed.

Parry was a thinker on music, which he connected, not only with life, but with other aspects of philosophy and science. When Parry was a young man the Darwinian controversy was in full swing. He became a follower of Herbert Spencer and decided to find out how far music, as well as the rest of life, followed the laws of evolution. These thoughts he embodied in his great book, *The Evolution of the Art of Music*, in which he proves, conclusively to most people, that Beethoven's Ninth Symphony, for example, is not an isolated phenomenon, but a highly developed stage of a process of evolution which can be traced back to the primitive folk-songs of our people.[b] I understand that there has grown up among our younger musicians a sort of musical fundamentalism, with its garden of Eden all complete; according to this theory we are to believe, I suppose, that a Beethoven symphony is not a development but a degenerate relic of angelic strains of some musical Adam and Eve. I suppose that these young people will say with Disraeli that they are on the side of the angels.

What about Parry as a composer? Potentially, I believe, he was among the greatest. But something stood in the way of complete realization. There is however one outstanding exception. I fully believe—and keeping the achievements of Byrd,

[b] (London: Kegan Paul, 1896; first published as *The Art of Music*, 1893).

Purcell, and Elgar firmly before my eyes,—*Blest Pair of Sirens* is the finest musical work that has come out of these islands.

Stanford in many ways was the opposite of Parry. Parry is sometimes musically inarticulate and clumsy. Stanford was occasionally too clever. His very facility sometimes betrayed him. He could, at will, adopt the technique of any composer he chose—as in *The Middle Watch*, where he beats Delius at his own game. But in such works as the Stabat Mater and the Requiem and some of his songs we find Stanford thinking his own beautiful thoughts in his own beautiful way. His very facility prevented him from knowing when he was genuinely inspired and when his work was routine stuff. Therefore we have to confess that some of his enormous output is dull and uninspired. But is this not true also of Beethoven and Bach? The great composer goes in for mass-production. He does not wait for the spark from Heaven to fall, otherwise he might, like the scholar gypsy, wander round the country for ever, always searching but never finding.[c] I believe that every composer can achieve something, even a small song, which no one else could do as well; but it must come out of a mass of often uninspired stuff; the composer must not stand waiting for a miracle to happen.

In 1952 we had occasion to celebrate the centenary of Stanford's birth. In any continental country a composer of Stanford's calibre would have been celebrated with performances in every opera house in the country. We have only two opera houses here, but even they could not give us an opportunity of hearing such splendid works, full of possibilities of popularity, as *Much Ado* and *Shamus O'Brien*. Instead they chose rather to shake the dead bones of *Norma* and Saint-Saëns's *Samson et Dalila*.

Stanford achieved a certain distinction as a conductor. He had of course no truck with the ideas of the temperamental director. His object was to present faithfully what the composer intended. For that reason he was labelled as 'academic' by certain silly journalists who complained that he 'lacked imaginative fancy'—which meant apparently that he gave his audiences what he believed the composer meant, and not what he thought he ought to have meant. Against this let me set the opinion of Eugene Goossens, himself a distinguished conductor, who as a student at the Royal College of Music had played the violin in the orchestra under Stanford's beat. Goossens told me that in his opinion Stanford was the finest interpreter of Brahms that he had ever heard.

---

[c] 'Thou waitest for the spark from heaven! ... Ah! do not we, wanderer! await it too?' Matthew Arnold, 'The Scholar-Gipsy', lines 171–80.

I have just mentioned the word 'academic'. It was the fashion among a certain class of journalist about fifty years ago to describe Parry, Stanford and others who ruled at the Royal College of Music as 'academic', which apparently meant that they founded the emotion of their music on knowledge, and not on mere sensation. To these critics, admiration of Brahms was equivalent to dry-as-dust pedantry. If they are alive today they must feel rather foolish when they see Brahms filling the house at a Promenade concert.

Stanford is best known to the general public by his arrangements of Irish melodies. He had made an exhaustive study of Petrie, Bunting, and other Irish collections, for he realized, as we all should, that vital art must spring from its own soil. I am far from saying that we have all got to write sham folk-songs; neither Parry nor Elgar, so far as I know ever used an actual English folk-song in their work. But we do feel that the same circumstances which produced our beautiful English folk-songs also produced their music, founded as it should be on our own history, our own customs, our own incomparable landscape, even perhaps our undependable weather and our abominable food. The youngest generation of composers profess not to believe in folk-song, but for the last fifty years we have been constantly in touch with it and they can no more help being influenced by it than by their own language.

If I might give a word of advice to young composers I would say 'learn the elements of your art at home; then, only then, when you feel sure of what you want to do, and feel the ability to do it, go and rub noses with the composers of other lands and see what you can learn from them. You may say that you do not want to be national, but that you want to be international. You will not achieve this by denying your own country from the start. If you subscribe to that extremely foolish description of music as a universal language, you will find that you have achieved nothing better than a standardized and emasculated cosmopolitanism which will mean nothing to you nor to those whose mannerisms you have been aping.'

The great universal figures of every art, such as Shakespeare, Bach, and Velasquez have also been the most intensely national. Shakespeare's clowns, even when they have Italian names and are nominally living in Italy, are purely English countrymen. Who could be more English than Dickens? And yet he has achieved popularity even in Russia. It was from the painting of that very English artist, Constable, that the whole French Impressionist movement grew. In this connection may I quote you a passage from an author who, so far as I know, knew little about music, and certainly knew nothing about folk song. Virginia Woolf writes as follows:

Masterpieces are not single and solitary births, they are the outcome of many years thinking in common, of thinking by the body of the people so that the experience of the many is behind the single voice.[d]

Now let us turn to Stanford as a teacher. We cannot consider him as a teacher without thinking of him as a man. He was a true Irishman, quarrelsome and at the same time lovable and generous. Though artistically we were poles apart, I had for him that affection which certain types of man seem to call up. He was intolerant and narrow-minded, and it was this, I think, which made him a good teacher. If a thing was wrong, it was wrong; if it was right it was right, and there was no question about it. It is fatal for a teacher to say, even mentally, to a pupil 'well perhaps you are right after all.' Stanford was often cruel in his judgements and the more sensitive among his pupils wilted under his methods and found comfort under a more soft-hearted teacher. I remember I once showed Stanford the slow movement of a string quartet. I had worked feverishly at it, and, like every other young composer, thought not only that it was the finest piece that had ever been written, and that my teacher would fall on his knees and embrace me, but that it was also my swan song. Now what would Parry have done in a case like this? He would have pored over it for a long time in hopes of finding something characteristic and, even if he disliked the piece as a whole, would try to find some point to praise. Stanford dismissed it with a curt 'All rot, me boy!' This was cruel but salutary. So far as I can remember, he was quite right. Luckily the piece was lost years ago.

Stanford's teaching was constructive. He was not content to criticize what his pupils brought him, but he set them tasks to perform in order to strengthen certain parts of their work. When I was with him at the Royal College he had just been back to school with Rockstro, studying all over again what was then known as modal counterpoint. This study had fascinated him, and partly for this reason and partly to counteract a growing tendency to Tchaikovskian lusciousness which he discovered among his pupils, he set them to work writing masses and motets in strict modal counterpoint. I was let off this discipline because Stanford found that I was too far gone in the modes already. Also, he found in my work too much seriousness and even stodginess; so he decided that I must write a waltz. True to my creed I showed him a modal waltz!

Stanford's own music is the music of an educated man. He had formed his style partly on the songs of his native land and partly on the songs of the great masters. His musical style might be compared with the literary style of Matthew

[d] *A Room of One's Own* (London: Hogarth Press, 1929), 98.

Arnold, and it was this sense of style that he passed on, often unconsciously, to his pupils. When I was Stanford's pupil I made the great mistake of fighting my teacher. A great deal of our meagre lesson time was occupied with the discussion of whether one of my progressions was damnably ugly or not, which time might have more profitably been spent on the larger issues. Anything crude or clumsy,—or 'ugly,' as he called it—was anathema to Stanford. He accused me once of all the crudities in Blow mentioned in Burney's History.

I had not read Burney, but probably if I had read it I should have found I had done just what Stanford accused me of. The way to get the best out of instruction is to surrender oneself, mind and soul, to one's instructor and to try to learn his methods without intruding one's own personality. Young students are much too fond of their own personalities. In the merest harmony exercises they insist on keeping all their clumsy progressions because that is what they 'felt', forgetting that art cannot mature unless the craft matures along side of it. Stanford would sometimes sigh deeply when I brought him my week's work and say he was hoping against hope! Nevertheless, his deeds were better than his words, and it was he who persuaded the Leeds Festival to perform my *Sea Symphony*.

The value of lessons with a great teacher cannot be computed in terms of what he said, or what you did, but in terms of some intangible contact with his mind and character. With Stanford I felt I was in the presence of a lovable, powerful and enthralling mind; this helped me more than any amount of technical instruction.

CHAPTER 73

Gerald Finzi: 1901–1956

THE LAST PIECE which I heard Gerald Finzi conduct was his Cantata, *In Terra Pax*. The end of that beautiful work contains a faint reminiscence of 'The First Nowell'. I believe that our purists opine that this is not a folk tune, however that may be, it is firmly rooted in our English hearts, and it seems inevitable that Finzi should make reference to it in a composition which gives us, so intensely, the spirit of the English Christmas.

In his early days Finzi was an enthusiastic country dancer, and even named his two favourite cats Rufty and Tufty. Later on, in his country home at Ashmansworth, he and his wife would organise summer country dance parties. I do not think that Finzi was a close student of folk song, his mind had turned more readily to other aspects of English music, but he could not help being influenced by it, like every other English composer who did not deliberately shut his ears to it.

Apart from the question of the direct influence of folk song on his music, there can be no doubt that the sacred spring from which he drank welled up from English poetry, and especially that of Bridges and Hardy. Indeed, in his settings of these two poets, he found the exact musical counterpart of the rhythm, the language and the thought of their poetry. This alone will, I believe, be enough to give his music the crown of immortality.

Source: *Journal of the English Folk Dance and Song Society*, 8/1 (1956), 57.

CHAPTER 74

Mr Gerald Finzi: A Many-Sided Man

GERALD FINZI'S LAST new work was the cantata *In Terra Pax*. This work is significant not only for its intrinsic beauty but because it seemed to give us hope of even better things to come. These hopes will not be fulfilled. *In Terra Pax* is characteristically founded on a poem by Robert Bridges. Finzi's music shows extraordinary affinity with this poet and with Thomas Hardy, both their language and their thought find an absolute counterpart in his settings.

No mention has been made in your obituary notice of Finzi's work as a musicologist. He was convinced that the English eighteenth-century composers were underrated, so he brought his imaginative scholarship to bear on the British Museum and other libraries where he discovered and made known to the world many hitherto hidden treasures.

Visiting the Finzis' house, with its wonderful view of the distant downs, was a happy experience. Gerald had a wide and critical knowledge of English literature, his wife is an accomplished artist and his two sons are fine musicians, so that a feeling of beauty without any self-consciousness has always pervaded the atmosphere of their home, in which there was always a welcome for their many friends and where discussion and hospitality flowered. Finzi had strong views on all that

Source: *The Times*, no. 53,652 (3 October 1956), 13.

was going on in the world, with which I did not always agree: and he expressed them in vigorous and clear-cut language. His interests were varied; he was, for instance, an enthusiastic fruit grower; indeed he was almost as keen on reviving forgotten varieties of apples as the works of forgotten English composers.

Finzi had a great sense of the social responsibilities of an artist. This led him, during the war, to found the Newbury String Players, a small body of amateur musicians, who, with a little professional help, have continued ever since to bring good music to the small villages of the neighbourhood which otherwise would have been without any such artistic experience.

Finzi's compositions range from the slightest of songs through the noble cantata *Dies Natalis*, to the large scale choral work *Intimations of Immortality*. He also wrote much purely instrumental music, including concertos for clarinet, violoncello and pianoforte. In all these works we find something absolutely personal, and in my opinion they will last on when other more showy but less truly original compositions are forgotten.

CHAPTER 75

Elgar Today

THE FIRST ELGAR which I ever heard was an early performance of the [Enigma] Variations. I had not the slightest idea what to expect, but I realized at once that I was listening to something which was quite new without being eccentric, universal and yet absolutely personal, and something which could only emanate from this country.

I had not the pleasure of intimate acquaintance with Elgar, but I should like to report one conversation which I had with him. We were sitting together listening to a rehearsal of Parry's *Symphonic Variations*. As your readers doubtless know, there is a curious, spiky—though entirely individual—sound about the orchestration of this work. I said to Elgar, 'I suppose most people would call this bad orchestration, but I do not agree'. He turned on me, almost fiercely, and said: 'Of course it's not bad orchestration—this music could be scored in no other way'. I think it is part of Elgar's greatness that he realized so fully that the style is the man.

Source: *The Musical Times*, 98/1372 (1957), 302.

PART V

Programme Notes on Vaughan Williams's Music

CHAPTER **76**

Heroic Elegy and Triumphal Epilogue

THE FIRST SECTION consists of a long melody given to the trombone, accompanied by a persistent syncopated figure on the strings. This melody is further developed by the horns and the section ends with a long-drawn cadence founded on the last bar of the melody. The theme of the middle section is given to the violins, divided into four parts, and repeated by the trumpets playing softly. After further development, the syncopated figure returns fortissimo, and the first section is repeated in shortened form. The coda is founded on the middle section, while the drum continues the syncopated figure of the opening.

Source: Programme note. Leeds Municipal Orchestra, 21 January 1905 (work first performed 1901). Reprinted in KC, 13.

CHAPTER 77

Pan's Anniversary

IN THE MUSIC to the choruses no attempt has been made to reproduce the Elizabethan style of music, but it is hoped that the music is appropriately simple. The music for the 'Masquers' Entry', the 'Pavan' and 'Galliard' are taken from sixteenth-century dances (Rogero, Mal Sims and Spagnoletta), arranged for orchestra by Mr G. von Holst. The entrances of the Thebans and Boeotians are two English folk tunes—'Bristol Town' and 'The Jolly Thresherman'. The morris dancers will be accompanied by their own music. The music for the Revels consists of four English folk tunes, 'Sellenger's Round', 'The Lost Lady', 'Maria Marten' and 'All on Spurn Point', arranged for orchestra by Mr G. von Holst. Some of these traditional melodies are from the composer's own manuscript collection, others ('Bristol Town' and 'The Lost Lady') are from the collection of Miss L. E. Broadwood, and are inserted by her kind permission. In the music of the choruses also, certain characteristic phrases from English folk music have been inserted.

Source: Programme note for first performance. Music for a masque by Ben Jonson. Chorus and orchestra of the Choral Union, conducted by Vaughan Williams. Stratford-upon-Avon, 24 April 1905. Reprinted in KC, 28–9.

CHAPTER 78

A Sea Symphony

THE FIRST SKETCHES for this work (namely, parts of the Scherzo and slow movement) were made in 1903, and it was gradually worked out during the next seven years. It was first produced at the Leeds Festival in 1910, and has since been performed (in a slightly revised form) at Oxford, Cambridge and Bristol.

There are two main musical themes which run through the four movements:

I. The harmonic progression to which the opening words for the chorus are sung.

II. A melodic phrase first heard at the words 'and on its limitless heaving breast, the ships'.

The plan of the work is symphonic rather than narrative or dramatic, and this may be held to justify the frequent repetition of important words and phrases which occur in the poem. The words as well as the music are thus treated symphonically. It is also noticeable that the orchestra has an equal share with the chorus and soloists in carrying out the musical ideas.

Source: Programme note. The Bach Choir and Queen's Hall Orchestra, conducted by Hugh P. Allen. Queen's Hall, London, 4 February 1913 (work first performed 1910). Reprinted in KC, 50.

The Symphony is written for soprano and baritone soli, chorus and orchestra. The two soloists sing in the first and last movements. The slow movement contains a solo for baritone (and also a long refrain for orchestra alone) while the Scherzo is for chorus and orchestra only. The words are selected from various poems of Walt Whitman to be found in *Leaves of Grass*, namely 'Sea Drift', 'Song of the Exposition', and 'Passage to India'.

CHAPTER 79

Phantasy Quintet

THIS 'PHANTASY' WAS written at the request of Mr W. W. Cobbett, as one of his series for various combinations of instruments.... It is in four very short movements, which succeed each other without a break. There is one principal theme (given out by the viola at the start) which runs through every movement—

I. Prelude (in slow 3/2 time).

II. Scherzo (this is a quick movement—the longest of the four).

III. 'Alla sarabanda.' (Here the 'cello is silent and the other instruments are muted.)

IV. Burlesca. (This movement is, for the most part, in the form of a 'basso ostinato'.)

Source: Programme note for first performance. London String Quartet. Aeolian Hall, London, 23 March 1914. Reprinted in KC, 60.

CHAPTER 80

A London Symphony

NOTE I

The title *A London Symphony* may suggest to some hearers a descriptive piece, but this is not the intention of the composer. A better title would perhaps be 'Symphony by a Londoner', that is to say, the life of London (including, possibly, its various sights and sounds) has suggested to the composer an attempt at musical expression; but it would be no help to the hearer to describe these in words. The music is intended to be self-expressive, and must stand or fall as 'absolute' music. Therefore, if listeners recognize suggestions of such things as the 'Westminster Chimes' or the 'Lavender Cry' they are asked to consider these as accidents, not essentials of the music. The work consists of the usual four symphonic movements, namely:

I. *Lento*, leading to *allegro risoluto*.
II. *Lento*.
III. *Scherzo* (Nocturne).
IV. *Maestoso alla marcia*, leading to Epilogue in which the theme of the opening Lento recurs.

Sources: Programme notes. First note written 1920. Second note written for performance by Liverpool Philharmonic Society, 1 December 1925 (original version of the work first performed 1914, with later revisions first performed in 1918, 1920 and 1934). Reprinted in KC, 71–2.

A London Symphony was first performed in the Spring of 1914, at one of the late Mr F. B. Ellis's concerts (conductor, Mr Geoffrey Toye); since then it has been revised, and the first performance of the revised version took place under Mr Albert Coates in May 1920.

NOTE 2

It has been suggested that this symphony has been misnamed, it should rather be called 'Symphony by a Londoner'. That is to say it is in no sense descriptive, and though the introduction of the 'Westminster Chimes' in the first movement, the slight reminiscence of the 'Lavender Cry' in the slow movement, and the very faint suggestion of mouth organs and mechanical pianos in the Scherzo give it a tinge of 'local colour', yet it is intended to be listened to as 'absolute' music. Hearers may, if they like, localize the various themes and movements, but it is hoped that this is not a necessary part of the music. There are four movements: The first begins with a slow prelude; this leads to a vigorous allegro—which may perhaps suggest the noise and hurry of London, with its always underlying calm. The second (slow) movement has been called 'Bloomsbury Square on a November afternoon'. This may serve as a clue to the music, but it is not a necessary 'explanation' of it. The third movement is a nocturne in form of a Scherzo. If the hearer will imagine himself standing on Westminster Embankment at night, surrounded by the distant sounds of the Strand, with its great hotels on one side, and the 'New Cut' on the other, with its crowded streets and flaring lights, it may serve as a mood in which to listen to this movement. The last movement consists of an agitated theme in three-time, alternating with a march movement, at first solemn and later on energetic. At the end of the finale comes a suggestion of the noise and fever of the first movement—this time much subdued—then the 'Westminster Chimes' are heard once more: on this follows an 'Epilogue' in which the slow prelude is developed into a movement of some length. The Symphony was finished in 1913, and first performed on March 27, 1914, under the direction of Mr Geoffrey Toye.

CHAPTER 81

A Pastoral Symphony

THE MOOD OF this Symphony is, as its title suggests, almost entirely quiet and contemplative—there are few *fortissimos* and few *allegros*. The only really quick passage is the *Coda* to the third movement, and that is all *pianissimo*.

In form it follows fairly closely the classical pattern, and is in four movements.

I. *Moderato.*—The opening subject is as follows:

This leads to a cadence which is frequently referred to later on (No. 2), and is followed by a new figure first played by the cor-anglais and taken up by the other

Source: Programme note for first performance. Orchestra of the Royal Philharmonic Society, conducted by Adrian Boult. Queen's Hall, London, 26 January 1922. Reprinted in KC, 86–9.

instruments (No. 3), which leads in its turn to a new subject in A minor (No. 4). Other tributary figures are No. 5 and No. 6.

No. 2

No. 3

Cor Anglais

No. 4

No. 5

No. 6   Oboe

After a cadence in A major a solo violin takes up the principal subject and develops it thus:

No. 7

There is no full re-statement of the principal subject, but Nos. 3 and 4 are recapit-ulated with slight variations, and the movement ends with a *Coda* founded on No. 1. II. *Andantino*.[a]—This movement commences with the following theme on the horn:

No. 8a

etc.

[a] This is the movement's original tempo direction; it was later changed to 'Lento moderato'.

followed by this passage on the strings—

No. 8b

which leads to a long melodic passage suggested by the opening subject:

No. 9

There is no definite second subject, but its place is taken by a fanfarelike passage on the trumpet (note the use of the true harmonic seventh, only possible when played on the natural trumpet):

No. 10

This leads to a resumption of Nos. 8 and 9, and at the end of the movement the two principal subjects are heard in combination (clarinet and horn).

III. *Moderato pesante.*—This movement is of the nature of a slow dance, and is chiefly founded on the following rhythmic figure:

No. 11

Other subjects in this movement are:

No. 12

No. 13

The following is the theme of a kind of *Trio* in quicker time:

No. 14

After this the opening recurs, followed again by the *Trio*; and the movement ends with a *Coda* (*presto* and *pianissimo*) founded on this subject:

No. 15a

and:

No. 15b

IV. *Lento—Moderato Maestoso.*—This movement starts with this introductory passage, unharmonized except for a drum-roll:

No. 16

The principal subject is as follows:

No. 17

given first to the wind, and then taken up by the strings.

The middle section of the movement is founded on the introductory passage (No. 16), after which the principal subject returns in shortened form, and the movement ends as it began, except that the introductory passage (No. 16) is accompanied, not by the drum, but by a high note held by the strings.

CHAPTER **82**

Flos Campi

WHEN THIS WORK was first produced two years ago, the composer discovered that most people were not well enough acquainted with the Vulgate (or perhaps even its English equivalent) to enable them to complete for themselves the quotations from the 'Canticum Canticorum', indications of which are the mottoes at the head of each movement of the Suite.

Even the title and the source of the quotations gave rise to misunderstanding.

The title 'Flos Campi' was taken by some to connote an atmosphere of 'buttercups and daisies', whereas in reality 'Flos Campi' is the Vulgate equivalent of 'Rose of Sharon' (*Ego Flos Campi, et Lilium Convallium*, 'I am the Rose of Sharon, and the Lily of the valleys').

The Biblical source of the quotations also gave rise to the idea that the music had an ecclesiastical basis. This was not the intention of the composer.

I
_____

Sicut Lilium inter spinas, sic amica mea inter filias ... Fulcite me floribus, stipate me malis, quia amore langueo. (As the lily among thorns, so is my

Source: Programme note written for a performance in 1927 (work first performed 1925). Reprinted in KC, 106–8.

love among the daughters.... Stay me with flagons, comfort me with apples; for I am sick of love.)

The opening theme:

Ex. 1

is played by the oboe, and is answered by the following:

Ex. 2

on the solo viola. Next comes the following theme (flute and viola):

Ex. 3

which is also used in later movements.

2

Jam enim hiems transiit; imber abiit, et recessit; Flores apparuerunt in terrâ nostrâ, Tempus putationis advenit; Vox turturis audita est in terrâ nostrâ. (For, lo, the winter is past, the rain is over and gone, the flowers appear on the earth, the time of the singing of birds is come, and the voice of the turtle is heard in our land.)

Over a murmuring accompaniment of voices and muted strings the viola plays the following melody:

Ex. 4

This is taken up by oboe and other wind instruments, and towards the end of the movement is sung by the chorus.

3

Quaesivi quem diligit anima mea; quaesivi illum, et non inveni ... Adjuro vos, filiae Jerusalem, si inveneritis dilectum meum, ut nuntietis ei quia amore langueo.... Quo abiit dilectus tuus, O pulcherrima mulierium? Quo declinavit dilectus tuus? et quaeremus eum tecum. (I sought him whom my soul loveth, but I found him not.... I charge you, O daughters of Jerusalem, if ye find my beloved, that ye tell him that I am sick of love.... Whither is thy beloved gone, O thou fairest among women? Whither is thy beloved turned aside? that we may seek him with thee.)

In this movement recitative-like passages on the viola alternate with answering passages for the trebles and altos of the chorus.

4

En lectulum Salomonis sexaginta fortes ambiunt, ... omnes tenentes gladios, et ad bella doctissimi. (Behold his bed [palanquin], which is Solomon's, three score valiant men are about it. ... They all hold swords, being expert in war.)

A march, of which the following are the principal subjects: Ex. 5 played by clarinet and bassoon, and Ex. 6 played by the viola.

Ex. 5

p marcato

Ex. 6

f risoluto

Later on Exs. 5 and 6, with their counterpoints, are heard in combination. The chorus does not enter till the end of this movement.

5

Revertere, revertere Sulamitis! Revertere, revertere ut intueamur te....
Quam pulchri sunt gressus tui in calceamentis, filia principis. (Return,
return, O Shulamite, return, return that we may look upon thee.... How
beautiful are thy feet with shoes, O Prince's daughter.)

A slow dance with these themes:

Ex. 7

(orchestra and chorus):

Ex. 8

(viola solo) accompanied by a persistent rhythm in the percussion. Towards the end
of the movement themes (Ex. 1) and (Ex. 3) reappear.

6

Pone me ut signaculum super cor tuum. (Set me as a seal upon thine heart.)

This movement is developed entirely out of the following theme:

Ex. 9

first by the orchestra, then by the chorus. This is interrupted towards the end by a
reminiscence of Exs. 1 and 2. The theme of the movement is then taken up again
softly by the chorus, flute and solo viola.

CHAPTER **83**

Piano Concerto

THE FIRST TWO movements of this Concerto were sketched in 1926, and the third movement in 1930. The work is dedicated to Miss Harriet Cohen. There are three movements: (1) *Toccata* leading to (2) *Romanza* leading to (3) *Fuga chromatica con Finale alla Tedesca*. There is no break between the movements.

(1) *Toccata*. The pianoforte starts off with the following figure:

No. 1

against which the orchestra plays the following theme:

No. 2

Source: Programme note for first performance. BBC Symphony Orchestra, Harriet Cohen (piano), conducted by Adrian Boult. Queen's Hall, London, 1 February 1933. Reprinted in KC, 138–9.

Then follows this figure on the pianoforte:

No. 3

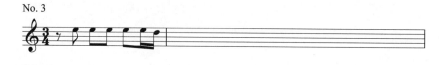

a development of which leads in its turn to this:

No. 4

etc.

Then the whole is repeated with slight modifications, the pianoforte and the orchestra as a rule changing places. After this comes a development of No. 3, which serves as an accompaniment to a new theme:

No. 5

3 etc.

An extension of No. 2 leads to a shortened recapitulation, and the movement, which is quite short, ends with a version of No. 5 canonically treated by pianoforte and orchestra. A short *cadenza* for pianoforte leads to

(2) *Romanza*. The principal theme is as follows:

No. 6

and is played by the pianoforte solo and repeated by the flute accompanied by pianoforte and strings. An additional theme is as follows (strings and muted horns):

No. 7

There is an episode in 3/2 time founded chiefly on the following:

No. 8

The opening themes are then heard again, but the movement is interrupted by the trombones, and a few bars of introduction lead to

(3) *Fuga chromatica con Finale alla Tedesca.* The subject of the fugue is:

No. 9

given out by the pianoforte. There is a counter-subject:

No. 10

After various episodes a *stretto* on a dominant pedal is reached, built up chiefly on an augmentation of part of the fugue subject:

No. 11

with which the subject and counter-subject of the fugue are combined. A *cadenza* for the pianoforte separates the fugue and the Finale, the subjects of which are the same as those of the fugue, but treated harmonically rather than contrapuntally, and finally there is another *cadenza* for the pianoforte, made up chiefly out of the episode (No. 8) in the slow movement. The *cadenza* ends with a quotation two bars long from a contemporary composer, added 'according to my promise'.[a] Then a few bars of *Allegro* bring the Concerto to an end.

[a] The quotation is from Bax's Third Symphony. In a revision of the score after the first performance this quotation was removed. As Vaughan Williams explained in a letter to Harriet Cohen, 'The "quotation" at the end of the work does not "come off"—*we* understand it but the audience does not.' See Michael Kennedy, *The Works of Ralph Vaughan Williams* (2nd edn, London: Oxford University Press, 1980), 236–7.

CHAPTER 84

Fourth Symphony

I

Two principal themes run through this Symphony:

and:

(Incidentally this is not the B A C H theme which in this key would run):

Source: Programme note for first performance. BBC Symphony Orchestra, conducted by Adrian Boult. Queen's Hall, London, 10 April 1935. Reprinted in KC, 148–50.

The (A) theme appears first as the tail-end of the opening subject of the first movement, thus:

Two other phrases complete the first group of subjects:

and the following version of (B):

Then follows a long *cantilena*, played by the upper strings, accompanied by repeated notes on the wind:

This leads to the key of D major and the following new theme:

which is expanded for about forty bars and is interrupted by a passage founded on the opening subject which eventually transforms itself into the following version of (A):

There is no complete recapitulation of the first subjects, but after a few bars suggestive of the opening, the *cantilena* passage follows immediately, this time in the bass, with a counter melody in the treble. This works up to a *fortissimo*. The music then dies away, and ends with a soft and slow repetition of the D major theme, this time in D flat.

II

The second movement has for its introduction a passage suggested by (B). The principal theme which follows is played by first violins over a *pizzicato* bass:

Then follow two episodes, during the second of which the introductory passage is also heard:

The first half of the movement ends with this cadence figure:

Then after another episode there is a shortened recapitulation. The final cadence figure extends itself into a *cadenza* for the flute, under which (A) is heard on the muted trombones.

III

The principal theme of the Scherzo is:

played on the bassoons. This is of course a version of (B). (A) is also heard in the course of the movement. Then over the following rhythmical accompaniment:

comes a theme which eventually takes this form:

The trio of the Scherzo is a *fugato* on this subject:

After a recapitulation of the Scherzo a long *crescendo* on a pedal leads direct to the Finale.

IV

This opens with a more energetic version of the cadence figure from the second movement:

This has, as a dependent theme, a melody for the wind over what is known in professional circles as an 'oompah' bass:

A further theme is the following:

which grows into this:

Instead of a development there is a long passage founded on the first three bars of the 'dependent' theme. Then a suggestion of the end of the first movement, and then another long pedal leading back to the recapitulation.

The subject of the fugal epilogue is (A), played first on the trombones and then heard both in its original form and inverted, combined with the other subjects of the finale. The work ends with a reference to the opening bars of the first movement.

The Symphony was sketched in the end of 1931 and the beginning of 1932, and was completed in 1934. It is dedicated to Arnold Bax.

CHAPTER 85

Five Tudor Portraits

IN MAKING A choral suite out of the poems of Skelton, I have ventured to take some liberties with the text. Certain omissions have been made necessary, partly by the great length of the original, partly from the fact that certain passages did not lend themselves to musical treatment, and partly that certain lines that look well when read cannot conveniently be sung.

I have occasionally, for musical reasons, changed the order of the lines; this seems to me legitimate, as there does not appear to be an inevitable sequence in Skelton's original order.

The first movement is a ballad telling of a certain Elinor Rumming who kept an alehouse in Leatherhead. The inn is still there ('The Running Horse') and a portrait of Elinor hangs on the outer wall.

The ballad is divided into five sections. The first describes Elinor herself, the second tells of the guests who came to the inn and the various shifts they were put to obtain their ale till they are at length driven out by the angry hostess. Then follows the episode of a visit of 'drunken Alice' (represented by a contralto). She succeeds apparently in obtaining a free drink, then she falls into a drunken slumber.

Source: Programme note for first performance. Norwich Festival: Festival Chorus, London Philharmonic Orchestra, conducted by Vaughan Williams. St Andrew's Hall, Norwich, 25 September 1936. Reprinted in KC, 154.

The fourth section introduces still another party of guests who join in a drinking chorus: 'With hey and with ho, sit we down a row.' Finally a few lines tell us that

'Thus endeth the geste
Of this worthy feast'.

The second movement is an Intermezzo, a love-song in praise of 'Pretty Bess', sung by the baritone solo, accompanied by the chorus.

The third (Burlesca) is a satirical epitaph on John Jayberd, the parish clerk of Diss, who was probably well known to Skelton and evidently cordially disliked by him. The words are written chiefly in monkish Latin with sudden unexpected interjections in English. The setting is for men's voices only.

The fourth movement (Romanza, for contralto solo and chorus of women's voices) is a lament sung by Jane Scroop, a pupil at the Abbey School of Carrow, near Norwich, for Philip, her sparrow, which had been killed by 'Gib, our cat'.

First there is a dialogue between Jane and her companions who may be supposed to enter in procession bearing the coffin and chanting the office. At first Jane laments her sparrow and cries for vengeance on all cats, wild and tame; then she summons all the birds of the air to take their part in the funeral ceremony; the robin to sing the requiem, the parrot to read the gospel, the peacock to sing the grail, and as a climax the phœnix to bless the hearse. Lastly the chorus sing their final farewell to Philip, while Jane softly murmurs portions of a Latin office for the dead.

There is no justification, I think, for describing these touching words as a 'parody'. Jane saw no reason, and I see no reason, why she should not pray for the peace of her sparrow's soul.

The last movement is entitled 'Scherzo' and is made up out of two poems, 'Jolly Rutterkin', and a song out of the play 'Magnificence'.

This fusion is, I hope, justified by the fact that the character who sings the song in the play has immediately before quoted a line from 'Jolly Rutterkin'. The setting is for baritone solo and chorus.

CHAPTER 86

Sixth Symphony

THIS SYMPHONY WAS begun probably about 1944 and finished in 1947. It is scored for full orchestra including saxophone. There are four movements: Allegro, Moderato, Scherzo and Epilogue. Each of the first three has its tail attached to the head of its neighbour.

FIRST MOVEMENT—ALLEGRO

The key of E minor is at once established through that of F minor, A flat becoming G sharp and sliding down to G natural at the half bar thus:

Ex. 1

Source: Programme note for first performance. Royal Philharmonic Society concert: BBC Symphony Orchestra, conducted by Sir Adrian Boult. Royal Albert Hall, London, 21 April 1948. Reprinted in KC, 180–3.

The last three notes of (1) are continued, rushing down and up again through all the keys for which there is time in two bars, all over a tonic pedal. Two detached chords

Ex. 2

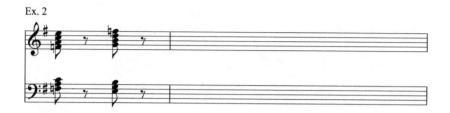

lead to a repetition of the opening bar, but this time the music remains in F minor and the rush up and down is in terms of the first phrase. While strings and wind remain busy over this the brass plays a passage which becomes important later on.

Ex. 3

The fussy semiquavers continue in the bass while the treble has a new tune in the cognate key of C minor.

Ex. 4

etc.

Then the position is reversed and the treble fusses while the bass has the tune. This leads us back to our tonic pedal and the instruments rush around as at the beginning. Thus ends the first section of the movement. The next section starts with this persistent rhythm:

Ex. 5

Over this trumpets, flutes and clarinets play a tune in cross-rhythm which starts thus

Ex. 6

This continues for a considerable time with some incidental references to Ex. 3 and is followed by a new tune while the persistent rhythm persists.

Ex. 7

Then we are given a further instalment of Ex. 6. The brass now plays Ex. 7 very loud and this brings us to what I believe the professional annotator would call the '*reprise* in due course'. As a matter of fact this *reprise* is only hinted at just enough to show that this is a symphony not a symphonic poem. But I am not sure that the 'due course' is well and truly followed when we find the tune Ex. 7 played for yet a third time (this time in E major) quietly by the strings accompanied by harp chords. To make an end and just to show that after all the movement is in E minor, there is an enlargement of the opening bar.

SECOND MOVEMENT—MODERATO

This leads on from the first movement without a break. The principal theme is based on this rhythm

Ex. 8

sometimes 'straight' and sometimes in cross-rhythm. A flourish follows, first on the brass loud, then on the woodwind loud and then soft on the strings.

Ex. 9

Between each repetition there is a unison passage for strings

Ex. 10

The strings continue softly, but before they have finished the trumpets enter with this figure taken from the opening theme

Ex. 11

The trumpets start almost inaudibly, but they keep hammering away at their figure for over forty bars, getting louder and louder. Meanwhile the rest of the orchestra have been busy chiefly with the melody though not the rhythm of the opening theme. Having reached its climax the music dies down. The cor anglais plays a bit of Ex. 10 and this leads direct to the third movement.

THIRD MOVEMENT—SCHERZO

This may be possibly best described as fugal in texture but not in structure. The principal subject does not appear at the beginning. Various instruments make bad shots at it and after a bit it settles down as Ex. 12. With this is combined a trivial little tune, chiefly on the higher woodwind (Ex. 13). An episodical tune is played on the saxophone and is repeated loud by the full orchestra (Ex. 14).

Ex. 12

Ex. 13

Ex. 14

(Constant Lambert tells us that the only thing to do with a folk tune is to play it soft and repeat it loud. This is not a folk tune but the same difficulty seems to crop up.)

When the episode is over, the woodwind experiment as to how the fugue subject will sound upside down but the brass are angry and insist on playing it the right way up, so for a bit the two go on together and to the delight of everyone including the composer the two versions fit, so there is nothing to do now but to continue, getting more excited till the episode tune comes back very loud and twice as slow. Then once more we hear the subject softly upside down and the bass clarinet leads the way to the last movement.

Fourth Movement—Epilogue

It is difficult to describe this movement analytically. It is directed to be played very soft throughout. The music drifts about contrapuntally with occasional whiffs of theme such as Ex. 15, with one or two short episodes such as this, on the horns (Ex. 16), and this on the oboe (Ex. 17):

Ex. 15

Ex. 16

Ex. 17

At the very end the strings cannot make up their minds whether to finish in E flat major or E minor. They finally decide on E minor which is, after all, the home key.

The composer wishes to acknowledge with thanks the help of Mr Roy Douglas in preparing the orchestral score.

CHAPTER **87**

Folk Songs of the Four Seasons

WHEN I UNDERTOOK to write a Folk Song Cantata for the Women's Institutes I set my mind to work to find some unifying idea which would bind the whole together. It was not long before I discovered the necessary link—the calendar. The subjects of our folk songs, whether they deal with romance, tragedy, conviviality or legend, have a background of nature and its seasons.

When the lovers make love the plough boys are ploughing in the spring and the lark is singing. When May comes round the moment is appropriate to celebrate it in song. The succession of flowers in the garden provides symbols for the deserted lover. The festivity of the Harvest Home is celebrated in the allegory of 'John Barleycorn'. The young maiden meets her dead lover among the storms and cold winds of autumn; and the joy of Christmas is set in its true background of frost and snow.

The songs which I have chosen come from various sources. Many of them are from my own collection, others from Cecil Sharp's *Folk Songs from Somerset*. I have been kindly allowed to use others from the collections of Lucy Broadwood and Fuller Maitland.

Source: Programme note for first performance. National Singing Festival of National Federation of Women's Institutes: London Symphony Orchestra, conducted by Sir Adrian Boult. Royal Albert Hall, London, 15 June 1950. Reprinted in KC, 185–6.

One of the tunes perhaps requires special notice: 'The Round'—or 'Rota'—'Summer is a-coming in' is not nominally a folk tune. It is supposed to have been composed in the thirteenth century by a monk—John of Forncete. It has long been a puzzle how this beautiful melody made its appearance amongst its clumsy contemporary monkish companions. The truth, I am sure, is that this is a folk tune and owes its freedom and grace to the fact that it was not bound by theoretical restrictions. At all events, I feel justified in including it in a collection of folk tunes.

We can imagine Brother John's delight when he discovered one day that this tune—(just like 'Early, early in the Spring' in this volume)—'went in canon'.

CHAPTER 88

Sinfonia Antartica

THIS WORK WAS suggested by the film *Scott of the Antarctic* which was produced by Ealing Studios a few years ago. Some of the themes are derived from my incidental music to that film. The Musical Director was Ernest Irving (he indeed composed three bars of the music himself). The *Sinfonia* is therefore gratefully dedicated to him.

A large orchestra is used, including a vibraphone, a wind machine and women's voices used orchestrally. There are five movements—*Prelude, Scherzo, Landscape, Intermezzo* and *Epilogue*. Each movement is headed by an appropriate quotation.

I. PRELUDE

> *To suffer woes which hope thinks infinite,*
> *To forgive wrongs darker than death or night,*
> *To defy power which seems omnipotent,*
> *Neither to change, nor falter, nor repent:*
> *This . . . is to be*

Source: Programme note for first performance. Hallé Orchestra, conducted by Sir John Barbirolli. Free Trade Hall, Manchester, 14 January 1953. Reprinted in KC, 211–13.

Good, great and joyous, beautiful and free,
This is alone life, joy, empire and victory.

Shelley, Prometheus Unbound

The opening subject starts as follows:

No. 1

This theme is used as a whole or in parts throughout the work. Then a few antarctic shimmerings form a prelude to a soprano solo without words, accompanied by a chorus of sopranos and altos (No. 2). This is followed by other themes of minor importance which lead up to a theme accompanied by deep bells, which was supposed in the film to be 'menacing'. It also is used frequently throughout the work. Then, after a repetition of the soprano solo, a trumpet flourish introduces the coda which is built up largely on the opening theme (No. 3).

No. 2   Soprano Solo

Chorus

No. 3   Trumpets

II. SCHERZO

There go the ships
And there is that Leviathan
whom thou hast made to take his pastime therein.

Psalm 104

The opening theme is as follows:

No. 4

This is followed by another little wisp of theme (No. 5). Then we get down to business with a *motif*, which as it is 'representative', must be thus designated. Those who wish may take it as representing whales (No. 6). The next section would, I suppose, be called by the official analyst the 'trio'. Its tune was used in the film to suggest penguins (No. 7).

No. 5

No. 6

No. 7 Trumpet   Trombone

The music ends softly on an indefinite chord for muted brass and celesta.

III. LANDSCAPE

> *Ye ice falls! Ye that from the mountain's brow*
> *Adown enormous ravines slope amain—*
> *Torrents, methinks, that heard a mighty voice,*
> *And stopped at once amid their maddest plunge!*
> *Motionless torrents! Silent cataracts!*

> Coleridge, *Hymn before Sunrise, in the Vale of Chamouni*

The music here is chiefly atmospheric, but the following themes may be noted:

No. 8 Muted Horns

No. 9

No. 10

In this movement there is a part for the organ (if there is one and at the right pitch). It leads without break to

IV. Intermezzo

Love, all alike, no season knows, nor clime,
Nor hours, days, months, which are the rags of time.

Donne, *The Sun Rising*

There are two main themes:

No. 11

Towards the end of the movement the bell passage reappears followed by some very soft music connected in the film with the death of Oates.

V. Epilogue

I do not regret this journey; we took risks, we knew we took them, things have come out against us, therefore we have no cause for complaint.

Captain Scott's last journal

The *Epilogue* starts with another flourish (No. 13). Then follows a march tune (No. 14), obviously suggested by the opening of the Prelude (No. 1).

No. 13

No. 14

Other themes follow leading to a big climax. The bell passage comes in again, suddenly very soft. The voices are heard again and the opening flourish, first loud and then soft, leads to a complete repetition of the beginning of the *Prelude*. Then the solo singer is heard again and the music dies down to nothing, except for the voices and the Antarctic wind.

CHAPTER 89

The Pilgrim's Progress

THE LIBRETTO OF this Morality is a free adaptation of Bunyan's allegory. The text is chiefly from Bunyan, with additions from the Psalms and other parts of the Bible. The words of Lord Lechery's song in Act III are by Ursula Wood.

For stage purposes a good deal of adaptation and simplification of the original has been necessary: thus, the Pilgrim's early domestic happiness has been omitted, his two companions, Faithful and Hopeful, do not appear, there are only three Shepherds; while Mr By-Ends has been provided with a wife. In Act II the House Beautiful and the House of the Interpreter have been merged into one, and an elaborate scene of initiation is built up from Bunyan's few hints. No explanation is given in the original as to how the Pilgrim escapes from Vanity Fair; the author merely says that 'he that overrules all things...so wrought it about that Christian, for that time, escaped them and went his way'. For this purpose the libretto has utilized the escape described later from Doubting Castle. Incidentally, the name Pilgrim is used throughout the libretto, as being of more universal significance than Bunyan's title.

Source: Programme note. Cambridge University Musical Society, Boris Ord (director), Dennis Arundell (producer). 23–27 February 1954 (first performed 1951). Reprinted in KC, 195–6.

CHAPTER 90

Tuba Concerto

THE FORM OF this concerto is nearer to the Bach form than to that of the Viennese School (Mozart and Beethoven) though the first and last movements each finish up with an elaborate cadenza which allies the concerto to the Mozart–Beethoven form. The music is fairly simple and obvious and can probably be listened to without much previous explanation. The orchestration is that of the so-called theatre orchestra consisting of woodwind, two each of horns, trumpets and trombones, timpani, percussion and strings.

Source: Programme note for first performance. London Symphony Orchestra Jubilee Concert, conducted by Sir John Barbirolli. Royal Festival Hall, London, 13 June 1954. Reprinted in KC, 216.

CHAPTER 91

Violin Sonata

THE *FANTASIA* BEGINS with a figure in the pianoforte left hand which after a few bars becomes the accompaniment to the principal theme, played by the violin; this, it will be noticed, is an augmentation of the opening pianoforte phrase. The pianoforte later takes up this theme, while the violin plays with the accompaniment figure and works up to a cadenza-like passage. A new subject appears for the pianoforte alone, which is repeated, more or less exactly, by the violin. The principal subject is then developed, with the relative positions of the two instruments reversed. This development continues on similar, but not identical lines with the opening. It leads to a still longer cadenza, then with a reference to the second subject, the movement finishes very softly.

The *Scherzo* is founded almost entirely on one figure which is first played on the pianoforte. Against this background two other themes appear, both played on the violin.

Tema con variazione: The theme is adapted from another work written several years ago, but discarded. It is given out by the pianoforte alone in three octaves without harmony, and is repeated, phrase by phrase, on the violin. Variation one

Source: Programme note. [Exact date of composer's note unknown.] First performed: Frederick Grinke (violin), Michael Mullinar (piano). BBC Home Service, 12 October 1954. Reprinted in KC, 218–9.

starts with an inversion of the theme against which the original is heard in the bass. In variation two, the theme is heard on the violin, accompanied in canon by the piano. Variation three is chiefly for unaccompanied violin, with double and triple stops. In variation four the pianoforte suggests the opening of the theme, against which the violin plays a free inversion of the whole. Variation five is a canon by inversion, founded on the theme. Variation six is a lively tune suggested by the theme, and played on the violin. The coda begins with a reminiscence of the opening *Fantasia*, against which the violin plays a melody suggested by the variation theme.

CHAPTER **92**

Eighth Symphony

THE SYMPHONY IS scored for what is known as the 'Schubert' orchestra: with the addition of a harp. Also there is a large supply of extra percussion, including all the 'phones and 'spiels known to the composer.

The *first movement*, as its title suggests, has been nicknamed 'seven variations in search of a theme'. There is indeed no definite theme. The opening section contains only a few isolated figures which are developed later, but that is all: here is a list of them.

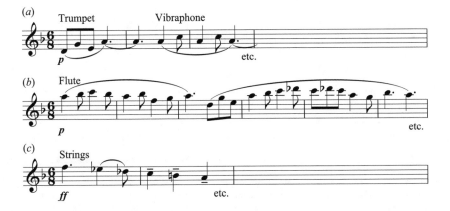

The second section is played presto, and (a), (b), and (c) are juggled with alternately by wind and strings.

In the third section a choral-like melody appears on the strings and harp which proves to be a descant of (a).

This leads to a cantabile phrase for oboe and solo violoncello which seems to be another variation of (a).

There is also another phrase suggested by (c).

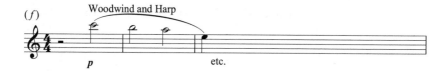

The fourth section, Allegretto 6/8, also starts with a variation of (a).

Source: 'The New Vaughan Williams Symphony', *Music and Musicians* 4/9 (1956), 8–9. First performance given by Hallé Orchestra, conducted by Sir John Barbirolli. Free Trade Hall, Manchester, 2 May 1956. Reprinted in KC, 221–5.

This gives way to still another variant of (a).

There is also a reference to (c).

The fifth section consists chiefly of the lengthening out of (a), starting with the violoncello and harp, the other instruments gradually joining in.

with another suggestion of (c).

We return to quick tempo in the sixth section which is chiefly occupied with (a) and a perversion of (b).

The seventh and last section is a repetition on a larger and more grandiose scale of the third section; starting softly, the music rises to a climax and then sinks down to softness, and the whole movement finishes with a reference to the opening.

I understand that some hearers may have their withers wrung by a work being called a symphony whose first movement does not correspond to the usual symphonic form. It may perhaps be suggested that by a little verbal jugglery this movement may be referred to the conventional scheme. Thus, the first section may be called the first subject; the second (presto) section can become the 'bridge passage'; the third section, starting at (d), may be described as the second subject. Sections four and five we will call the development, the allegro will be the reprise of the first subject, though this, I admit, will be skating over rather thin ice: but there will be no difficulty in referring the final section to the recapitulation and coda. Thus all wounds will be healed and honour satisfied.

The *second movement* (*Scherzo*) is, as its title suggests, for wind instruments only, namely, flute, piccolo, two oboes, two clarinets, three bassoons (third ad lib.), two horns, two trumpets and three trombones.

Under an accompaniment of repeated chords the bassoons have a tune, starting thus:

This is repeated by flute and piccolo while the bassoons have occasional scales. This leads to another tune, on the trumpet (b), with a sequel played by the higher wind instruments (c).

A figure out of this section suggests a fugato which is started by the bassoons and carried on with various devices, such as stretto, augmentation, etc., by the rest of the band.

There is a short trio in 6/8 time.

(e)

Bassoons

p

etc.

There is no complete recapitulation of the scherzo, its place being taken by a short stretto and a few bars of coda. I think I may claim precedence for this idea of the truncated recapitulation in the third movement of Brahms's Clarinet Quintet.

In the *third movement* (*Cavatina*) the strings take over, thus giving the wind a well-earned rest. The violoncello start off with a cantilena twelve bars long, which begins thus:

(a)

Violoncelli

p cantabile

etc.

This leads to a short episode of which we shall hear more later.

(b)

1st Violins

etc.

Then the violins take up (a) again, with occasional pizzicato scales in the bass: this leads to an important second section in triple time.

(c)

1st Violins

p cantabile

etc.

A development follows founded on this figure.

(d)

1st Violins

p

etc.

This development also contains a cadenza-like passage for the solo violin. Then comes the orthodox recapitulation of the opening theme, this time given to violas, cellos and basses, which leads to a shortened version of (c), and an arpeggio figure, based on (d), for a solo violoncello ends the movement.

The *fourth movement, Toccata,* besides full strings and wind, commandeers all the available hitting instruments which can make definite notes, including glockenspiel, celesta, xylophone, vibraphone, tubular bells and tunable gongs. These last are ad lib.: according to the score they are 'not absolutely essential but highly desirable'.

After a short, rather sinister exordium (a), the trumpet gives out the principal theme ((b) and (c)), surrounded by all the tunable percussion.

There are thus two sections, each of which is repeated by full orchestra. Then comes another tune, given to strings and horns.

This returns us safely to the principal theme: indeed, we shall soon discover that this movement is a modified rondo. Music (b) and (c) recur at intervals, surrounded by episodes. The first episode is built up on this theme.

(e)

1st Violins

pp   etc.

The second is characterized by the voice of the xylophone, and third episode introduces vibraphone and celesta. The fourth episode consists of a resumption of (d) accompanied by glissandi on all the available percussion instruments. This leads to a final, and perhaps rather portentous statement of (b) and (c)—the symphony ends with a reference to the sinister exordium.

CHAPTER 93

Ninth Symphony

THIS SYMPHONY WAS begun, except for a few vague sketches, early in 1956, and was finished, so far as a composition ever is finished, in November 1957. It was written chiefly in London, but partly in Majorca and partly at Ashmansworth, the home of Gerald and Joyce Finzi. It is dedicated to the Royal Philharmonic Society, and was first played at a concert on 2 April 1958 by the Royal Philharmonic Orchestra conducted by Sir Malcolm Sargent.

The usual symphony orchestra is used, with the addition of three saxophones and flügel horn. This beautiful and neglected instrument is not usually allowed in the select circles of the orchestra and has been banished to the brass band, where it is allowed to indulge in the bad habit of vibrato to its heart's content. While in the orchestra it will be obliged to sit up and play straight. The saxophones, also, are not expected, except possibly in one place in the scherzo, to behave like demented cats, but are allowed to be their own romantic selves. Otherwise the orchestration is normal, and is, the composer hopes, sound in wind and strings.

There are four movements, as is usual in a symphony. The first movement, *Allegro Moderato*, is not in strict sonata form but obeys the general principles of statement, contrast and repetition, which is the basis of all musical form.

Source: 'The Music of my New Ninth Symphony: An Analysis of this Month's Premiere', *Music and Musicans*, 6/8 (1958), 12-13. Reprinted in KC, 231–6.

The opening subject is this:

No. 1

Trombones and Tuba

It is played by the trombones and tuba, and then repeated a fifth higher by the other brass, surrounded by an E pedal in four octaves. This theme occurred to the composer after playing some of the organ part of the opening of Bach's St Matthew Passion. Those who are curious about these matters can doubtless trace the connection. This section finishes with a cadential passage founded on the Neapolitan sixth played by the saxophones against a minor tonic chord on the strings.

No. 2

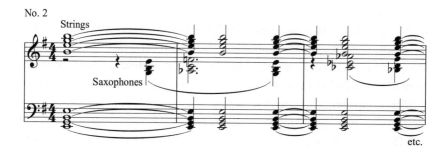

The opening is repeated, with a counter-theme after this pattern.

No. 3

Then follows what is apparently a second subject, played on three clarinets.

No. 4

Surely there is something wrong here? The second subject should be in G major? But all will be explained before long. This theme, 4, gradually unfolds itself with passing references to 1, till G major is reached. The correct key for the second subject at last; but, oh dear, it is not a new subject at all but a version of 4, developed and extended. Never mind, Haydn often does much the same, and what is good enough for the master is good enough for the man. We now successfully return to the home key, E, but major this time, not minor. But alas, there is no sign of the first subject, instead another version of 4 develops into a rhapsodical passage on the solo violin accompanied by harp and pizzicato strings. Surely there is something wrong again, here? Well, it's Joseph Haydn to the rescue once more: the fact is the composer had forgotten all about the first subject, so he adds it now, very softly, hoping it doesn't intrude. This is the end of the movement, except for the saxophone cadence, *à la Napolitaine*.

The second movement, *Andante Sostenuto*, seems to have no logical connection between its various themes. This has led some people to think it must have a programme since apparently programme music need not be logical. It is quite true that this movement started off with a programme, but it got lost on the journey— so now, oh no, we never mention it—and the music must be left to speak for itself—whatever that may mean.

Here is the opening theme:

It is played on the flügel horn (senza vibrato!).

There is a footnote in the score that it must never be played on the cornet, and if the flügel horn unfortunately is not available, the passage must be played on the French horn. This theme is borrowed from an early work of the composer's, luckily long since scrapped, but changed so that its own father would hardly recognize it.[a]

The episode which follows is a strong contrast; a barbaric march theme, 6, against which there is a counter-theme, 7:

[a] A reference to *The Solent* (composed 1902-03).

No. 6

No. 7

A sudden modulation to B flat minor brings back a version of 5, followed by a romantic episode in triple time, played chiefly by the strings.

No. 8

etc.

followed by another theme:

No. 9

and

No. 10

Then a menacing stroke on the gong brings back a reminiscence of 5. Why is a gong in the orchestra always supposed to be menacing? To the unmusical hearer a note on the gong means dinner; this perhaps often is menacing enough, as a well-known parody of a hymn reminds us. Anyhow, the gong stroke gives a sinister aspect to this theme. Then a quick crescendo leads to a restatement of 6, played by the full force of the orchestra, which dies down again to softness, and the flügel horn and its tune are once more heard, this time with a counter subject below it on the clarinet.

The third movement, *Allegro Pesante*, is a scherzo. After a few preliminary side-drum taps the opening theme is announced on three saxophones:

No. 11

etc.

A repetition of this in a higher octave leads to a new theme, 12, and then to 13:

No. 12

No. 13

Indeed, this is a movement of juxtaposition, not of development. A cadenza-like passage on the three saxophones leads to the most important of the subsidiary themes:

No. 14

The composer, to his delight, discovered that by a little jugglery this tune could be made to go in canon; he could not resist the temptation. For some time the music has been loud; it now dies down to introduce the recapitulation, which is not exact, but takes the form of a fugato on this theme:

No. 15

The various subsidiary themes are introduced in turn as counterpoints to the fugue subject. All well mannered orchestral fugues must be interrupted by a choral; this duly happens, thus:

No. 16   3 Saxophones

(This is where the demented cats come in.)

The well-mannered choral, after its first statement, should of course be combined with the fugue subject. The composer tried this, but found the result so dull that he scrapped it and substituted a simple repetition of the choral with rather fuller instrumentation. Then, as a climax, comes a restatement of the opening theme, II, at half the speed, for full orchestra, thus:

No. 17

This leads to another saxophone cadenza, and lastly, the first saxophone plays its little tune very softly accompanied by the side drum. When the tune is finished the side drum goes on by itself and quietly taps itself to death.

Only a very short pause separates the scherzo from the last movement, *Andante Tranquillo*. This final movement is really two movements, played without break, and connected by three short phrases which recur throughout:

No. 18

No. 19

No. 20

etc.

We start off with a long cantilena played by the violins,

No. 21

It is answered by the violas and a florid counterpoint on the clarinet adds its quota. This leads to the first of the before-mentioned connecting phrases.

This in its turn leads to another new tune:

No. 22

etc.

It is played on the horn, to an accompaniment of Verdi-like arpeggios on the woodwind. This is repeated and extended and leads to a loud repetition of 18, which in its turn leads to the two other connecting links, 19 and 20, both soft. Then 'all that again' as Purcell would say, but differently coloured. This leads to a loud statement of 20 which, however, soon softens down and is followed by an episode, 23, which divides the two sections of the movement.

No. 23

The second half starts with this tune played on the violas, under a high pedal G.

No. 24

This tune develops itself, at first it is soft, but gradually wakes up and becomes loud and contrapuntal. The three connecting themes are also heard, then 24 is blared out by the full orchestra in two-part harmony, we hear a suggestion of 19, and the movement ends with the saxophones once more in their Neapolitan vein, but this time with the final chord of E major.

PART VI

Programme Notes on
the Music of Other Composers

CHAPTER 94

Bach Cantatas

THE POLICY OF performing the cantatas of Bach (especially the more intimate ones) with a chorus of three hundred in a hall capable of holding over two thousand, may seem to some to be hazardous. Truly, the ideal way to give such music is by a small choir in a small building. But where are these ideal circumstances to be found?—not apparently in the concert-rooms of London.[1] It seems then to be a question of three hundred voices or no cantatas; for the third course, that of keeping the majority of the chorus silent in all except the noisier numbers, is unthinkable in the case of a society like the Bach Choir, which lives through the enthusiasm of its members; and surely, if the Bach Choir is to be true to its name, it cannot cut out of its scheme those works which contain most of the essence of Bach. It is hoped, therefore, that the beauty of these cantatas will make itself felt under any conditions and in any circumstances, provided that the performers bring their minds and their hearts to the work. This brings us face to face with another problem—in what language are the cantatas to be sung? The Bach Choir have no unreasoning prejudice against the German language, but it is difficult to sing from the heart in any language

---

Source: Programme note. Bach Choir, conducted by Vaughan Williams. Central Hall, Westminster, 14 December 1921.

[1] The present programme was arranged before the welcome news came that Dr Whittaker proposes to bring his Newcastle Choir to London to sing Bach.

but one's own; therefore, English must be the language of an adequate rendering,[2] provided that the English translation used has (1) any relation to the German original, (2) any relation to the English language as it exists outside opera libretti. At present only a handful of such translations exist, and the choice is thereby limited. It remains for some enthusiastic Bach lover to put this right, and arrange for the publication of many of the cantatas in a version in which they can be widely used.

The large chorus requires a (comparatively) large orchestra to support it. This occasionally upsets the orchestral balance and has necessitated a slight modification of the instrumental detail. In one case also where Bach (probably for safety) directed trombones to play with the voices throughout, the conductor has ventured to substitute some unobtrusive horn parts; in another case an obbligato for the obsolete 'violoncello piccolo' has necessitated a slight rearrangement of the string parts.

Three complete cantatas will be performed tonight—

   I.   'Jesus took unto Him the Twelve' *(Jesus nahm zu sich)*, which was Bach's 'trial piece' on his installation as Cantor at Leipzig in 1723. This is, so far as is known, the first performance in England.

  II.   'Stay with us' *(Bleib' bei uns)*, written for the 'Second Easter Festival', probably in 1736.

 III.   'The Sages of Sheba' *(Sie Werden aus Saba)*, an Epiphany cantata dating from 1724 (?).

There will also be sung the chorus, 'Now praise my soul' (taken from the cantata *Gottlob, nun geht*). The chorus is founded on the choral 'Nun lob' mein Seel', and was composed early in the Leipzig period.[3]

At the end of the programme the choral 'Jesu, joy of man's desiring', will be sung by special request.

The instrumental part of the programme will consist of the short organ prelude in C (as an introduction to 'Now praise my soul'), the Concerto in D for pianoforte, violin and flute (No. 5 of the 'Brandenburg' concertos) and the French suite in E major for pianoforte solo.

---

[2] It seems to be a sound principle that no singer should sing in any language with which both he and his audience are not familiar. Perhaps an exception may be found in the case of liturgical music such as the Roman Mass, in which the English equivalent is thoroughly familiar to the audience.

[3] This chorus will be sung in the version edited and translated by Sedley Taylor, whose name lives in the grateful remembrance of so many generations of Cambridge musicians.

CHAPTER 95

British Choral Music and Dvořák, *Stabat Mater*

TO THE ENGLISH musician William Byrd was, up till a few years ago, little more than a name; indeed, to the average man he was not even a name. Now, owing to the unceasing efforts of Dr Fellowes, we have changed all that, and we can perform his works without having recourse to the forgotten recesses of the British Museum manuscript room. One thing that Dr Fellowes has discovered for us is, that the art of combining orchestra and voices was not unknown to the Elizabethan composers.

To the ordinary concert goer the name of Charles Burke will be even more unfamiliar than that of Byrd, and this is not surprising. Up to the age of fifty-nine Burke had no opportunity of developing, or even realizing, the music which was latent in him. Then (about fifteen years ago) he came under the influence of Holst at Morley College. Holst, besides teaching him the technique of his art also encouraged in him the love of fine tunes, so that he naturally turned to the ancient hymn melodies of his native country, which he already knew and loved, to exercise his newly acquired art. Before Burke died, he had the opportunity of hearing his

Source: Programme note. Works performed: Byrd, 'Christ is risen again'; Charles Burke, *St Patrick's Prayer*, Fantasia on Two Irish Hymn Melodies; Holst, Choral Hymns from *Rig Veda*; Dvořák, *Stabat Mater*. Bach Choir and British Symphony Orchestra, conducted by Vaughan Williams. Queen's Hall, London, 7 April 1922.

simple and beautiful work performed by his fellow students at Morley College. Tonight, however, will be its first performance in a public concert room.

There is, luckily, no need at the present day to appraise the art of Gustav Holst. The *Hymn of Jesus* and *The Planets* have taught us what to expect of him, and in these earlier Hymns from the *Rig Veda* we find exactly the same characteristics; the mystical point of view expressed with a wonderful power of direct and forcible utterance. The texts of these hymns are free adaptations by the composer himself from the Sanskrit originals. It is a mistake to suppose that because the words are of eastern origin the music is a study in orientalism; it is the mysticism, and not the orientalism, of the Vedic Hymns which Holst emphasizes in his music: we feel it in the appeal to the unseen forces behind nature in the 'Battle Hymn', in the mystery of that to which even the Gods bow in the 'Hymn to the Unknown God', in the majestic triumph of the funeral hymn.

The mental contrast between Holst and Dvořák is extreme. Holst has evidently reached his mystical outlook through deep thought; Dvořák took religion as he found it and expressed it näively, warmly, occasionally sentimentally, but above all musically. It has been urged that this setting of the *Stabat Mater* has no direct connection with the poem. This is partly true. In listening to the *Stabat Mater* we must not think of Jacopone de Todi, we must not even think of the austere ritual of Westminster Cathedral or the Vatican Chapel, but of some small country church in Bohemia all suffused with the warm, almost Italian, colouring of its surroundings, with the choir singing, the congregation murmuring their responses, and the simple-minded peasant boy moved to tears by what he listens to, perhaps without altogether understanding it; add to this, that the peasant boy happens to be a musical genius and is able to pour out his feelings in exquisite melody, tempered occasionally by the recollection that he has been well grounded in counterpoint, and has been approved of by Brahms.

CHAPTER 96

Bach, St Matthew Passion

IT MAY SEEM to some an hopeless task to present Bach's St Matthew Passion in a London concert room, because if we listen to it as a concert piece we shall entirely mistake its purpose. The essence of the 'Passion' form is the recital of the Gospel story as a church service interspersed with reflective solos and choruses and the well-known choral melodies of the Lutheran church (many of which happily belong to the English church as well, so that here we are on familiar ground) and it is in this spirit that it must be performed and listened to.

However, in transferring a work from the Thomaskirche in 1729 to a London concert room in 1923, certain adaptations and compromises are inevitable. To start with, the only possible language in which the Gospel history can be recited to an English audience is that of the 'Authorized Version' of 1611; anything else would be an insult both to Bach and to the Bible. To do this it is necessary to alter a few notes of Bach's recitative, and in a few cases to

Source: Programme note. Bach Choir, London Symphony Orchestra, conducted by Vaughan Williams. Queen's Hall, London, 7 March 1923.

sacrifice some of Bach's subtlety of phrasing, but the compromise cannot be avoided.[1]

Bach's original chorus for his cantatas and passions consisted of not more than forty voices. What then are we to do when we have a chorus of three hundred? It seems ridiculous and outside the bounds of dramatic propriety to give the words of the Apostles or the questioners of St. Peter to more than a few voices; these numbers have therefore been assigned to a semi-chorus. One exception, however, has been made: the words 'truly this was the Son of God', belong not to 'the Centurion and they that were with him', but are the triumphant outcry of the whole world.

In a performance such as today's, another question arises. In Bach's time the Passion was divided into two parts with a long interval (and a Sermon) between the parts. When such conditions no longer obtain, are we justified in making certain omissions? There seems to be no object in performing the whole of the Passion merely to be able to say (like the man who proposed to go down a coal mine) that we have done so. A few cuts are made in today's performance of certain arias which, according to the standard which Bach himself has set, do not reach the high level of the rest (though for any other composer we should consider them as great music), of others which require a virtuoso obbligato on an obsolete instrument, and of parts of the narrative which are not essential to the course of the story. Also certain 'da capo's' have been abbreviated, in connection with which we may quote the wise sentence of Hubert Parry, 'The only respect in which Bach falls under the spell of convention, was in following without sufficient consideration the principle of repetition familiar through the direction "da capo".' It is as though when he had carried out his artistic scheme with all the technical richness and care in detail he could muster up a certain point, he felt he had done all that was required of him and wrote 'da capo al fine'.

---

[1] Alas! Compromise in the other direction is also unavoidable in one or two cases; 'Weissage' cannot be fitted to 'Prophesy unto us' and the wonderful orchestral illustration of 'bete' cannot be sung to the word 'yonder', so we must perforce substitute 'Now tell us' for 'Prophesy unto us', and 'Go yonder and pray' for 'Go and pray yonder'. On the other hand the words 'Memorial of her' fit exactly musically to 'Was sie gethan hat', the word 'memorial' being given the climax instead of 'her', thus avoiding the usual awkward transposition 'of her—for a memorial'.

CHAPTER 97

Dvořák, 'New World' Symphony

Form in Music

Music, like everything else, must have design and symmetry and pattern, otherwise it will be unintelligible. This pattern or symmetry is produced chiefly by the statement and re-statement at certain points in the design of certain phrases or melodies which balance other parts of the whole structure.

The form of a piece of music has been compared to an arch, the principal parts in whose structure are the supporting pillars, which are equal and opposite, and the keystone which they support. In music, in the same way, we start with some salient phrase or tune, which leads on to a contrasting phrase or tune and finally leads back to a repetition of the opening. This at its simplest shape can be seen in folk-tunes and simple pieces, but the same principle applies to the more elaborate structure of a Brahms Symphony or a Bach Concerto.

Symphony 'From the New World', Dvořák (1841–1906)

Antonín Dvořák was born of Bohemian peasant stock and was brought up among the beautiful folk-tunes of his native land. In 1892 he visited America and determined

Source: Programme note. Leith Hill Musical Festival Orchestra, conducted by Vaughan Williams. Dorking, April 1924.

to crystallize his impressions in music; so he composed this 'New World' Symphony, in the ordinary four separate parts or movements, the tunes of which were suggested by the people and sights of the United States. It is not to be wondered at that Dvořák, loving his own native melodies so much, should be attracted by the gay and beautiful tunes of the negro population of America; and this influence is apparent throughout the work.

In the first part or movement after a few bars of introduction we hear this theme:

Ex. 1 Horns

obviously, with its syncopated rhythm, suggested by the negro idiom (we now are all too familiar with the formula under the name of 'rag-time'). This is the 'first subject', or base of the arch; when we get to the 'second subject', or keystone, we find the following:

Ex. 2 2nd Violins

Does not this inevitably suggest a negro fiddler? Later we have:

Ex. 3 Flute

which is a close variant of the well-known 'spiritual' 'Swing low, sweet chariot'.

And so the movement goes on its way, extending and repeating itself and achieves that symmetry without which no music can be intelligible.

The next movement (after a few bars of introduction) gives us a new aspect of America. The famous tune of this movement (played on the 'cor anglais') is obviously an idealisation of those popular American melodies of which 'Swanee River' is the best-known example. To the great composer 'all roads lead to Rome', and it is interesting to see to what heights even this type of sentiment can rise at the hands of a great master. This tune is too well known to need quotation. As a landmark we may notice the phrase which marks the opening of the episodal section of the movement, from which we gradually return to the first melody.

Ex. 4

In the third movement Dvořák seems for a moment to forget the 'New World' and to be back among his native Bohemian songs and dances, but, before the end, a reminder of the 'other side' comes in the shape of the theme (Ex. 1) of the first movement.

In the last movement we are back among the outlines and rhythms of America, as the following quotations will prove:

Ex. 5

Ex. 6

CHAPTER 98

Elgar, Introduction and Allegro for String Orchestra

T HIS WORK IS written for the unusual combination of solo string quartet and full string orchestra. It is very characteristic of the composer, full of unmistakeable Elgarian melody, especially the big tune in D major which comes in the middle of the Allegro, and it goes without saying brilliantly and gratefully written for the instruments. In the Introduction the composer seems to be considering his themes one by one and wondering what use he will make of them. The only subject stated at any length in the Introduction is the quiet melody which later appears as No. 4.

With the Allegro we get into our stride. The opening subject is as follows:

No. 1

etc.

Then follows a quick passage in semiquaver[s] in which the solo quartet alternates with the full orchestra (No. 2), and this in turn leads to the big tune in D

Source: Programme note. Leith Hill Musical Festival Orchestra, conducted by Vaughan Williams. Dorking, April 1931.

major already referred to (No. 3). The quiet tune (No. 4), which played so large a part in the Introduction now appears in shortened form and only as a tail piece to No. 3. The composer has good reasons for this truncation as we shall see later.

No. 2

No. 3

No. 4

Then by all the rules of the game there should follow a 'development' of the themes already heard, but this 'development' has in a sense already taken place in the Introduction; it is therefore time for something new which takes the form of a fugue on this subject:

No. 5

and it is this fugue which leads us back safely to the normal and expected repetition of the main themes of the movement. These all follow in their expected order except No. 4 which now, instead of being a mere coda, becomes a long extended melody.

We now understand what Elgar was doing when he dwelt so lovingly on that theme in his Introduction. These discoveries make musical analysis a fascinating subject. It is only when the composer's last note is heard that everything falls into its place and the surprises become the inevitable.

CHAPTER **99**

Gordon Jacob, Passacaglia on a Well-known Theme

THE MUSICAL FORM known as 'passacaglia', which is first cousin to the 'chaconne' and 'ground' of Purcell, has always been a favourite device with composers. The violin chaconne and the organ passacaglia of Bach are well known. The Variations in C minor of Beethoven and the Finale of Brahms' Fourth Symphony are also in the passacaglia form, though not so called, and we find the form used even by such extreme modernists as von Webern.

The device consists in a melodic or rhythmical pattern which persists without interruption throughout the piece, usually in the bass, surrounded by simple or complex figuration as the composer desires.

The 'well-known' theme on which Gordon Jacob founds his passacaglia is the tune 'Oranges and Lemons', whose bell-like character is well suited to contrapuntal treatment.

One example must suffice to show the various possibilities which the composer has found in his theme:

Source: Programme note. Leith Hill Musical Festival Orchestra, conducted by Vaughan Williams. Dorking, April 1932.

CHAPTER 100

Weber, *Der Freischütz* Overture

WEBER'S *FREISCHÜTZ* OVERTURE is a typical product of the Teutonic romantic movement of the early nineteenth century. The story, with its wolf's glen, its flaxen-haired maidens and its magic bullets, one of which, at the climax of the opera, apparently goes crooked and hits the villain instead of the heroine, leaves a modern Anglo-Saxon audience, alas! cold. But we must remember that out of this farrago evolved the great supernatural music dramas of Richard Wagner. Not only in his choice of subjects but in the actual texture of the music Weber was the direct forerunner of Wagner. The dramatic tension engendered by tremolando strings and heavy drum notes, which we find in the introduction of this overture became almost a bad habit with Wagner at tragic situations. Weber's famous passage for four horns in *Der Freischütz* certainly foreshadows an equally famous passage for four horns in *Tristan* and there can be little doubt that if Weber had not written the well known melody (No. 3) Wagner would never have thought of Tannhäuser's song in praise of Venus. Whether this is a subject for rejoicing or regret is a matter of individual taste.

Source: Programme note. Leith Hill Musical Festival Orchestra, conducted by Vaughan Williams. Dorking, April 1932.

The Overture starts with a slow introduction, the principal feature of which is the passage for four horns mentioned above.

No. 1

Then follows an allegro in C minor, the first subject being

No. 2

and the second subject in E flat the famous tune

No. 3

Besides this there are references to the slow introduction and the Overture ends with a brilliant version of No. 3.

CHAPTER 101

Brahms, Choruses from the Requiem

THIS YEAR THE Leith Hill Musical Festival, in common with the rest of Europe, celebrates the 100th anniversary of the birth of Johannes Brahms, which took place at Hamburg on May 7th, 1833. Brahms is the last of the group of great German composers which for 150 years made the terms 'classical' and 'Teutonic' synonymous in music. In this group none has been more essentially Teutonic than Brahms, and of his works none is more essentially Teutonic than the German 'Requiem'.

The words which Brahms has set have, of course, nothing to do with the Roman rite—Brahms calls it 'Ein deutsches Requiem'. It was to be for the German people what the 'Missa pro defunctis' is for the Latins. Brahms chose words from the Lutheran Bible to illustrate the mysteries of death and the future life.

One difficulty attends us who try to perform this work in England. Our English Bible means more to us, even more than Luther's Bible means to the German, and we would not alter a single word. But in translating a foreign language certain technical difficulties are continually occurring in the fitting of words to notes which makes it impossible to use our English text exactly as it stands. To give one example out of many: 'For all flesh is as grass' becomes in German, 'Denn alles Fleisch es ist

Source: Programme note. Leith Hill Musical Festival Orchestra and Chorus, conducted by Vaughan Williams. Dorking, April 1933.

wie Gras', two syllables too many, so we have perforce to sing, 'Behold all flesh is as the grass' and so on throughout the work. The text given below is that which will be sung tonight with all the deviations from the authorized version made necessary by the music.

Four numbers have been selected for performance today.

The opening chorus, 'Blessed are they that mourn', needs no comment, the orchestral accompaniment is subdued and the violins are silent. Then follows the famous 'Funeral March' as it has been called, though indeed it is in triple not in march time. After a short introduction the lower voices sing softly, but menacingly, 'All flesh is as grass' and the sopranos join in with 'the grass withereth'. (Nos. 1a and 1b).

No. 1a

Be - hold, all flesh is as the grass

No. 1b

For lo, the grass with'r - eth

After a big orchestral crescendo the voices join together once more to declare in their loudest tones the mortality of man. The next section may be described technically as the Trio of the march; a quiet homily on the words 'Be patient therefore'.

Once again the chorus proclaim that man will perish as the grass, but this time triumph supervenes and in a great fugal chorus (not strictly a fugue) the chorus, headed by the basses, march rejoicing to Zion (No. 2). The soft ending to this number on the words 'Joy everlasting' should be specially noticed.

No. 2

The re - deem - ed of the Lord shall re - turn a - gain, and

come re - joic - ing, come re - joic - ing un - to___ Zi - on

The next movement to be sung tonight, 'How lovely is thy dwelling-place', is too well-known to need comment. It is Brahms in his most lyrical and gracious mood. In the sixth number, 'Here on earth', Brahms challenges comparison with other great composers in eschatological descriptiveness. Think for a moment of the realistic trumpets in Verdi's 'Tuba mirum', the overwhelming 'Et expecto', in Bach's B minor Mass or, in a different connection, the final scene of Wagner's *Dusk of the Gods*. Brahms, with the simplest of means, achieves perhaps the most striking effect of all; besides, whereas Wagner ends his great epic in a mood of pessimism, Brahms ends with a blazing chord of C major, 'O death where is thy sting?' Some hearers, indeed, have been led to mistake this climax for the end of the work and have inopportunely applauded, but for Brahms this moment is the starting point for an ascription of praise led off by the altos in the mighty fugue 'Worthy art thou' (No. 3).

No. 3

This is one of the most dramatic moments of all music and is none the less so for being brought about by a so-called academic device.

CHAPTER 102

George Dyson, *The Canterbury Pilgrims*

JUST AS BRAHMS went to the Lutheran Bible to appeal to his fellow countrymen in one mood, so Dyson in a very different mood goes to the great English classic Chaucer to help him to suggest that side of England which is shrewd and gay. In Dyson's music the brilliant, witty and sympathetic word pictures of Chaucer receive their musical counterpart, and just as certain phrases stand out in the poet and have become household words, so in Dyson's music the Monk, the Nun, the Scholar, the Merchant, the Shipman, the wife of Bath, the poor Parson and the Host stand before us in musical notation till at last the procession fades away into silence with the opening words of the Knight's tale. This end is a real inspiration and the theme which accompanies it is of great originality from the very reason that it appears to us strangely familiar. There is no space here to write a dissertation on originality as opposed to mere novelty, but this much may be said: that whatever is truly new and original brings with it that strange feeling of being already known.

Source: Programme note. Leith Hill Musical Festival Orchestra and Chorus, conducted by Vaughan Williams. Dorking, April 1933.

The Knight's Tale

Other striking and appropriate themes are the following:

The Clerk of Oxenford

The Shipman

etc.

The Wife of Bath

SELECT BIBLIOGRAPHY
OF FOLK SONG COLLECTIONS

Vaughan Williams often refers to individual folk song collections in this book. References for these publications are given below, listed alphabetically by the editor(s) of each volume.

Baring-Gould, S. *Songs of the West* (London: Patey & Wills, 1889).

Broadwood, John. *Sussex Songs* (published privately, 1843).

Broadwood, Lucy. *English Traditional Songs and Carols* (London: Boosey, 1908).

———— and J. Fuller Maitland. *English County Songs* (London: Leadenhall Press, 1893).

Gilbert, Davies. *Some Ancient Christmas Carols* (London: J. Nichols, 1822).

Kidson, Frank. *Traditional Tunes* (Oxford: C. Taphouse, 1891).

Leather, Ella Mary. *Folklore of Herefordshire* (London: Sidgwick & Jackson, 1912).

Moffatt, Alfred and Frank Kidson. *The Minstrelsy of England* (London: Bayley & Ferguson, 1901).

Sandys, William. *Christmas Carols, Ancient and Modern* (London: Beckley, 1833).

Sharp, Cecil. J. *Folk-Songs of English Origin Collected in the Appalachian Mountains*, 2 vols. (London: Novello, 1919, 1921).

———— and Charles L. Marson. *Folk-Songs from Somerset*, 5 series [4th and 5th series ed. Cecil J. Sharp] (London: Simpkin, Marshall, Hamilton, Kent, 1904–1909).

Stainer, John and H. R. Bramley. *Christmas Carols New and Old* (London: G. Routledge, 1871).

Stanford, Charles Villiers. *The National Song Book* (London: Boosey, 1906).

INDEX